Security Management Services

Security Management Services

Shailendra Sengar

ANMOL PUBLICATIONS PVT. LTD.
NEW DELHI-110 002 (INDIA)

ANMOL PUBLICATIONS PVT. LTD.
H.O.: 4374/4B, Ansari Road, Darya Ganj,
New Delhi-110 002 (India)
Ph.: 23278000, 23261597
B.O.: No. 1015, Ist Main Road, BSK IIIrd Stage
IIIrd Phase, IIIrd Block
Bangalore - 560 085 (India)
Visit us at: www.anmolpublications.com

Security Management Services

First Published, 2008

ISBN 978-81-261-3441-0

PRINTED IN INDIA

Printed at Mehra Offset Press, Delhi.

Contents

Preface

This Encyclopaedic Series of Career and Vocational Guidance Covers careers, describing jobs, places of employment, working conditions, qualifications, education and training. This has been developed to aid career and counsellors and job placement coordinators in planning activities for students and potential students about career vocational education programs. It contains a career and vocational guidance model which clarifies what career and vocational guidance services mean and what planners should include in their activities. The model shows an interrelatedness among major thrusts with career development being a central theme of vocational guidance. All of the thrusts depicted in the model represent essential services that should be available to students in career and vocational education programs. The encyclopaedia deals with various sections which correspond to the major thrusts identified in the model: (1) career development; (2) recruitment; (3) guidance and counselling; (4) placement; (5) follow-up and follow-through; and (6) consultation. Each section contains an outline of the perceived needs of the topic, an overview of the topic relative to career and vocational guidance, and some suggested activities and strategies that may be useful in meeting student needs.

It also contains current information about occupations, employment trends, and job searching. Materials on career decision-making, internships, and salaries are also located in each volume. This Series of Encyclopaedia helps students assess their potential for various careers.

Shailendra Sengar

1

Career in Security Services

Police Officer

Police officers maintain law and order. They protect people and property. Officers investigate and try to prevent crime. They are also called to accidents and emergencies.

Work Activities: Police officers have a number of responsibilities. These include:

- maintaining law and order
- protecting people and property from harm
- investigating and preventing crime
- dealing with emergency situations.

All new recruits spend at least two years as a probationary constable. This includes working on the beat with an experienced officer, getting to know a particular area and the people who live there. During this period the probationer learns how best to judge situations and gains experience in activities like:

- interviewing suspects
- investigating suspicious incidents
- taking statements from witnesses
- informing next of kin of injuries or death.

Police officers take control of situations such as traffic accidents, break-ins, street fights and domestic incidents. They use their skills to communicate effectively with other officers, other services and members of the public. They must provide the action, advice and sympathetic leadership expected of them by the public. They also complete accurate reports and other documents.

Police officers can work on the beat, on foot or in a patrol car, or apply to join a specialist unit. Uniformed officers can specialise in dog handling, the traffic/motorway section, underwater search units, the mounted police or the river police. Not all forces have an underwater or a mounted unit.

A local policing unit/station is usually managed by an inspector and a team of sergeants. Incidents are reported directly to the station or are diverted to the police from 999 calls. Most police stations have a control room, where police officers provide radioed backup to officers on the beat.

The Criminal Investigation Department (CID) offers the opportunity to work as a detective. Officers can specialise in one of a number of areas like:

- fraud
- drugs
- nationality (immigration)
- special operations (surveillance)
- intelligence and information gathering
- child protection.

Competition for some CID specialities can be severe.

Personal Qualities and Skills: You should enjoy working with people. You need to be able to deal with people of all ages and from a variety of backgrounds. Verbal and written communication skills are important.

It is important that you can handle difficult situations with sensitivity. Good judgement is an essential quality. Decision making skills and initiative are also important. Close attention to detail will help you to solve crimes and spot suspicious events or circumstances.

As a police officer you must act quickly and keep calm in emergencies. You will also need to concentrate for long periods of time. The job demands you to be fit and active.

All entrants to the police must pass medical and eyesight tests, although most forces accept people who wear contact lenses or glasses. Your colour vision may be tested. There are no minimum height requirements, although your height to weight ratio may be checked.

For some police forces you need a driving licence.

Pay and Opportunities: Police officers are paid on a rising scale. The pay rates given below are approximate. Police constables on appointment earn £20,397 a year. After two years, or on joining at the age of 22 or above, they earn £24,090 a year. Sergeants earn £32,025 rising to £35,991 after five years. Inspectors earn £41,034-£46,320 a year.

Police officers work 40 hours a week, which may include shifts, evenings, weekends and public holidays. They may be required to work paid overtime to cover special events or emergencies. About 140,000 police officers are employed throughout the UK. Each police force is responsible for its own recruitment. There is fierce competition for places.

The following information is sourced from government statistics. The government's definition of types of job is slightly different to that used in this programme. For this type of job, the most relevant Government-defined occupation is 'Police officers (sergeant and below)'.

In 2001 there were 17,100 people working as 'Police officers (sergeant and below)' in Scotland. 79 in every 10,000 employees working in Scotland were employed as 'Police officers (sergeant and below)'.

Entry Routes and Training: The minimum age for entry to the police force is 18 years 6 months.

Whether you have Standard Grades or a degree you will undergo the same Standard Entrance Test.

This will include tests of:

- language
- information handling
- numeracy

You will also have to undergo a fitness test, a range of individual and group assessments, an interview and a medical examination.

You must tell the police force to which you apply about any convictions or juvenile offences.

If you are accepted you will undergo a lengthy training programme which prepares you for a career in the police force. Training takes place on the job with block release to the Police College at Tulliallan.

All entrants work as a probationary constable for at least the first two years. During this time you will receive ongoing training. You will also spend time with specialist departments such as CID and Traffic.

Some police forces operate cadet training schemes for young people, but opportunities are very limited and a cadetship does not guarantee a place as a probationary constable.

Many further education colleges run courses aimed at school leavers who want to enter public/uniformed services but who can't apply until they are 18. Successful completion of such a course does not, however, guarantee employment in the public/ uniformed services.

Qualifications: The usual requirement for entry to the Police Service is a good general education and a pass in the Police Standard Entrance Test. If you have Standard Grades (1-3) and/or Highers you may be at an advantage. English and Maths are useful subjects.

However, entry requirements vary—check with individual forces for their specific requirements.

Adult Opportunities: Experience as a volunteer special constable may be helpful when applying for a paid position.

Relevant work experience, for example in the forces or community, is viewed very positively. Maturity and life experience is viewed as an asset. The entry requirements are the same for all ages up to the specified limit.

Graduates (any discipline) can apply to join the police service through the Accelerated Promotion Scheme for Graduates. Applicants are expected to show some evidence of community involvement.

5% of police officers work part-time.

Police and Detectives

Significant Points: Police and detective work can be dangerous and stressful.

Competition should remain keen for higher paying jobs with State and Federal agencies and police departments in affluent areas; opportunities will be better in local and special police departments that offer relatively low salaries or in urban communities where the crime rate is relatively high. Applicants with college training in police science or military police experience should have the best opportunities.

Nature of the Work: People depend on police officers and detectives to protect their lives and property. Law enforcement officers, some of whom are State or Federal special agents or inspectors, perform these duties in a variety of ways, depending on the size and type of their organization. In most jurisdictions, they are expected to exercise authority when necessary, whether on or off duty.

Uniformed police officers have general law enforcement duties, including maintaining regular patrols and responding to calls for service. They may direct traffic at the scene of an accident, investigate a burglary, or give first aid to an accident victim. In large police departments, officers usually are assigned to a specific type of duty. Many urban police agencies are involved in community policing—a practice in which an officer builds relationships with the citizens of local neighbourhoods and mobilizes the public to help fight crime.

Police agencies are usually organized into geographic districts, with uniformed officers assigned to patrol a specific area, such as part of the business district or outlying residential neighbourhoods. Officers may work alone, but, in large agencies, they often patrol with a partner. While on patrol, officers attempt to become thoroughly familiar with their patrol area and remain alert for anything unusual. Suspicious circumstances and hazards to public safety are investigated or noted and officers are dispatched to individual calls for assistance within their district. During their shift, they may identify, pursue and arrest suspected criminals; resolve problems within the community; and enforce traffic laws.

Public college and university police forces, public school district police and agencies serving transportation systems and facilities are examples of special police agencies. These agencies have special geographic jurisdictions and enforcement responsibilities in the United States. Most sworn personnel in special agencies are uniformed officers; a smaller number are investigators.

Some police officers specialize in such diverse fields as chemical and microscopic analysis, training and firearms instruction, or handwriting and fingerprint identification. Others work with special units, such as horseback, bicycle, motorcycle or harbour patrol; canine corps; special weapons and tactics (SWAT); or emergency response teams. A few local and special law enforcement officers primarily perform jail-related duties or work in courts. Regardless of job duties or location, police officers and detectives at all levels must write reports and maintain meticulous records that will be needed if they testify in court.

Sheriffs and deputy sheriffs enforce the law on the county level. Sheriffs are usually elected to their posts and perform duties similar to those of a local or county police chief. Sheriffs' departments tend to be relatively small, most having fewer than 50 sworn officers. Deputy sheriffs have law enforcement duties similar to those of officers in urban police departments. Police and sheriffs' deputies who provide security in city and county courts are sometimes called bailiffs.

State police officers (sometimes called *State troopers* or *highway patrol officers*) arrest criminals Statewide and patrol highways to enforce motor vehicle laws and regulations. State police officers are best known for issuing traffic citations to motorists. At the scene of accidents, they may direct traffic, give first aid and call for emergency equipment. They also write reports used to determine the cause of the accident. State police officers are frequently called upon to render assistance to other law enforcement agencies, especially those in rural areas or small towns.

State law enforcement agencies operate in every State except Hawaii. Most full-time sworn personnel are uniformed officers who regularly patrol and respond to calls for service. Others work as investigators, perform court-related duties, or carry out administrative or other assignments.

Detectives are plainclothes investigators who gather facts and collect evidence for criminal cases. Some are assigned to interagency task forces to combat specific types of crime. They conduct interviews, examine records, observe the activities of suspects and participate in raids or arrests. Detectives and State and Federal agents and inspectors usually specialize in investigating one of a wide variety of violations, such as homicide or fraud. They are assigned cases on a rotating basis and work on them until an arrest and conviction occurs or until the case is dropped.

Fish and game wardens enforce fishing, hunting and boating laws. They patrol hunting and fishing areas, conduct search and rescue operations, investigate complaints and accidents and aid in prosecuting court cases.

The Federal Government maintains a high profile in many areas of law enforcement. *Federal Bureau of Investigation (FBI) agents* are the Government's principal investigators, responsible for investigating violations of more than 200 categories of Federal law and conducting sensitive national security investigations. Agents may conduct surveillance, monitor court-authorized wiretaps, examine business records, investigate white-collar crime, or participate in sensitive undercover assignments. The FBI investigates organized crime, public corruption, financial crime, fraud against the Government, bribery, copyright infringement, civil rights violations, bank robbery, extortion, kidnapping, air piracy, terrorism, espionage, interstate criminal activity, drug trafficking and other violations of Federal statutes.

U.S. Drug Enforcement Administration (DEA) agents enforce laws and regulations relating to illegal drugs. Not only is the DEA the lead agency for domestic enforcement of Federal drug laws, it also has sole responsibility for coordinating and pursuing U.S. drug investigations abroad. Agents may conduct complex criminal investigations, carry out surveillance of criminals and infiltrate illicit drug organizations using undercover techniques.

U.S. marshals and deputy marshals protect the Federal courts and ensure the effective operation of the judicial system. They provide protection for the Federal judiciary, transport Federal prisoners, protect Federal witnesses and manage assets seized from criminal enterprises. They enjoy the widest jurisdiction of any Federal law enforcement agency and are involved to some degree in nearly all Federal law enforcement efforts. In addition, U.S. marshals pursue and arrest Federal fugitives.

Bureau of Alcohol, Tobacco, Firearms and Explosives agents regulate and investigate violations of Federal firearms and explosives laws, as well as Federal alcohol and tobacco tax regulations.

The U.S. Department of State *Bureau of Diplomatic Security special agents* are engaged in the battle against terrorism. Overseas, they advise ambassadors on all security matters and manage a complex range of security programmes designed to protect personnel, facilities and information. In the United States, they investigate passport and visa fraud, conduct personnel security investigations, issue security clearances and protect the Secretary of State and a number of foreign dignitaries. They also train foreign civilian police and administer a counter-terrorism reward programme.

The *Department of Homeland Security* employs numerous law enforcement officers under several different agencies, including *Customs and Border Protection, Immigration and Customs Enforcement* and the *U.S. Secret Service. U.S. Border Patrol agents* protect more than 8,000 miles of international land and water boundaries. Their missions are to detect and prevent the smuggling and unlawful entry of undocumented foreign nationals into the United States; to apprehend those persons violating the immigration laws; and to interdict contraband, such as narcotics.

Immigration inspectors interview and examine people seeking entrance to the United States and its territories. They inspect passports to determine whether people are legally eligible to enter the United States. Immigration inspectors also prepare reports, maintain records and process applications and petitions for immigration or temporary residence in the United States.

Customs inspectors enforce laws governing imports and exports by inspecting cargo, baggage and articles worn or carried by people, vessels, vehicles, trains and aircraft entering or leaving the United States. These inspectors examine, count, weigh, gauge, measure and sample commercial and noncommercial cargoes entering and leaving the United States. Customs inspectors seize prohibited or smuggled articles; intercept contraband; and apprehend, search, detain and arrest violators of U.S. laws. *Customs agents* investigate violations, such as narcotics smuggling, money laundering, child pornography and customs fraud and they enforce the Arms Export Control Act. During domestic and foreign investigations, they develop and use informants; conduct physical and electronic surveillance; and examine records from importers and exporters, banks, couriers and manufacturers. They conduct interviews, serve on joint task forces with other agencies and get and execute search warrants.

Federal Air Marshals provide air security by fighting attacks targeting U.S. airports, passengers and crews. They disguise themselves as ordinary passengers and board flights of U.S. air carriers to locations worldwide.

U.S. Secret Service special agents protect the President, Vice President and their immediate families; Presidential candidates; former Presidents; and foreign dignitaries visiting the United States. Secret Service agents also investigate counterfeiting, forgery of Government checks or bonds and fraudulent use of credit cards.

Other Federal agencies employ police and special agents with sworn arrest powers and the authority to carry firearms. These agencies include the Postal Service, the Bureau of Indian Affairs Office of Law Enforcement, the Forest Service and the National Park Service.

Working Conditions: Police and detective work can be very dangerous and stressful. In addition to the obvious dangers of confrontations with criminals, police officers and detectives need to be constantly alert and ready to deal appropriately with a number of other threatening situations. Many law enforcement officers witness death and suffering resulting from accidents and criminal behaviour. A career in law enforcement may take a toll on their private lives.

Uniformed officers, detectives, agents and inspectors are usually scheduled to work 40-hour weeks, but paid overtime is common. Shift work is necessary because protection must be provided around the clock. Junior officers frequently work weekends, holidays and nights. Police officers and detectives are required to work at any time their services are needed and may work long hours during investigations. In most jurisdictions, whether on or off duty, officers are expected to be armed and to exercise their authority whenever necessary.

The jobs of some Federal agents such as U.S. Secret Service and DEA special agents require extensive travel, often on very short notice. They may relocate a number of times over the course of their careers. Some special agents in agencies such as the U.S. Border Patrol work outdoors in rugged terrain for long periods and in all kinds of weather.

Training, Other Qualifications and Advancement: Civil service regulations govern the appointment of police and detectives in most States, large municipalities and special police agencies, as well as in many smaller jurisdictions. Candidates must be U.S. citizens, usually must be at least 20 years of age and must meet rigorous physical and personal qualifications. In the Federal Government, candidates must be at least 21 years of age but less than 37 years of age at the time of appointment. Physical examinations for entrance into law enforcement often include tests of vision, hearing, strength and agility. Eligibility for appointment usually depends on performance in competitive written examinations and previous education and experience. In larger departments, where the majority of law enforcement jobs are found, applicants usually must have at least a high school education and some departments require a year or two of college coursework. Federal and State agencies typically require a college degree. Candidates should enjoy working with people and meeting the public.

Because personal characteristics such as honesty, sound judgment, integrity and a sense of responsibility are especially important in law enforcement, candidates are interviewed by senior officers and their character traits and backgrounds are investigated. In some agencies, candidates are interviewed by a psychiatrist or a psychologist or given a personality test. Most applicants are subjected to lie detector examinations or drug testing. Some agencies subject sworn personnel to random drug testing as a condition of continuing employment.

Before their first assignments, officers usually go through a period of training. In State and large local departments, recruits get training in their agency's police academy, often for 12 to 14 weeks. In small agencies, recruits often attend a regional or State academy. Training includes classroom instruction in constitutional law and civil rights, State laws and local ordinances and accident investigation. Recruits also receive training and supervised experience in patrol, traffic control, use of firearms, self-defense, first aid and emergency response. Police departments in some large cities hire high school graduates who are still in their teens as police cadets or trainees. They do clerical work and attend classes, usually for 1 to 2 years, at which point they reach the minimum age requirement and may be appointed to the regular force.

Police officers usually become eligible for promotion after a probationary period ranging from 6 months to 3 years. In a large department, promotion may enable an officer to become a detective or to specialize in one type of police work, such as working with juveniles. Promotions to corporal, sergeant, lieutenant and captain usually are made according to a candidate's position on a promotion list, as determined by scores on a written examination and on-the-job performance.

Most States require at least two years of college study to qualify as a fish and game warden. Applicants must pass written and physical examinations and vision, hearing, psychological and drug tests similar to those taken by other law enforcement officers. Once hired, officers attend a training academy lasting from 3 to 12 months, sometimes followed by further training in the field.

To be considered for appointment as an FBI agent, an applicant must be a graduate of an accredited law school or a college graduate with one of the following: a major in accounting, electrical engineering, or information technology; fluency in a foreign language; or three years of related full-time work experience. All new agents undergo 18 weeks of training at the FBI Academy on the U.S. Marine Corps base in Quantico, Virginia.

Applicants for special agent jobs with the U.S. Secret Service and the Bureau of Alcohol, Tobacco and Firearms must have a bachelor's degree, a minimum of three years' related work experience, or a combination of education and experience. Prospective special agents undergo 11 weeks of initial criminal investigation training at the Federal Law Enforcement Training Centre in Glynco, Georgia and another 17 weeks of specialized training with their particular agencies.

Applicants for special agent jobs with the DEA must have a college degree with at least a 2.95 grade point average or specialized skills or work experience, such as foreign language fluency, technical skills, law enforcement experience, or accounting experience. DEA special agents undergo 14 weeks of specialized training at the FBI Academy in Quantico, Virginia.

U.S. Border Patrol agents must be U.S. citizens, be younger than 37 years of age at the time of appointment, possess a valid driver's license and pass a three-part examination on reasoning and language skills. A bachelor's degree or previous work experience that demonstrates the ability to handle stressful situations, make decisions and take charge is required for a position as a Border Patrol agent. Applicants may qualify through a combination of education and work experience.

Postal inspectors must have a bachelor's degree and 1 year of related work experience. It is desirable that they have one of several professional certifications, such as that of certified public accountant. They also must pass a background investigation, meet certain health requirements, undergo a drug screening test, possess a valid State driver's license and be a U.S. citizen between 21 and 36 years of age when hired.

Law enforcement agencies are encouraging applicants to take postsecondary school training in law enforcement-related subjects. Many entry-level applicants for police jobs have completed some formal postsecondary education and a significant number are college graduates. Many junior colleges, colleges and universities offer programmes in law enforcement or administration of justice. Other courses helpful in preparing for a career in law enforcement include accounting, finance, electrical engineering, computer science and foreign languages. Physical education and sports are helpful in developing the competitiveness, stamina and agility needed for many law enforcement positions. Knowledge of a foreign language is an asset in many Federal agencies and urban departments.

Continuing training helps police officers, detectives and special agents improve their job performance. Through police department academies, regional centers for public safety employees established by the States and Federal agency training centers, instructors provide annual training in self-defense tactics, firearms, use-of-force policies, sensitivity and communications skills, crowd-control techniques, relevant legal developments and advances in law enforcement equipment. Many agencies pay all or part of the tuition for officers to work toward degrees in criminal justice, police science, administration of justice, or public administration and pay higher salaries to those who earn such a degree.

Employment: Police and detectives held about 842,000 jobs in 2004. About 80 percent were employed by local governments. State police agencies employed about 12 percent and various Federal agencies employed about 6 percent. A small proportion worked for educational services, rail transportation and contract investigation and security services.

According to the U.S. Bureau of Justice Statistics, police and detectives employed by local governments primarily worked in cities with more than 25,000 inhabitants. Some cities have very large police forces, while thousands of small communities employ fewer than 25 officers each.

Job Outlook: The opportunity for public service through law enforcement work is attractive to many because the job is challenging and involves much personal responsibility. Furthermore, law enforcement officers in many agencies may retire with a pension after 25 or 30 years of service, allowing them to pursue a second career while still in their 40s or 50s. Because of relatively attractive salaries and benefits, the number of qualified candidates exceeds the number of job openings in Federal law enforcement agencies and in most State police departments—resulting in increased hiring standards and selectivity by employers.

Competition should remain keen for higher paying jobs with State and Federal agencies and police departments in more affluent areas. Opportunities will be better in local and special police departments, especially in departments that offer relatively low salaries, or in urban communities where the crime rate is relatively high. Applicants with college training in police science, military police experience, or both should have the best opportunities.

Employment of police and detectives is expected to grow about as fast as the average for all occupations through 2014. A more security-conscious society and concern about drug-related crimes should contribute to the increasing demand for police services. However, employment growth will be hindered by reductions in Federal hiring grants to local police departments and by expectations of low crime rates by the general public.

The level of government spending determines the level of employment for police and detectives. The number of job opportunities, therefore, can vary from year to year and from place to place. Layoffs, on the other hand, are rare because retirements enable most staffing cuts to be handled through attrition. Trained law enforcement officers who lose their jobs because of budget cuts usually have little difficulty finding jobs with other agencies. The need to replace workers who retire, transfer to other occupations, or stop working for other reasons will be the source of many job openings.

Earnings: Police and sheriff's patrol officers had median annual earnings of $45,210 in May 2004. The middle 50 percent earned between $34,410 and $56,360. The lowest 10 percent earned less than $26,910 and the highest 10 percent earned more than $68,880. Median annual earnings were $44,750 in Federal Government, $48,980 in State government and $45,010 in local government.

In May 2004, median annual earnings of police and detective supervisors were $64,430. The middle 50 percent earned between $49,370 and $80,510. The lowest 10 percent earned less than $36,690 and the highest 10 percent earned more than $96,950. Median annual earnings were $86,030 in Federal Government, $62,300 in State government and $63,590 in local government.

In May 2004, median annual earnings of detectives and criminal investigators were $53,990. The middle 50 percent earned between $40,690 and $72,280. The lowest 10 percent earned less than $32,180 and the highest 10 percent earned more than $86,010. Median annual earnings were $75,700 in Federal Government, $46,670 in State government and $49,650 in local government.

Federal law provides special salary rates to Federal employees who serve in law enforcement. Additionally, Federal special agents and inspectors receive law enforcement availability pay (LEAP)—equal to 25 percent of the agent's grade and step—awarded because of the large amount of overtime that these agents are expected to work. For example, in 2005, FBI agents entered Federal service as GS-10 employees on the pay scale at a base salary of $42,548, yet they earned about $53,185 a year with availability pay. They could advance to the GS 13 grade level in field nonsupervisory assignments at a base salary of $64,478, which was worth $80,597 with availability pay. FBI supervisory, management and executive positions in grades GS-14 and GS-15 paid a base salary of about $76,193 and $89,625 a year, respectively, which amounted to $95,241 or $112,031 per year including availability pay. Salaries were slightly higher in selected areas where the prevailing local pay level was higher.

According to the International City-County Management Association's annual Police and Fire Personnel, Salaries and Expenditures Survey, average salaries for sworn full-time positions in 2004 were as follows:

	Minimum annual base salary	*Maximum annual base salary*
Police chief	$72,924	$92,983
Deputy chief	61,110	76,994
Police captain	60,908	75,497
Police lieutenant	56,115	67,580
Police sergeant	49,895	59,454
Police corporal	41,793	51,661

Total earnings for local, State and special police and detectives frequently exceed the stated salary because of payments for overtime, which can be significant. In addition to the common benefits—paid vacation, sick leave and medical and life insurance—most police and sheriffs' departments provide officers with special allowances for uniforms. Because police officers usually are covered by liberal pension plans, many retire at half-pay after 25 or 30 years of service.

Police Jobs

Growing concerns over the quality of life especially with crime, increased government revenues in a strong global economy and a shortage of qualified candidates have contributed to a demand for police and other law enforcement candidates through out the world. A more security-conscious society and growing concern about drug-related crimes, also contribute to the increasing demand for police services. This has opened a gateway of opportunities for the Indians, who look forward to a successful career as Police officers.

Career Opportunities

Exciting and rewarding opportunities exist for Indians to specialize in the many diverse areas of police work, such as the Criminal Investigation Department, Firearms Unit, Dogs Section, Air Operations and more. At national and international level, one can join the Police Force as:

Police Officers/Detectives

Police and detectives enforce laws, catch criminals, collect evidence and testify in court.

Criminal Investigation Department (CID)/Federal Bureau of Investigation (FBI)

Their main role is to investigate serious crime and to act upon intelligence, which can lead to the arrest and prosecution of persistent offenders.

Dog Handler

Officers aiming to become dog handlers go through a rigorous evaluation procedure and receive intensive training once selected for this role.

Firearms Unit

They are trained in the use of firearms and are drafted in to support operations, which require armed assistance.

Fraud Investigation Unit

It deals with company business fraud, major deceptions and corruption allegations and also provides assistance and guidance for area detectives on various matters pertaining to fraud investigation.

Special Branch

Special Branch exists primarily to acquire intelligence for the protection of national security, in particular protection against terrorism, espionage, sabotage, proliferation of weapons of mass destruction and from actions intended to overthrow democracy by political, industrial or violent means.

Traffic Unit

They ensure road safety by enforcing traffic laws, including those relating to speeding and drink driving.

Forensic Expert

Forensic Science is rapidly progressing in the new millennium. The modern crime detection technique keeps the investigators one step ahead of criminals.

Related Occupations

Police and detectives maintain law and order, collect evidence and information and conduct investigations and surveillance. Workers in related occupations include correctional officers, private detectives and investigators.

Eligibility

Different countries have various selection procedures for recruiting Police Personnel. However, the candidate must be a graduate and Getting hired for a law enforcement position demands a graduate degree and include lots of tests & evaluations. These tests are administered in a sequence to be determined by the respective law enforcement agency of the country.

The Police—A Team Strengthened by Differences

Becoming a Police Officer is not merely a job it's a way of life! For that reason it takes a special sort of person to meet the demands that modern policing places upon them and to achieve the high standards that the public expect and deserve. Anyone who can meet those demands will embark upon a career that is both rewarding and stimulating.

Recruitment and Training

To become a Police Officer, candidates must be aged over 18 with good health and eyesight and have a high standard of physical fitness. There are no minimum restrictions on height requirements.

Applicants need to have a good general education but formal academic qualifications are not normally required. What is required is the potential to become a Police Officer after undergoing a period of comprehensive training.

All Police Officers go through the same basic training programme and serve their first two years as probationary constables.

Specialist Posts: A Police career offers a variety of opportunities at all ranks. Uniformed officers serving a diverse community are a vital part of the Police service and after successfully completing two years as a probationary constable, Police Officers can apply to move into specialised units such as CID, traffic, horses and dog section and child protection.

Advancement

Officers are entitled to take the promotion examination to become a Sergeant after their probationary period and officers of exceptional ability can apply for the accelerated promotion scheme which gives an opportunity to rise quickly through the various ranks.

University graduates with the potential to reach high rank can be considered for a place on the Accelerated Promotion Scheme for Graduates.

The Police—Serving the Community

Whatever work the police do—from directing traffic to football crowd security, from preventing organised crime to detective work with hi-tech scientific back-up—they do for us. Their duty is based around the needs of the community to be protected from crime, the effects of crime and the fear of crime.

In Britain, policing has developed over the centuries into today's professional police service, serving the community, preventing crime and apprehending criminals. For many years there was no such thing as a 'police force'—it was the duty of everyone in the country to catch criminals. There was not always law and order.

The police in Britain deal with about six million 999 emergency calls a year and are faced with more and more complicated crimes. Recent developments to help them target resources and meet the ever-changing challenges of protecting society include:

taking a fresh look at how to prevent and tackle crime;

working in closer partnership with the community;

streamlining its own management structures; and

using the latest technology

The support and consent of the public are essential to effective policing.

Police Forces

There are 43 police forces and more than 127,000 police officers in England and Wales—about one for every 400 people.

The size of individual forces depends on both population and area. Where fewer people live, one force can cover a larger area, for example Devon and Cornwall.

At the head of each force is the Chief Constable (except in London, where the Metropolitan Police and the City of London Police are each headed by a Commissioner). A Chief Constable is responsible for the day to day management of policing in the area and for overall command of the operations the police carry out on the public's behalf. To keep policing in tune with local needs, the areas are broken down into Divisions, each under the leadership of a Superintendent. Each Divisional headquarters controls a network of local stations. Home beat, crime prevention and other community officers work from individual police stations, which also have their own criminal investigation department (CID), police cells and communications centres.

To create a police service that reflects the community it serves, forces encourage women and people from ethnic minority communities to apply for jobs. Of the 127,000 or more police officers in England and Wales, more than 18,500 are women and more than 2,300 officers are from ethnic minorities. In 1995, Pauline Clare of Lancashire Constabulary became the first women Chief Constable. In 1997, Wiltshire Constabulary became the second force to appoint a woman as Chief Constable. In May 1996 Tariq Ghaffur became the first ethnic minority officer to be appointed as an Assistant Chief Constable, with Lancashire Constabulary.

London's Metropolitan Police is the largest single force. Each of its five areas is about the size of a complete force elsewhere in the country. Its headquarters are at New Scotland Yard. The name Scotland Yard had become so strongly linked in the public's imagination with the Metropolitan Police that when they built a new centre they took the name with them. Each area of London has its own operational and administrative responsibilities. The City of London has its own police force.

Police Constables

Police Constable (PC) is the key rank in the police service. Nearly three-quarters of all the police officers in England and

Wales are police constables. PCs do the bulk of what people usually think of as police work—patrolling the streets on foot or in cars, answering calls for assistance, giving advice to the public, dealing with disturbances, handling enquiries, dealing with arrested people at the police station. PCs have to deal with a whole range of crimes, from violent offences and burglary to shoplifting and car crime.

It is the constable who meets the public and usually has to make the first—often vital—decisions on the spot at an incident. Constables need an understanding of the community in which they serve, they need good communication skills and have to be hardworking and understanding.

All police officers start their careers as PCs and many stay as PCs because it gives them the chance to be in touch with the public and be involved with front-line policing all the time.

To join the police, a candidate must be:

aged over 18½;

of a high standard of physical fitness, with good health and eyesight; and

a British citizen, a Commonwealth citizen with no restrictions on his or her stay here, or a citizen of the Irish Republic.

All police officers go through the same basic training programme, serving for their first two years as a probationary constables. They train at one of the six national police training centres. Metropolitan Police Officers train at the Hendon Training Establishment. The Police Staff College at Bramshill trains officers for promotion and to become effective leaders in the police service.

Personal and Protective Services

On the Job:

- Protective services workers are those who work as a team to protect people and property from harm. Personal service workers provide personal services such as home care, childcare or cosmetic services. In all cases, they work with the public.

- Many personal services workers are self-employed. Many childcare workers operate home-based centers. Hairstylists and barbers often lease a chair in a salon.
- Advancement into management positions for personal and protective services workers is common, but usually after significant work experience. In police or fire departments, passing an exam is required for most promotions.
- Protective services workers, like police officers, firefighters or security guards, often work long and irregular hours. Their jobs are dangerous and complex, requiring them to work and sometimes live, as a team.
- Personal service workers are less likely to work evening and night shifts but often work weekend hours.

What Skills Do You Need?

- Critical-thinking abilities and patience to handle hectic and stressful situations.
- Decisiveness for making good on-the-spot judgments about people and situations.
- Listening and speaking skills to effectively understand and relay information.
- People-orientation skills for dealing with a wide variety of people in varied situations.
- Selective attention for protective services workers to notice details about things going on around them.
- Stamina for workers who have to stand for long periods of time or endure long, stressful work shifts.
- Time management skills to adequately provide services to the public within time constraints.

Job Outlook: Good

There's always a need for police officers, firefighters and security guards. Public demand for hairstylists and childcare workers is also consistently high. Layoffs of certain protective service occupations, like firefighters, are rare because they are considered essential. Experts say when budget cuts do occur, it usually means less equipment and not fewer jobs. So even if the economy slows, there will still be openings. Turnover is high, especially in personal services. A large number of people in personal and protective services enter and leave jobs each year because of burnout, low pay or the desire for additional education.

Most occupations in this field require less than 2 years of school or on-the-job training with good opportunities to gain work-related skills.

Career Opportunities in Security

While the information contained in this brochure will be of interest to anyone who wants to learn more about the field of security, it has been prepared primarily for the following categories of individuals: o Individuals seeking to pursue a degree in security management, asset protection, or a related discipline.

- o Individuals entering the security field after obtaining a degree in security management, asset protection, or a related discipline.
- o Individuals already in the security field who seek a management-track position after obtaining a degree in security management, asset protection, or a related discipline.
- o Individuals transitioning from other careers into the public or private security field who seek a management-track position.

This booklet has been extensively revised in light of the security environment which exists as a result of the September 11, 2001, attacks and subsequent events.

Information from a number of security specialties has been compiled to give the reader a better idea of the prerequisites for entering management-track supervisory and non-supervisory positions in those specialties.

In addition to the entry-level data, there is information concerning the duties of mid-level management and non-management personnel in those specialties.

Unless otherwise indicated, in dealing with these specialties the following terminology has been used:

- o "Management" refers to the direction of activity at the second-line supervisory level or above.
- o "Non-management" refers to non-supervisory line positions, first-line supervisor positions and staff positions.
- o "Entry-level" refers to management-track supervisory and nonsupervisory positions.
- o "Mid-level" refers to management and non-management level positions at the branch, area, region, or division level.
- o "Executive-level" refers to management positions in charge of corporate or agency-level activities.

What is Security?

A Dynamic Industry: Security is one of the fastest-growing professional careers worldwide. A career in the security field provides a multitude of opportunities.

These opportunities range from entry-level security officer positions to investigators specializing in specific areas and managers and directors of security at major corporations and organizations around the world.

The demand for heightened security is being increased by theft of information, workplace violence, terrorism and economic crime.

The security industry in the U.S. is a $100 billion a year business and growing. Opportunities exist at all levels within the security industry.

All businesses, no matter how small, have security concerns such as fraud, theft, computer hacking, economic espionage, or workplace violence. All organizations need to protect themselves from activities that disrupt their normal operations. Each specialty within the security field has its own requirements and issues. Shoplifting continues to be a problem for retail organizations, while hospitals face privacy rights issues and hotels have to reconcile fire and safety regulations with security requirements. In addition, government and private industry have differing security needs. Individuals wishing to pursue a career in a security specialty field should become more knowledgeable of the latest trends, issues and concerns within that specialty.

A Diverse Industry

In today's downsizing corporate world and changing environment, it is essential for students and individuals seeking career changes to be able to identify opportunities in the security marketplace. Women, minorities and physically challenged individuals are becoming valuable resources for organizations in need of security professionals.

Students seeking careers in security should pursue course work in security, computer science, electronics, business management, law, police science, personnel and information management. Information from various security specialties has been compiled to give you a better idea of the credentials and requirements for entering a particular industry. In addition to the entry-level information, demographics associated with security professionals in each industry, as well as desired requirements for entering into a management position, are provided.

Proprietary or Contract Security

Proprietary security personnel are employed directly by the organization whose assets are being protected. As a general rule, proprietary security operations occur in businesses, institutions and agencies large enough to warrant full-time attention to the issues of assets protection. The security services industry provides security products and services under contract to an organization.

Equipment suppliers include a wide range of firms that sell, install and maintain equipment such as access control, intrusion detection, protective lighting and closed circuit television systems. There are other contract firms that provide uniformed security officers, conduct investigations, perform risk assessments, design security systems, transport high-value shipments, protect high-risk personnel and offer other security services.

Law Enforcement vs. Security

Law enforcement focuses on reaction to crime and the enforcement of public laws and ordinances. Security professionals, on the other hand, are more proactive and focus on identifying and preventing a problem before it occurs. In addition, security personnel are more likely to be involved in protecting assets and carrying out an organization's policies and procedures than in enforcing criminal statutes.

Public or Private Arenas

Many people think of the security field as being synonymous with the private sector and to a large extent, that is true. However, there are many security opportunities in government agencies, particularly at the federal level. Public sector security personnel perform many of the same functions as their proprietary counterparts in the private sector.

Academic Programmes in Security

A number of colleges and universities offer security education programmes of one degree or another at the associate, baccalaureate, or graduate level. Some of these offer a major in security management, asset protection, or a similar discipline while others offer an area of concentration, a minor or a series of courses in security.

Some institutions, particularly at the community college level, may offer weekend seminars in selected security topics.

Security is a business function and is not a subset or spin-off of the criminal justice system. Students seeking careers in security should pursue course work in security management, business, computer science, law, terrorism studies, emergency management and personnel and information management.

Students should also seek involvement in internships, co-ops or work study programmes with security employers. In addition, students should seek out security professionals who work in the security specialties or disciplines the student may wish to pursue, with a view to learning more about the specialty through activities such as site visits and networking.

Certifications

Certifications from ASIS International (ASIS): Certification is a significant voluntary investment in a security professional's future and it offers an edge in the increasingly competitive security job market. Companies, contractors and governments are now taking additional steps to ensure that they are hiring or working with the most skilled and knowledgeable individuals.

Board certifications from ASIS offer them a screening tool that has the backing and credibility of the leading organization in the world for security professionals. And for individuals, certifications could make the difference when bidding on contracts, applying for jobs, or transitioning to private security. Certifications are objective means of distinguishing competent security practitioners from those who claim to be. The three board-certified designations of ASIS all meet stringent, internationally accepted requirements for education, experience and examination. Being certified allows you to:

- demonstrate your knowledge and skills
- gain instant professional credibility
- differentiate yourself from others
- enhance your personal and professional development
- increase your earnings potential

ASIS Offers three Certifications: Certified Protection Professional (CPP) is the preeminent designation awarded to individuals whose primary responsibilities are in security management and who have demonstrated advanced knowledge in security solutions and best business practices. CPPs must have nine years of security experience, with at least three of those years in responsible charge of a security function; or a bachelor's degree and seven years of experience, with at least three of those years in responsible charge of a security function. Eligible individuals must then pass an examination.

Professional Certified Investigator (PCI) is a technical designation awarded to those individuals whose primary responsibilities are to conduct investigations and who have demonstrated in-depth operational knowledge and competence in this area. PCIs must have a high school diploma or GED equivalent and five years of investigations experience, two of which must be in case management. Eligible individuals must then pass an examination.

Physical Security Professional (PSP) is a technical designation awarded to those individuals whose primary responsibilities are to conduct physical security surveys, design integrated security systems, or install, operate, or maintain those systems and who have demonstrated in-depth operational knowledge and competence in this area. PSPs must have a high school diploma or GED equivalent and five years of physical security experience. Eligible individuals must then pass an examination.

Other Certifications: In addition to ASIS certifications, a number of specialized security and security-related certifications are offered by other organizations. A select few are mentioned in this booklet, if appropriate to an industry sector.

Certified Fraud Examiner (CFE) offered by the Association of Certified Fraud Examiners.

Certified Healthcare Protection Administrator (CHPA) offered by the International Association of Healthcare Security and Safety Professionals (IAHSSP).

Certified Information Systems Security Professional (CISSP) offered by the International Information Systems Security Certification Consortium (ISC).

Certified Lodging Security Supervisor (CLSS) and Certified Lodging Security Director (CLSD) offered by the Educational Institute of the American Hotel and Lodging Association (AH&LA),

Global Information Assurance Certificate (GIAC) offered by SANS Institute.

Industrial Security Professional (ISP) offered by the National Classification Management Society (NCMS).

Security Disciplines: The security field is divided into a number of specialized disciplines. In a large organization, a security professional may work full-time in one of these disciplines. In smaller organizations, a security professional may need to have some proficiency in each of them. These disciplines may be found in most of the security specialty areas.

Physical Security focuses on the protection of people, property and facilities through the use of security forces, security systems and security procedures. Physical security personnel oversee proprietary or contract uniformed security operations, identify security system requirements, assess internal and external threats to assets and develop policies, plans, procedures and physical safeguards to counter those threats. Physical security can include the use of barriers, alarms, locks, access control systems, protective lighting, closed circuit televisions and other state-of-the-art security technology.

Information Security involves safeguarding sensitive information. Although information security has traditionally been associated with protection of U.S. Government classified information, it can also include privacy data, proprietary information, contractual information and intellectual property. Information security deals with issues such as who should access the data and how the data is stored, controlled, marked, disseminated and disposed of.

Personnel Security deals with ensuring the integrity and reliability of an organization's workforce. Personnel security encompasses background investigations, drug testing and other pre-employment screening techniques, as well as adjudication of results and granting security clearances and other information access privileges.

Information Systems Security involves maintaining the confidentiality, reliability and availability of data created, stored, processed and/or transmitted via automated information systems. Information systems security personnel develop procedures and safeguards to protect against hackers and other unauthorized efforts to access data, viruses and a number of other threats to information systems.

Homeland Security—In the aftermath of September 11, 2001, there has been significant emphasis on "homeland security." The term has been applied to activities ranging from, but not limited to, the protection of U.S. airspace to the response to chemical or biological attacks and from protection against cyber attacks to the security of rail lines and seaports from terrorist attacks. Unfortunately, there is little consensus on exactly what the term means. Since "homeland security" has such a broad connotation, it is treated in this booklet as an emerging crosscutting discipline rather than a security specialty.

Critical Infrastructure Protection (CIP) is another cross-cutting specialty that has emerged in recent years. Many would describe it as protecting the information systems that control elements of the infrastructure, such as petroleum pipelines, telecommunications systems and nuclear power plants, from terrorist attacks.

Others consider it as covering the protection of not only the information systems that operate and control the infrastructure, but the infrastructure itself, whether it be a bridge, a telephone switching centre or a food processing plant. Due to the varying connotations applied to CIP and the extensive scope of the infrastructure, it too is treated in this booklet as an emerging cross-cutting discipline rather than a security specialty.

Security Speciality Areas

To the average person the idea of a career in security may be unappealing. The tendency for many people is to think only in terms of uniformed security officers on patrol, monitoring alarms, or controlling access to a facility. Those who may be interested in a career as a security professional need to understand that a wide range of administrative, technical, supervisory and managerial opportunities also exist in the security field.

To gain entrance into the security field at the non-management entry-level, there are some typical prerequisites. They include having a high school education or above, having no criminal record, being 18+ years of age and having obtained or be in the process of obtaining some general security knowledge or experience. For example, many states require a certain amount of training before an individual can be employed as an armed or unarmed security officer. Many of the duties performed by individuals in these positions are likely to be similar, regardless of the security industry sector in which the individual is employed. Those duties can include such activities as routine patrolling, public relations, controlling access to facilities and basic report writing.

Duties performed in entry-level management-track positions can vary significantly, depending upon the specialty. Duties performed in mid-level positions, regardless of the specialty, may include typical responsibilities such as planning, organizing, staffing, controlling, budgeting, coordinating, presenting, directing and writing reports. In addition to these functions, mid-level positions may include specialty-specific responsibilities. The following areas represent some of the specialties within the security field. Each specialty area provides a brief description of the specialty in addition to prerequisites for entering management-track supervisory and non-supervisory positions in those specialties. In addition to the entry-level data, there is information concerning the duties of mid-level management and non-management personnel in those specialties.

Banking and Financial Services Security

Careers in this field include those associated with banking (including retail banking, mortgage, credit/debit cards, internet banking, commercial and consumer lending), stock brokerages, insurance companies and other financial institutions. As a key component to the critical infrastructure of every nation, the financial services industry is regulated by various government agencies. Financial institution security directors and managers must deal with a wide variety of concerns including theft, fraud, workplace violence, information security, investigations, executive protection, business continuity and physical security in order to adequately protect their institution. Security managers must be effective leaders within their organization and able to successfully influence change.

Because of the increasing complexity of the financial services industry, companies continue to seek the best and the brightest from law enforcement agencies, colleges and universities and from within other private sector companies, both within and outside of the financial services sector.

Entry-level: management positions in financial services generally require a degree in business, finance, or criminal justice from an accredited institution as well as three to five years experience either in law enforcement or security. The salary range for entry-level positions is $35,000 to $65,000, depending on many factors.

Mid-level: management positions, requiring expertise in multiple security disciplines, generally require a bachelor's degree in an appropriate discipline, as well as three to seven years of demonstrated success in the field. Professional certifications such as the CPP and CFE are often desired as an indicator of professionalism and qualifications. The salary range for mid-level management positions is $40,000 to $100,000.

Commercial Real Estate Security

Security in the commercial real estate industry provides opportunities not only in commercial high-rise office buildings but also in residential buildings and shopping malls. Commercial real estate ranges from the environment in which people spend their working hours to where they live and where they shop. Each venue has challenges and aspects that while not unique to the security industry, must be addressed in an appropriate and cost effective manner. Regardless of the venue, the primary focus is on personnel and asset protection. This is accomplished by solid liaison with local law enforcement, knowledge of staffing requirements and electronic security systems. All vulnerable areas of a facility must be identified and protected with appropriate resources

Entry-level: Management positions generally require a degree in security or criminal justice from an accredited institution as well as one to two years experience in law enforcement or security. The salary range for entry-level positions is $40,000 to $50,000, depending on many factors.

Mid-level: Management positions, requiring expertise in multiple security disciplines, generally require a security or criminal justice degree in an appropriate discipline, as well as five to seven years of demonstrated success in the field.

Professional certifications such as the CPP and CFE are often desired as an indicator of professionalism and qualifications.

Cultural Properties

Museum and Cultural Properties' common denominator is making a unique contribution to the public by collecting, preserving and interpreting the things of this world. Their numbers include both governmental and private museums of anthropology, art history and natural history, aquariums, arboreta, art centers, botanical gardens, children's museums, historic sites, nature centers, planetariums, science and technology centers, zoos, libraries and archives. Protection and security service careers in cultural properties provide paths to security operations (security and/or law enforcement officers, investigators, supervisors and managers), technical services (physical and electronic security specialists), fire protection specialists, health and safety services, administrative (payroll, recruiting, training) and visitor services.

Entry-level: Management positions desire an associate's or bachelor's degree. Protection-related and/or liberal arts & humanities fields of study are acceptable. Past work experience in public service or educational tourism is desirable. Salary levels range generally between $20,000 to $40,000 per year.

Mid-level: Management positions desire a bachelor's degree appropriate to the chosen career path. Operations managers = security or criminal justice related. Technical managers = electrical and/or locksmith related. Health and Safety`= science related. Administrative = liberal arts and business related. Three to five years related work experience is normally a pre-requisite for mid-level management positions.

Educational Institution Security

The primary objective of an educational institution security programme is to educate the campus community on the potential for crime both on and off-campus. The central themes of a campus crime prevention programme are awareness, self-protection and prevention. Educational institution security has been a growing concern throughout the 1990s. With increasing publicity about campus crime, it is likely that the trend will continue. The level of violence on and around educational institutions has brought about a need for security at public and private educational institutions at both the elementary and secondary school levels. Many educational institutions operate a commissioned police department which makes police academy training or law enforcement certification a requirement. Interested college students can often enter this field by working for campus security departments on a part-time basis.

Entry-level: Management positions do not require an academic degree; however, a degree, general security experience, specialty-specific experience and professional certification are all desired. The salary range is from the low $40,000's to $50,000.

Mid-level: Management positions also do not require an academic degree; however, a degree, general security experience, specialty-specific experience and professional certification are all desired.

Gaming/Wagering Security

As the world of gaming continues to grow and change, one thing has always remained true: at its core, gaming is entertainment. With advancing technology in the gaming and wagering industry and the tremendous growth of the industry itself, comes new opportunities and responsibilities for security practitioners. Gaming's entertainment value requires security practitioners to provide adequate security while allowing guests and gamblers to experience this unique and ever-changing environment.

Entry-level: Management positions require a high school diploma or equivalent and a minimum of one year experience in law enforcement, security, or surveillance systems operation, with Emergency Management Training (EMT) certification and a license to carry a firearm, if applicable. Previous gaming experience is preferred. Salary range is approximately $8 to $15 per hour (or $16,640 to $31,200 per year) depending on qualifications, certifications, licensing and gaming jurisdiction.

Mid-level: management positions require a minimum of two to three years in law enforcement, casino security, or surveillance systems operation, as well as EMT certification and a license to carry a firearm, if applicable. A degree in criminal justice or a related field and a CPP or other ASIS certification are preferred.

Government/Industrial Security

Government/industrial security professionals protect a variety of special categories of classified information in accordance with the National Industrial Security Programme (NISP). The NISP is a security partnership between the Government and industry that was created to safeguard Federal Government classified information that is released to contractors, licensees and grantees of the U.S. Government. Personnel within this specialty must meet the requirements, restrictions and other safeguards within the constraints of applicable law and the Code of Federal Regulations, necessary to prevent unauthorized disclosure of classified information released by U.S. Government departments and agencies to their contractors.

Entry-level: Management positions require an academic degree from an accredited institution and three to five years experience in the government or industrial security field, preferably in a supervisory role. Necessary specialty-specific training or experience includes successful application of security regulations and some exposure to security budgetary issues. Professional certifications or a documented record of involvement in professional security activities or training and education are a plus. Other prerequisites include a proven, positive track record in problem solving and customer relations. The salary range is from $55,000 to $75,000, depending on a variety of factors.

Mid-level: Management positions require a baccalaureate or advanced degree from an accredited institution and five to 10 years experience in the government or industrial security field with supervisory or previous managerial experience. Necessary specialty-specific training or experience includes professional certification (CPP, PCI, PSP, ISP, CFE, etc.) preferred, or a documented record of professional security training from U.S. Government-sponsored training sessions. Other preferred prerequisites include a proven track record in problem solving, policy development, customer relations, successful application of security regulations and budgetary development.

Healthcare Security

Security in the healthcare industry provides opportunities not only in hospitals, but also in long-term care facilities, clinics and nursing homes. The healthcare industry is a multi-faceted, challenging field, which includes dealing with immobile, unconscious, emotionally disturbed and distraught patients and their families and providing security to gift shops, cafeterias, parking lots, pharmacies and emergency departments. Employee investigation plays a substantial role in asset protection. The work environment is oriented toward patient protection and service and may also include safety and community emergency management. Security opportunities may include being a security supervisor, security director, or public relations person in charge of interacting with the medical community as well as patients.

Entry-level: Management positions require a bachelor's degree in security or a related field, or equivalent experience. Two years of security supervisory experience are required and experience in health care security or customer service is desired. In addition, training and experience in business management and human resources are desired. Salary range is $30,000 to $50,000.

Mid-level: Management positions require a bachelor's degree in security or a related field, or equivalent experience. A master's degree is desired. Five years as a senior supervisor or entry-level manager are required and experience in healthcare security or customer service is desired. In addition, training and experience in business management and human resources are desired. The CHPA and CPP are preferred designations.

Information Systems Security

Information Systems Security (ISS) is an important and constantly growing security career field which reflects today's reliance on data communications, the Internet and e-commerce. Systems security professionals are responsible for safeguarding hardware, software applications and business processes while ensuring that authorized users comply with established security policies and procedures. Depending on their assignments, systems security professionals will also be directly or indirectly responsible for the business continuity and disaster recovery plans of their organizations.

The technical complexity of systems security requires a thorough knowledge of threats against computer operations, networking (including TCP/IP, UDP and ICMP protocols) and internal and network perimeter defenses. Systems security professionals are expected to understand common defenses such as firewalls, intrusion detection/prevention, anti-virus, router access control lists and methods to control attacks across all seven layers of the ISO Open Systems Interconnect (OSI) Model. Systems security professionals will find opportunities in both commercial and Government organizations; most Government opportunities will require a security clearance appropriate to the sensitivity of the organization and data processed.

Entry-level: Managers traditionally require a four-year degree in computer science or a related field, at least four years of experience in systems security and evidence of success in the career field. Desired certifications include the CPP, CISSP and/ or SANS GIAC. Additional vendor certifications for particular security products are also helpful. Typical job titles include Security Analyst, Security Consultant, Network Security Specialist and Security Team Leader. Salary range is $40,000 to $80,000, depending on organization and location.

Mid-level: Managers normally require a four-year degree (or graduate degree depending on the organization), at least 10 years of experience in direct computer security roles and evidence of success in at least two different types of organizations. Desired certifications include the CPP, CISSP, SANS GIAC and other related industry and vendor certifications. Some mid-level managers have recently added IT audit skills to their resumes which reflects the current emphasis on compliance programmes. Job titles include Network Security Manager, Information Assurance Manager, Chief Information Security Officer, or IT Audit Manager.

Investigations

The process of investigation is an important function in both the public and private sectors. It is a very broad field and includes many sub-specialties. Background investigation is an important aspect and involves gathering information used to determine the level of trust that should be granted to an individual. In the case of an organization, the term "due diligence" is generally used and is usually performed prior to a merger, acquisition, or establishment of a significant business agreement. In the commercial sector, investigators determine the facts in cases of theft, employee misconduct, computer system abuse, sabotage, threats and potential workplace violence.

They also ferret out fraud, waste, abuse, financial mismanagement and corporate ethics violations. Investigators use a variety of tools and techniques such as interviewing, evidence collection and processing, physical and technical surveillance, computer forensics, database searches and crime analysis algorithms. Like most security measures, an effective investigations programme serves both as a deterrent to crime and a response once a crime has been committed.

Entry-level: Management positions generally prefer a four-year degree. Criminal Justice and criminology are popular but a business degree is acceptable. Two-year degrees can help the entry-level aspirant. Depending on the position, no experience may be required but specialty areas usually require at least one to two years in the respective area. Experience from police or security investigations is taken into consideration. Salary range is $35,000 to $55,000, depending on many factors.

Mid-level: Management positions, requiring expertise in multiple investigative and business disciplines, generally require a degree in an appropriate discipline, as well as five or more years of demonstrated success in the field. Professional certifications such as the PCI and CFE are often desired as an indicator of professionalism and qualifications. Mid-level investigative managers may expect a salary range from $60,000 to $85,000.

Lodging and Hospitality Security

Since the terrorist attacks in 2001, the lodging industry has increased its interest in and dedicated additional resources to, the security function. Hotel owners and property managers are cognizant of the need to protect their guests and assets, in order to have their properties perceived as safe havens. To meet this need, there is increased emphasis on recruiting and hiring knowledgeable security professionals. Lodging security's primary focus is on the protection of life and, secondarily, the protection of assets. Hotel security positions generally pay well and include excellent benefits. The work environment is professional, demanding and complex, while routine responsibilities include extensive interaction with guests and employees. The industry is slowly rising from its post-September 11, 2001, slump and the outlook, in general, looks promising with career opportunities continuing to expand.

Entry-level: Management positions often require a certificate in security management and/or a bachelor's degree, as well as one to three years of general employment, plus one year of lodging-specific security service. The CLSS designation is preferred but not required. The salary range, depending on the size of the property, is $35,000 to $50,000.

Mid-level: Management positions require a bachelor's degree, three to five years of general employment, plus one year of lodging-specific security service. In addition, successful managers should be computer proficient, articulate and possess excellent interpersonal skills. The CLSD and CPP designations are preferred.

Manufacturing Security

Manufacturers make products which, in turn, are sold either to wholesalers, distributors, or directly to consumers. Professionals within the manufacturing security specialty are responsible for issues involving not only sales transactions, but transport issues, ordering and purchasing of raw materials and the protection of resources against loss or theft. Manufacturers are becoming increasingly aware of the potential for loss. Prevention of loss can be accomplished only through employing competent security directors and managers who can help integrate the security function into the total operation rather than allowing it to remain isolated. Depending on the products being manufactured, individuals in this specialty may work in a variety of environments, including exposure to varying weather conditions and involvement with chemical processing areas.

Entry-level: Management positions generally require at least an associate's degree and often a bachelor's degree. Most positions require two-plus years of general security experience and may require some specialty-specific training or experience. A CPP designation is preferred for many positions. The salary range for most positions is $30,000 to 50,000.

Mid-level: Management positions generally require a bachelor's degree and five-plus years of general security experience and may require some specialty-specific training or experience. A CPP designation is required or desired for many positions.

Retail Loss Prevention

The most common perception of the general public regarding the function of retail loss prevention (LP) departments is that they are primarily involved in the recruitment of store detectives or "shoplifter catchers". While it is true that many retailers hire store detectives to prevent and apprehend shoplifters, the responsibilities of LP professionals and the role they play in the overall profitability of the company makes this one of the most critically important functions within retail organizations. Retail companies are plagued by theft and fraud from both internal and external sources.

Entry-level retail loss prevention positions generally involve undercover shoplifting apprehensions, LP or safety auditing and many other such functions and can lead to rapid advancement into more lucrative positions of responsibility. Retail LP positions offer valuable work experience. Part-time work as a store detective is an excellent job while in college.

Retail LP managers have responsibility for overseeing the store detectives and also addressing and resolving internal theft concerns. Depending on the size of the stores and the company, an LP manager may be responsible for the LP functions within a single store, or responsible for overseeing LP at a number of locations within a chain.

Entry-level: Management positions generally require an undergraduate degree from an accredited institution as well as three to five years experience in retail loss prevention. Salary range is $25,000 to $38,000, depending on many factors.

Mid-level: Management positions, requiring expertise in multiple security disciplines, require an undergraduate degree in an appropriate discipline, as well as five to eight years of demonstrated success in the field in relevant retail-related LP functions. The CPP and CFE are the preferred designations.

Security Engineering and Design

Architects and engineers create environments for people to work and live in. These environments are created in response to programme, budgetary, legal and aesthetic requirements. To date, security has often been incorporated into design as an afterthought. Today, managers have learned that they must contain costs and work with knowledgeable professionals who can design security into either a new facility or the renovation of an older one. The costs of incorporating security features and systems skyrocket if security, like any other building feature or system, is considered after a facility is built or renovated. Inadequate security in today's climate increases the potential for loss. Reduction of loss can be accomplished through the employment of knowledgeable security professionals, who may also be licensed professional architects and engineers that practice in the field of security. This expertise can help integrate the security function into an environment at the conceptual stage while working with rapid technology innovations. The discipline is to determine the functional requirements and to let the experts handle the options.

Entry-level: Positions for security consultants to architecture/engineering firms as well as architects and engineers generally require at least a bachelor's degree. Most security-related positions require some minimal experience in the field. For advancement, security design and/or engineering training as well as some specialty-specific training or experience could be required. The salary range for most positions is $30,000 to $60,000.

Mid-level: Positions generally require a bachelor's degree and five to seven years of security and/or engineering experience beyond the area of study and should require some additional specialty-specific training or experience. Professional licensing for engineers and architects should factor heavily for a mid-level position and a PSP certification would be appropriate to indicate proficiency. Licensed and certified professionals tend to have a more global view of projects, which allows them to integrate security better with other elements of building and site design. The CPP designation is not required, but it certainly is a plus.

Security Sales, Equipment and Services

This security specialty can be stimulating, challenging and financially rewarding. New security-related products and services have resulted from emerging threats and evolving high technology and the number of companies offering various security services has grown as a result. Sales positions can range from products such as barriers, alarm systems, sophisticated biometrics, closed circuit television (CCTV), biological detection equipment and risk management software, to uniformed security services. Sales and service personnel may be employed by a product manufacturer to sell that particular company's products or by an independent dealer that represents a variety of products. Entry-level positions may involve making sales calls, handling advertising queries, staffing and organizing sales booths, demonstrating products and providing input on government proposal requests. In addition to typical management functions, mid-level management responsibilities may include directing and motivating sales personnel, organizing sales and marketing campaigns, preparing and presenting proposals, conducting briefings and managing a trade show booth.

Entry-level: Management positions may call for a college degree, depending on the size and nature of the employer. It's recommended that broad-based education and experience be achieved in areas such as accounting, industrial engineering, management, marketing, human resources, communications, statistics, or labour relations. The nature and extent of the desired education and experience and the entry-level salary range can vary depending on the type of product or service being provided, the size of the vendor and other factors.

Mid-level: Management positions require the experience to perform a wide range of functions as indicated above. The ability to effectively deal with a range of people and the capability to present information verbally and in writing are particularly important.

Transportation Security

Security in the transportation industry extends throughout all passenger and cargo modes including aviation, trucking, buses, railroads and maritime. It is further differentiated in asset based and non-based carriers, infrastructure, shippers, receivers, tourism and business travelers. Infrastructure includes seaports, airports, airplane hangers, warehouses, passenger terminals, highways and intermodal container transfer facilities. It is a multi-faceted and challenging endeavor that touches the core of our economy—our transportation system. Today, terrorism and cargo theft present a greater threat within our global supply chain than any time in recent history. Passengers feel the tension of heightened security. Airlines and airports are heightening security to prevent terrorist acts.

Ports and terminals are taking steps to control access. Railroads and trucking companies are implementing security policies that mitigate risk. Sophisticated cargo theft occurs in all modes. Transportation security professionals are challenged with the requirement to protect critical transportation infrastructure without hindering the free flow of commerce and passengers. This industry employs professionals in both government and private sector organizations.

Entry-level: Management positions may require a two-year or four-year degree in security or law enforcement, depending on the nature of the position. For many positions, experience in investigations may be desired, if not required. Cargo security experience and knowledge of security systems, such as CCTV and intrusion detection systems, can also be a requirement. Coursework in distribution and logistics is a plus for companies transporting cargo. Exposure to passenger transportation is a plus for companies with business or tourist travel movement. Salaries can range from $30,000 to $50,000.

Mid-level: Management positions will typically require a bachelor's degree or equivalent professional experience. Depending on the nature of the position, experience in investigations, security systems, security force management and cargo security operations will also be required. Experience in distribution and logistics operations will be considered. Operational experience in public or private sector passenger systems is a plus. Knowledge of Federal Government security initiatives is preferred.

Utility and Nuclear Security

Utility operations refer to gas, water, electric and nuclear power plants. Even though sources of power differ; there are common facilities to all utility operations. Electric sources include fossil fuel (gas, oil and coal), water and nuclear generation. Each facility maintains transmission and distribution systems that facilitate bulk transfers of electric, gas and/or water over long distances and a system of smaller pipes and wires designed to distribute the commodity to the end user. Utility security professionals take appropriate measures and perform a range of duties for the protection of people, property, information and other assets in the event of crime, natural disaster, technological emergency, resource shortage, civil disturbance, war, or terrorist activity.

Entry-level: Management positions generally require an associate's degree, preferably in security and five years of security or law enforcement experience. The salary range is $50,000 to $70,000. A CPP (or other ASIS designation) is also preferred.

Mid-level: Management positions generally require a bachelor's degree, preferably in security or business administration and 10 years of security or law enforcement experience. A CPP (or other ASIS designation) is preferred. [Some of the information for this specialty was extracted from Utility Security Operations Management, authored by Clay Higgins and sponsored by the ASIS Utility Security Committee, 1989.]

ASIS International

ASIS International (ASIS) is the preeminent organization in the world for security management professionals who are responsible for protecting people, property and information. For more than 50 years, security professionals have relied on ASIS to provide them with the resources they need to increase their effectiveness and productivity. This has led to consistent growth, so that today, membership in ASIS exceeds 33,000 individuals around the world.

The uniqueness of ASIS allows it to embrace all facets of security, from access control and personnel protection to information technology and global terrorism. Given the interrelatedness of security threats today, this ability to involve all industries and all functions is imperative. Security professionals in varying industries and with different responsibilities need to be able to communicate with each other. ASIS affords them this opportunity.

Founded in 1955 as the American Society for Industrial Security, ASIS has since increased both its size and reach significantly. In 2002, the organization changed its name to ASIS International, reflecting both its worldwide membership and the fact that security has become a global issue that demands a strategic direction based on this broadened view. ASIS also expanded its mission to encompass the establishment, development and promotion of excellence in the security profession.

ASIS provides a wealth of professional development opportunities for its members and other security practitioners through its educational programmes. The organization also offers cutting-edge information resources, such as comprehensive library and career services, unmatched security-related publications, indispensable industry guidelines and studies and the leading periodical in the security industry. Furthermore, ASIS advocates for security and security professionals, aggressively communicating the role, value and concerns of its members and the industry to the business community, government officials, news media and the general public.

Over the years, ASIS has worked effectively to raise the bar for the security profession.

More than a quarter of a century ago, ASIS established a certification programme-the Certified Protection Professional (CPP)-acknowledged worldwide as the highest credential awarded a security professional. Since then, two other certifications-the Professional Certified Investigator (PCI) and the Physical Security Professional (PSP)-have been introduced. Other initiatives include developing relationships with graduate schools of business in order to have security recognized as a business discipline, spearheading the creation of security guidelines to help the private sector safeguard its operations and infrastructure and ensuring that the body of knowledge of the security profession continues to evolve to confront rapidly changing threats worldwide.

ASIS members tackle today's security challenges and anticipate the challenges of tomorrow. And, despite the multiplicity of voices and expertise, all are focused on one common goal: to advance security worldwide.

ASIS members benefit from numerous products and services, all of which are designed to enhance the professional development of security management practitioners and to advance the industry as a whole. For new members, the primary reasons for joining include networking, access to up-to-date information and the opportunity to build a professional reputation within the industry. Annual dues are $150; for full-time students, $25.

ASIS members also receive a subscription to Security Management magazine, the leading magazine in the security industry, which features in-depth analysis and breaking news on a range of critical issues.

Members also have access to the ASIS Career Centre, enabling you to search for jobs online by location, category, or level. All job postings are security-related. In addition, there are a variety of free and fee-based services, ranging from resume critiques, motivational tips and tactics, to career coaching.

Security Jobs

Employment of security officers is expected to grow faster than the average for all occupations through 2012 as concern about crime, vandalism and terrorism continue to increase the need for security. Numerous job openings, all across the world, will stem from employment growth attributable to this desire, for increased security. In addition to full-time job opportunities, the limited training requirements and flexible hours attract many persons seeking part-time or second jobs.

The Demand for guards will also grow as private security firms increasingly perform duties, such as monitoring crowds at airports and providing security in courts, which were formerly handled by government police officers.

Career Opportunities

The security field can be divided into specialized disciplines that provide numerous career options.

Physical Security

Physical security personnel oversee proprietary or contract uniformed security operations, identify security system requirements, assess internal and external threats to assets and develop policies, plans, procedures and physical safeguards to counter those threats.

Information Security

It deals with issues such as who should access the data and how the privacy data, proprietary information, contractual information and intellectual property is stored, controlled, marked, disseminated and disposed of.

Personnel Security

Personnel security encompasses background investigations, drug testing and other pre-employment screening techniques, as well as adjudication of results and granting security clearances and other information access privileges.

Information Systems Security

Information systems security personnel develop procedures and safeguards to protect against hackers and other unauthorized efforts to access data, viruses and a number of other threats to information systems.

Related Careers

Many Professions are closely related to this industry, like Bailiffs, School Bus Drivers, Correctional Officers and Jailers, Criminal Investigators and Special Agents, Fire Inspectors, Police Detectives, Private Detectives and Investigators Sheriffs and Deputy Sheriffs, Delivery Services.

The Employers look for:

- Social Perceptiveness
- Critical Thinking
- Important Abilities
- Oral Expression
- Sound Localization
- Response Orientation
- Night Vision
- Selective Attention

Eligibility: International Recruiters usually prefer individuals who are high school graduates or hold an equivalent certification. Many jobs require a driver's license and a formal training course. For positions as armed guards, employers often seek people who have had responsible experience in other occupations.

Security Service Personnel

The Security Service's main responsibility is to protect national security and the economic well-being of the country and to support the police and other law enforcement agencies in their work against serious crime.

Main areas of work for Security Service personnel include: anti-terrorism (national and international); anti-espionage; serious crime prevention; and counter-proliferation—the disruption of attempts to acquire materials, technology and expertise which could be used to develop chemical, biological or nuclear weapons programmes.

They also advise on protective security for key national infrastructure such as power, water and transport systems.

There is a wide variety of roles within the service, including:

Surveillance officers observe and report on the movements and actions of those under investigation. Often trained in a specialist role, officers work in teams and liaise with the police or other agencies and may provide evidence in court. Work can be on a mobile or static basis.

Security service generalists (graduate entrants), who may also be known as desk officers, operate in teams and assess and investigate threats in one of the areas mentioned above. Identifying targets from intelligence data, they decide on the most appropriate method to conduct an investigation. Later in their careers, they may also be involved in policy work, training other staff and a variety of other roles.

Linguists work within the Service's language unit. They translate and transcribe incoming intelligence information and interpret its political and cultural context. The information may be classed as secret and take the form of intercepted telephone calls, emails or post.

Developed vetting investigation officers carry out the security vetting of new staff and also review security clearances of existing employees. They produce written reports from their findings and make recommendations.

IT specialists providing protection and IT support to the government's computer systems, networks and communication systems. Posts exist within applications management, communications networks, development, integration and testing, quality management, service desk, security, server management and telecommunications engineering. The Security Service also employs people in a wide range of support roles. These include administrative positions, security guards, building maintenance and services personnel and other technician roles.

Security Officer

Significant Points: Opportunities for most jobs should be favorable, but competition is expected for higher paying positions at facilities requiring longer periods of training and a high level of security, such as nuclear power plants and weapons installations.

Because of limited formal training requirements and flexible hours, this occupation attracts many individuals seeking a second or part-time job.

Some positions, such as those of armored car guards, are hazardous.

Nature of the Work: Guards, who are also called security officers, patrol and inspect property to protect against fire, theft, vandalism, terrorism and illegal activity. These workers protect their employer's investment, enforce laws on the property and deter criminal activity or other problems. They use radio and telephone communications to call for assistance from police, fire, or emergency medical services as the situation dictates. Security guards write comprehensive reports outlining their observations and activities during their assigned shift. They may also interview witnesses or victims, prepare case reports and testify in court.

Although all security guards perform many of the same duties, specific duties vary based on whether the guard works in a "static" security position or on a mobile patrol. Guards assigned to static security positions usually serve the client at one location for a specific length of time. These guards must become closely acquainted with the property and people associated with it and often monitor alarms and closed-circuit TV cameras. In contrast, guards assigned to mobile patrol duty drive or walk from location to location and conduct security checks within an assigned geographical zone. They may detain or arrest criminal violators, answer service calls concerning criminal activity or problems and issue traffic violation warnings.

Specific job responsibilities also vary with the size, type and location of the employer. In department stores, guards protect people, records, merchandise, money and equipment. They often work with undercover store detectives to prevent theft by customers or store employees and help in the apprehension of shoplifting suspects prior to arrival by police. Some shopping centers and theaters have officers mounted on horses or bicycles who patrol their parking lots to deter car theft and robberies. In office buildings, banks and hospitals, guards maintain order and protect the institutions' property, staff and customers. At air, sea and rail terminals and other transportation facilities, guards protect people, freight, property and equipment. They may screen passengers and visitors for weapons and explosives using metal detectors and high-tech equipment, ensure nothing is stolen while being loaded or unloaded and watch for fires and criminals.

Guards who work in public buildings such as museums or art galleries protect paintings and exhibits by inspecting people and packages entering and leaving the building. In factories, laboratories, government buildings, data processing centers and military bases, security officers protect information, products, computer codes and defense secrets and check the credentials of people and vehicles entering and leaving the premises. Guards working at universities, parks and sports stadiums perform crowd control, supervise parking and seating and direct traffic. Security guards stationed at the entrance to bars and places of adult entertainment, such as nightclubs, prevent access by minors, collect cover charges at the door, maintain order among customers and protect property and patrons.

Armored car guards protect money and valuables during transit. In addition, they protect individuals responsible for making commercial bank deposits from theft or bodily injury. When the armored car arrives at the door of a business, an armed guard enters, signs for the money and returns to the truck with the valuables in hand. Carrying money between the truck and the business can be extremely hazardous for guards. Because of this risk, armored car guards usually wear bulletproof vests.

All security officers must show good judgment and common sense, follow directions and directives from supervisors, accurately testify in court and follow company policy and guidelines. Guards should have a professional appearance and attitude and be able to interact with the public. They also must be able to take charge and direct others in emergencies or other dangerous incidents. In a large organization, the security manager is often in charge of a trained guard force divided into shifts; whereas in a small organization, a single worker may be responsible for all security.

Gaming surveillance officers and gaming investigators act as security agents for casino managers and patrons. They observe casino operations for irregular activities, such as cheating or theft, by either employees or patrons. To do this, surveillance officers and investigators often monitor activities from a catwalk over one-way mirrors located above the casino floor. Many casinos use audio and video equipment, allowing surveillance officers and investigators to observe these same areas via monitors. Recordings are kept as a record and are sometimes used as evidence against alleged criminals in police investigations.

Working Conditions: Most security guards and gaming surveillance officers spend considerable time on their feet, either assigned to a specific post or patrolling buildings and grounds. Guards may be stationed at a guard desk inside a building to monitor electronic security and surveillance devices or to check the credentials of persons entering or leaving the premises. They also may be stationed at a guardhouse outside the entrance to a gated facility or community and use a portable radio or cellular telephone that allows them to be in constant contact with a central station. The work usually is routine, but guards must be constantly alert for threats to themselves and the property they are protecting. Guards who work during the day may have a great deal of contact with other employees and members of the public. Gaming surveillance often takes place behind a bank of monitors controlling several cameras in a casino, which can cause eyestrain.

Guards usually work at least 8-hour shifts for 40 hours per week and often are on call in case an emergency arises. Some employers have three shifts and guards rotate to equally divide daytime, weekend and holiday work. Guards usually eat on the job instead of taking a regular break away from the site. More than 1 in 7 guards worked part time and many individuals held a second job as a guard to supplement their primary earnings.

Employment: Security guards and gaming surveillance officers held more than 1.0 million jobs in 2002. More than half of jobs for security guards were in investigation and security services, including guard and armoured car services. These organizations provide security services on a contract basis, assigning their guards to buildings and other sites as needed. Most other security officers were employed directly by educational services, hospitals, food services and drinking places, traveller accommodation (hotels), department stores, manufacturing firms, lessors of real estate (residential and nonresidential buildings) and governments. Guard jobs are found throughout the country, most commonly in metropolitan areas. Gaming surveillance officers worked primarily in gambling industries; traveller accommodation, which includes casino hotels; and local government. Gaming surveillance officers were employed only in those States and Indian reservations where gambling has been legalized.

A significant number of law enforcement officers work as security guards when off-duty to supplement their incomes. Often working in uniform and with the official cars assigned to them, they add a high profile security presence to the establishment with which they have contracted. At construction sites and apartment complexes, for example, their presence often prevents trouble before it starts.

Training

Most States require that guards be licensed. To be licensed as a guard, individuals must usually be at least 18 years old, pass a background check and complete classroom training in such subjects as property rights, emergency procedures and detention of suspected criminals. Drug testing often is required and may be random and ongoing.

Many employers of unarmed guards do not have any specific educational requirements. For armed guards, employers usually prefer individuals who are high school graduates or hold an equivalent certification. Many jobs require a driver's license. For positions as armed guards, employers often seek people who have had responsible experience in other occupations.

Guards who carry weapons must be licensed by the appropriate government authority and some receive further certification as special police officers, which allows them to make limited types of arrests while on duty. Armed guard positions have more stringent background checks and entry requirements than those of unarmed guards because of greater insurance liability risks. Compared to unarmed security guards, armed guards and special police typically enjoy higher earnings and benefits, greater job security, more advancement potential and usually are given more training and responsibility.

Rigorous hiring and screening programmes consisting of background, criminal record and fingerprint checks are becoming the norm in the occupation. Applicants are expected to have good character references, no serious police record and good health. They should be mentally alert, emotionally stable and physically fit in order to cope with emergencies. Guards who have frequent contact with the public should communicate well.

The amount of training guards receive varies. Training requirements are higher for armed guards because their employers are legally responsible for any use of force. Armed guards receive formal training in areas such as weapons retention and laws covering the use of force.

Many employers give newly hired guards instruction before they start the job and also provide on-the-job training. An increasing number of States are making ongoing training a legal requirement for retention of certification. Guards may receive training in protection, public relations, report writing, crisis deterrence and first aid, as well as specialized training relevant to their particular assignment.

Guards employed at establishments placing a heavy emphasis on security usually receive extensive formal training. For example, guards at nuclear power plants undergo several months of training before being placed on duty under close supervision. They are taught to use firearms, administer first aid, operate alarm systems and electronic security equipment and spot and deal with security problems. Guards authorized to carry firearms may be periodically tested in their use.

Although guards in small companies may receive periodic salary increases, advancement opportunities are limited. Most large organizations use a military type of ranking that offers the possibility of advancement in position and salary. Some guards may advance to supervisor or security manager positions. Guards with management skills may open their own contract security guard agencies.

In addition to the keen observation skills required to perform their jobs, gaming surveillance officers and gaming investigators must have excellent verbal and writing abilities to document violations or suspicious behaviour. They also need to be physically fit and have quick reflexes because they sometimes must detain individuals until local law enforcement officials arrive.

Surveillance officers and investigators usually do not need a bachelor's degree, but some training beyond high school is required; previous security experience is a plus. Several educational institutes offer certification programmes. Training classes usually are conducted in a casino-like atmosphere using surveillance camera equipment.

Other Qualifications

Job Outlook: Opportunities for security guards and gaming surveillance officers should be favorable. Numerous job openings will stem from employment growth attributable to the desire for increased security and from the need to replace those who leave this large occupation each year. In addition to full-time job opportunities, the limited training requirements and flexible hours attract many persons seeking part-time or second jobs. However, competition is expected for higher paying positions that require longer periods of training; these positions usually are found at facilities that require a high level of security, such as nuclear power plants or weapons installations.

Employment of security guards and gaming surveillance officers is expected to grow faster than the average for all occupations through 2012 as concern about crime, vandalism and terrorism continue to increase the need for security. Demand for guards also will grow as private security firms increasingly perform duties-such as monitoring crowds at airports and providing security in courts-which were formerly handled by government police officers and marshals. Because enlisting the services of a security guard firm is easier and less costly than assuming direct responsibility for hiring, training and managing a security guard force, job growth is expected to be concentrated among contract security guard agencies. Casinos will continue to hire more surveillance officers as more States legalize gambling and as the number of casinos increases in States where gambling is already legal. Additionally, casino security forces will employ more technically trained personnel as technology becomes increasingly important in thwarting casino cheating and theft.

Earnings: Median annual earnings of security guards were $19,140 in 2002. The middle 50 percent earned between $15,910 and $23,920. The lowest 10 percent earned less than $13,740 and the highest 10 percent earned more than $31,540. Median annual earnings in the industries employing the largest numbers of security guards in 2002 were as follows:

Elementary and secondary schools	$24,470
General medical and surgical hospitals	24,050
Local government	22,120
Traveller accommodation	21,390
Investigation and security services	17,910

Gaming surveillance officers and gaming investigators had median annual earnings of $23,110 in 2002. The middle 50 percent earned between $19,620 and $28,420. The lowest

10 percent earned less than $15,930 and the highest 10 percent earned more than $35,170.

Security and Protective Services Pathway

The Security and Protective Services pathway contains a variety of careers based on specific knowledge, skill-sets and necessary educational requirements. Those who enter careers in this pathway tend to have strong interests in the safety and security of people, places and things. These workers might be guarding millions of dollars or standing by a security camera in your favourite mall watching for shoplifters. You might find them sitting in front of a computer tracing a criminal who is trying to break into your checking account.

These workers are often part of a private security force and even include private investigators who are great at tracking down missing people, missing money, or a very valuable antique diamond necklace that was stolen!

A Guide for Your Career Plans in Protective Services

Sadly, the world is not always as safe as you might like it to be. Most people are content to play by the rules, but there are always some who decide to go against the grain. Making sure that violent, harmful, or immoral incidents stay relatively low is the job of protection agencies, law enforcement officials and the judicial process. Protection services like these are crucial to the well being and functionality of any society.

Protection Services Careers are Becoming Increasingly Complex

Thanks to increased global connectivity, Internet access and wireless communication, the world can conduct business with phenomenal ease regardless of where a person is. Unfortunately, these conveniences also translate to the world of crime. A career criminal with modest computer skills on the other side of the world can rob you of your funds without ever meeting you. Recent studies suggest that incidents of cyber crime will only increase as the years progress. As a result, you will need to study up on the latest advances in crime and crime fighting if you want to be successful in this career.

Protection against Large Scale Disasters

Crime fighting is only one half of what protection services do. Natural disaster relief and crisis control are both crucial components of this industry. Hurricanes, earthquakes, terrorist attacks and epidemics are usually pretty unpredictable. Making sure that people receive aid and assistance in a timely, organized fashion is an involved and detailed process.

Crime and Natural Disasters will Remain Fixtures in our Society

Because crime and natural disasters will never be 100% eradicated, you can be sure that after your studies, there will be plenty of protection services careers from which to choose. Whether you opt to study crime fighting or crisis control, you will be helping to make the world a safer and more enjoyable place. There are few jobs that offer comparable levels of inner fulfilment and satisfaction.

Articles and Information

What does it mean to study Protective Services?

If you're interested in law enforcement and public safety and you like shielding others who are weak or vulnerable, then a career in protective services could be right for you. You can take the social work path or the security services route to a career in protective services.

What kind of person succeeds at Protective Services?

Do you already know CPR and first aid? Do you watch television shows or read books about family or public safety? If you're the kind of person who's sensitive to security issues, then you have the sort of "radar" that will help you succeed in a protective services career.

Why study Protective Services?

Most people who thrive in protective services careers thrive on the knowledge that what they do is important to other people's welfare. Since 40% of government jobs go to those with social work degrees, many branches of protective services lead to jobs with state or local government agencies or non-profits like shelters for abused women. Alternatively, you might study security management to find a job providing private or business security.

Studying for Careers in Protective Services

Those who work in child protective services tend to be trained social workers. Social workers need a bachelor's degree in social work (BSW) to practice. If you want to run a protective services agency, you'll need to get a master's (MSW). If you want to work in business or personal protective services, you'll need to study security management and get your bachelor's degree.

What's it like to have a Protective Services career?

Either of these protective services careers tends to mean a standard 40-hour work week. The casework can be demanding and emotionally draining in child protective services. You'll work under pressure and understaffing is common. If you've studied for a either protective services career, a good part of your time will be spent in meeting with clients and with staff. Salaries average $35,000, but vary greatly. Today, protective services are in high demand.

Protective Services Careers—Future Outlook

The reason that most people sleep soundly at night is because they have faith in the system. They know that people are out there trying to stop bad things from happening. And should they happen, there are other people out there to manage the situation accordingly. Careers such as law enforcement, disaster relief, doctors and firefighters are just some of the more popular paths people follow. If you have a burning desire to guard, serve and watch over others, you might consider a career in protection services. Your skills will always be in demand.

Protection Services Careers

Bad things happen. This is one of those sad facts of life. However, the frequency and severity of crises, violent acts, cyber-crimes, terrorist attacks and epidemics is relatively low thanks to the efforts of devoted individuals with a career in protection services. Working around the clock, they try to head off and prevent crimes and disasters from taking place. In addition, they rehearse first responder drills so that if a tornado hits or a traffic accident occurs, they can provide immediate assistance. Depending on which field of protection services you decide to enter, you might study areas as diverse as first aid, crowd control, hostage negotiation, urban planning, computer programming and cyber-crime. Society needs people like you to monitor and fix every potential chink in the armor.

Studies show that crime is going down (or is it up)?

Whichever way the studies go, your job is never really over. After all, the most powerful weapons against crises are prevention and preparation. Thus your career is truly full time regardless of what a study says about the level of criminal activity or the likelihood of another earthquake. But the rewards are worth it. Every peaceful day that passes is proof of a job well done.

General Career Information: Protective Services Jobs

Even in the most well-ordered society, danger is a potential threat that every person faces. Violence, terrorism, natural disasters, cyber crimes, diseases. The list is endless and frightening. Fortunately, there are people out there who work around the clock to ensure relative safety for all. Protective services careers are crucial to the sustainability and security of modern society.

What are protective services careers?

Broadly speaking, protective services jobs focus on preventing and treating things like crime, disease and crises. Law enforcement agencies and disaster relief organizations are the most popular career paths for some people. If you have ever considered joining this field, now is as good a time as any. The world is not becoming safer, so your skills will certainly be appreciated.

What to Study: Your exact career path will dictate what type of studies you must pursue. If you want to work in law enforcement, you'll need to study at the appropriate academy. For disaster relief, you'll need to study medical treatment and crisis management. If you plan to work in a high tech field (like cyber crime prevention), you'll need to master computers and programming languages. As you can see, the work (and thus the studies) are extremely diverse.

Hard work with many rewards: Earthquakes, criminals and viruses don't take predictable vacations and neither will you. Much of your work will be around the clock or at strange hours. However, the rewards are tremendous. Every safe day is a victory. Every healthy citizen is a testament to your hard work and dedication. You might not receive a standing ovation at the end of every work week, but your efforts will be appreciated all the same.

If you are passionate about helping others, have a genuine desire to serve and protect and enjoy a job with many challenges, you'd be hard pressed to find a better industry than protection services.

Job Openings & Education Requirements—General Outlook

Projected job growth varies widely by education and training requirements. Protective Services Education is essential in getting a high-paying job. In fact allmost all of the highest paying occupations require a college degree.

Job openings stem from both employment growth and replacement needs. Replacement needs arise as workers leave occupations. Some transfer to other occupations while others retire, return to school, or quit to assume household responsibilities. Replacement needs are projected to account for 60 percent of the approximately 58 million job openings between 2000 and 2010. Thus, even occupations with little or no change in employment still may offer many job openings.

Jobs requiring an associate degree are projected to grow 32 percent over the 2000-10 period and jobs requiring a postsecondary vocational award grow 24.1 percent. Employment in occupations requiring an associate degree is projected to increase faster than any other occupational group categorized by education or training.

The largest number of job openings will be among occupations requiring short-term on-the-job training. Almost two-thirds of the projected job openings over the 2000-10 period will be in occupations that require on-the-job training and arise mostly from replacement needs. Occupations requiring work-related training are projected to increase 12.4 percent. These jobs will account for 37.3 million of the projected 57.9 million total job openings through 2010. However, many of these jobs typically offer low pay and benefits; this is more true of jobs requiring only short-term on-the-job training, which will account for 24.8 million openings.

Jobs requiring a bachelor's degree and which usually offer higher pay and benefits, will account for about 7.3 million job openings through 2010. Employment in occupations requiring at least a bachelor's degree is expected to grow 21.6 percent. Most of these openings will result from job growth.

How to get required education for your Protective Services career?: The right education is important for your career. Protective Services Education always depends on learning & going to school. You should consider that except for financial considerations, the public or private nature of a university should not be a factor in selecting a graduate programme. High quality programmes exist in both types of institutions.

Of more importance is the institution's commitment to the graduate programme. This commitment is found in its willingness to maintain a first-class faculty and to provide excellent facilities for advanced study, including libraries, laboratories, computers and other equipment.

Another important factor to consider in many disciplines is the presence of strong departments in other fields relevant to your interests so that you can have access to scholars and courses in disciplines related to your own. Selecting the right school that offers the required degree for your education is a large investment of time, money and effort. A consequent & careful evaluation of campus-based or online schools is important.

Find schools that meet your interests: Go to the Protective Services School Directory and select the appropriate category, country or state. You will then find a list of Protective Services Schools matching your interests.

Gather information from all schools: Upon request every Protective Services School listed in the directory will provide you with information and details. In the directory just click on the link for each school or on the button "Complimentary Information" to request more information about its educational programmes, finacial aid, admission requirement, etc.

Contact all Protective Services Schools that meet your interests: the more information you receive from schools, the better a decision you will make about your education!

Security Force Officer-White Sands, Las Cruces, NM

The Security Force Officer is primarily responsible to perform protective service work such as guarding Government owned or leased buildings and property, protecting Government equipment and material and controlling access to Government owned or leased buildings and property by employees and visitors. The Security Force Officer will protect and prevent loss of materials or processes, which are important for national defense, public health or safety, or their value as national treasures. The Security Force Officer does not act in the capacity of a law enforcement officer and has no arrest or apprehension powers. The Security Force Officer is armed with a side arm and automatic weapons as designated in the government Statement of Work.

Essential Duties and Responsibilities: Reasonable accommodations may be made to enable individuals with disabilities to perform the essential functions of this position.

- o Required to follow all company personnel and safety policies and perform all assigned duties in a safe work manner.
- o May be required to work other than normal duty hours, which may include evenings, weekends and/or holidays.
- o Other duties may be assigned.
- o Will arrive at work 30 minutes prior to guard mount, in proper uniform and carrying needed, issued equipment.
- o Will be armed with a pistol and an automatic weapon and will be required to exercise force up to and including deadly force.

- o Will draw assigned weapon.
- o Will participate in Guard Mount, receive assigned post and copy any extra instructions.
- o Will carry out general and special orders for post assigned.
- o Will communicate via radio, telephone and orally according to general and special orders.
- o Required to interact with public, contractor and military personnel.
- o Required to operate effectively in a foreign nation environment, sensitive to cultural differences.
- o Will provide access control and conduct walking and motorized security guard functions.
- o Will be responsible for cleanliness of uniform and equipment assigned.
- o `Will follow applicable standard operating procedures and Army regulations pertaining to security of weapons, buildings, personnel, government property and equipment.
- o Will not remove firearms from installation, required to turn in after shift.
- o Successfully complete all training and have obtained all required permits, licenses, certifications and security clearances for the site.
- o Pass written test on trained subjects with an 80% or better.

Qualifications: To perform this job successfully, an individual must be able to perform each essential duty satisfactorily. The requirements listed below are representative of the knowledge, skill and/or ability required. Reasonable accommodations may be made to enable individuals with disabilities to perform the essential functions.

Education and/or Experience

- o Must be at least 21 Dears of age.
- o Minimum of a high school diploma or GED. Completion of a bona fide law enforcement course of instruction.
- o Experience with a civilian police force, military police force, or civilian security guard organization.

Certificates, Licenses, Registrations

- o U. S. citizenship
- o A valid state drivers license
- o Must speak, read, write and understand English.
- o Must be able to obtain a secret clearance if required by position.
- o Honorably discharged/retired from the military preferably as a MP.
- o Be able to meet any Federal requirements to work as an Armed Security Guard.

Language Skills: Ability to read, analyze and interpret general business periodicals, professional journals, technical procedures, or government regulations. Ability to write reports, business correspondence and procedure manuals. Ability to effectively present information and respond to questions from groups of managers, clients, customers and the general public.

Mathematical Skills: Ability to apply concepts such as fractions, percentages, ratios and proportions to practical situations.

Reasoning Ability: Ability to define problems, collect data, establish facts and draw valid conclusions. Ability to interpret basic supervision policies and procedures and be capable of making decisions affecting security at the assigned site.

Physical Demands: The physical demands described here are representative of those that must be met by an employee to successfully perform the essential functions of this job. Reasonable accommodations may be made to enable individuals with disabilities to perform the essential functions.

While performing the duties of this job, the employee if frequently required to stand; walk, use hand to finger, handle, or feel objects, tools, or controls; reach with hands and arms; and talk and hear. The employee may occasionally sit for prolonged periods of time at a desk, or table. The employee may stand for prolonged periods of time.

Must be able to occasionally travel by designated transportation *i.e.* aircraft, vehicle, mass transit system.

Must pass physical agility test as prescribed by the government.

Work Environment: The work environment characteristics described here are representative of those an employee encounters while performing the essential functions of this job. Reasonable accommodations may be made to enable individuals with disabilities to perform the essential functions.

The employee may occasionally work in a temperature-controlled office environment.

The employee will regularly stand duty at a gate control guard station. The employee will regularly be exposed to extreme heat or cold weather conditions and unpredictable crisis situations. Will be occasionally exposed to fumes or airborne particles, toxic or caustic chemicals and loud noise.

Project Manager/Chief of Security FLETC (NM)

The Project Manager/Chief of Security (PM/CS) is the central point of authority and responsibility for all activities associated with armed and unarmed contract guard services on specific programmes. The PM/CS is responsible for implementing corporate policies and procedures through key management personnel at the job sites.

Supervisory Responsibilities: Has complete authority over assigned personnel to ensure the accomplishment of quality work.

Essential Duties and Responsibilities: Reasonable accommodations may be made to enable individuals with disabilities to perform the essential functions of this position

- o Assures that all provisions of the contract are clearly understood by subordinate managers and by the personnel actually performing the work.
- o Administers the contract through transition and/or phase-in activities.
- o Plans and directs all work within the Contract Management Office.
- o Establishes policies and procedures at the Contract Management Office level.

- o Modifies the organization as needed.
- o Ensures personnel and other adequate resources are available to satisfy the needs of the contract.
- o Interfaces with customer personnel.
- o Ensures timely submission of all contractually required reports.
- o Required to implement and support the Safety Management System and ensure that all company personnel adhere to all applicable safety policies and perform all assigned duties in a safe work manner.
- o May be required to work other than normal duty hours, which may include evenings, weekends and/or holidays.
- o Other duties may be assigned.

Qualifications: To perform this job successfully, an individual must be able to perform each essential duty satisfactorily. The requirements listed below are representative of the knowledge, skill and/or ability required. Reasonable accommodations may be made to enable individuals with disabilities to perform the essential functions.

Education/Experience

- o Minimum of a Bachelors in Criminal Justice, law enforcement, criminal justice or a related discipline or a minimum of ten (10) years experience in law enforcement or a security related area.
- o Previously fully commissioned by a local LEA.

  Three (3) years of progressively responsible general experience gained in analytical decision making and administrative work and activities.
- o Three (3) years of law enforcement or security-related supervisory responsibility.
- o Knowledge of criminal law and traffic code regulations and legal applications relative to the state specific site.
- o Knowledge and/or experience in project management and business rules.
- o Other Skills

- o Strong personnel management skills; excellent written, verbal and interpersonal skills.
- o Superior knowledge, analytical, persuasion and problem solving skills relative to health, safety, environmental and business matters.
- o Ability to manage multiple, high priority tasks simultaneously.

  Capable of assimilating and critically evaluating information.

Language Skills: The ability to read, analyze and interpret general business periodicals, professional journals, technical procedures, or government regulations. The ability to write reports, business correspondence and procedure manuals. To ability to effectively present information and respond to questions from groups of managers, clients, customers and the general public.

Certificates, Licenses, Registrations

- o U.S. Citizen
- o Valid state drivers
- o DOD Secret Security Clearance
- o Federal, State, local, or military service approved recognized basic law enforcement or physical security academy certificate.

Mathematical Skills: Ability to work with mathematical concepts such as probability and statistical inference and fundamentals of plane and solid geometry and trigonometry. Ability to apply concepts such as fractions, percentages, ratios and proportions to practical situations.

Reasoning Ability: Ability to define problems, collect data, establish facts and draw valid conclusions.

Physical Demands: The physical demands described here are representative of those that must be met by an employee to successfully perform the essential functions of this job. Reasonable accommodations may be made to enable individuals with disabilities to perform the essential functions.

While performing the duties of this job, the employee if frequently required to stand; walk; use hand to finger, handle, or feel objects, tools, or controls; reach with hands and arms; and talk and hear. The employee must be able to sit for prolonged periods of time at a desk, table, or computer terminal; move in a confined office space. May be required to stand for prolonged periods of time while making presentations or attending meetings.

Must be able to occasionally travel by public transportation *i.e.* aircraft, vehicle, mass transit system.

Work Environment: The work environment characteristics described here are representative of those an employee encounters while performing the essential functions of this job. Reasonable accommodations may be made to enable individuals with disabilities to perform the essential functions.

The employee will normally work in a temperature-controlled office environment, with frequent exposure to electronic office equipment.

During visits to areas of operations, may be exposed to extreme cold or hot weather conditions. Is occasionally exposed to fumes or airborne particles, toxic or caustic chemicals and loud noise.

Security Officer/Guard

Security officers/guards provide a protection service for property, people, cash and other valuables. Many officers/guards are static—permanently based at one site. Mobile guards patrol different locations by van or work on armoured 'cash in transit' vans. Most employers only recruit applicants aged 21 years and over.

Work Activities: Security officers and guards are responsible for protecting premises, cash and valuable products/ commodities. The most common security work is as a static guard based permanently on industrial or commercial premises. Static security officers:

- patrol inside and outside premises
- check that windows and doors are locked

- make certain that unauthorised persons do not enter the grounds
- keep the risk of accidents to a minimum.

Many security officers use closed-circuit television or other surveillance equipment. Most have two-way radios so they can keep in touch with other on-duty guards or their security control centre. In emergency situations immediate assistance can then be arranged. Some officers patrol with dogs.

Mobile officers patrol premises by van. They may be allocated several different properties to protect. These officers concentrate on:

- checking the outside of buildings
- making sure that all doors and windows are safely secured
- checking that nothing has been disturbed.

Officers who accompany cash in transit--and security van drivers—make sure that money and valuable items are taken safely from one place to another. They must keep in regular radio contact with their headquarters.

Personal Qualities and Skills: As a security officer or guard you must be honest and alert. Good observational skills, reliability and the ability to deal with aggressive people are also necessary.

This job requires common sense and a practical approach. You must be able to react quickly to situations without putting yourself in unnecessary danger.

You must be in good physical condition and willing to wear a uniform, if required. You may need to wear protective clothing and a steel helmet.

Pay and Opportunities: Pay rates for security officers vary depending on employer and duties. The pay rates given below are approximate. Security officers earn around £12,000 a year, rising to around £18,000-£25,000 for experienced officers.

Security officers work a basic 39-42 hour week, including nights and weekends. Those involved in transporting cash and valuables generally work daytime only. Overtime is a fairly common feature for all security officers.

Employers throughout the UK are private security firms, commercial and industrial establishments, property estate owners, government departments, shops and warehouses.

Experienced officers and guards may progress to supervisory level posts or to central control duties.

The following information is sourced from government statistics. The government's definition of types of job is slightly different to that used in this programme. For this type of job, the most relevant Government-defined occupation is 'Security guards and related occupations'.

In 2001 there were 12,100 people working as 'Security guards and related occupations' in Scotland. 56 in every 10,000 employees working in Scotland were employed as 'Security guards and related occupations'.

Entry Routes and Training: Employers usually recruit people who are at least 18 years old and some have a minimum age limit of 21.

Training generally takes place both on-and off-the-job. Initial training should cover the following:

- general duties
- assignment instructions
- report and record keeping
- patrolling
- fire safety
- civil and criminal law
- major incidents
- relevant electrical devices
- legal powers
- health and safety

Specialist training in professional dog handling may also be available. There are a variety of relevant training courses available. For example, there is an SVQ in Security, Safety and Loss Prevention at level 2 that can be taken while in employment. You normally have to tell the employer about any criminal convictions.

Qualifications: No educational qualifications are usually required for entry to this job, although some employers prefer some Standard Grades including Maths and English.

Adult Opportunities: Applicants with police, prison officer, firefighter or HM Forces background have an advantage.

Modern Apprenticeships may be available in some areas.

The Security Industry Training Organisation Ltd. (SITO) offers a wide range of security-related courses at all levels. These include short courses and distance learning programmes.

Skills for Security offers two City & Guilds courses by distance learning. CG7295 Certificate of Knowledge for the Professional Security Officer and CG7296 Advanced Security Officer. A list of training providers is available from the Security Industry Authority (SIA) website.

- 3% of security officers are self-employed.
- 12% of security officers work part-time.
- 4% have flexible hours

Porter/Security Attendant

Porters/security attendants work in students' halls of residence, offices and some private apartment blocks. They have a range of duties related to the maintenance and security of the building. Security duties may include making patrols and monitoring visitors. The job often involves general caretaking work.

Work Activities: Porters/security attendants have a number of duties connected with the maintenance and security of buildings, such as students' halls of residence, offices and some private apartment blocks.

Security is an important part of the work. Porters are often based in offices or at desks close to a building's main entrance. They monitor visitors and may be responsible for checking entrance passes. Some porters keep and issue keys. Most porters patrol the site, making sure that the building, equipment and grounds are secure. They may have to open and lock gates, doors and barriers. Security duties also involve looking after firefighting and other safety equipment.

Portering services often include general caretaking work. Porters supervise the operation of heating systems and carry out general maintenance jobs. Most porters have some cleaning duties. This can involve using heavy electrical cleaning and polishing machines.

Collecting and disposing of refuse is also usually part of the work. When there are deliveries to the building, porters check in and sign for goods and move items to the appropriate place. Porters also move furniture as required, set up rooms for meetings or other functions and erect and take down equipment.

Personal Qualities and Skills: You need to be mature and trustworthy. You should be reliable with a conscientious attitude to security and safety. This work suits those with practical ability. Good hand skills are needed for using tools and equipment.

Lifting and carrying is involved so you need to be fit and active. You should also be prepared to spend long periods on your feet.

It is important for you to be able to work without close supervision. You may spend quite a lot of your time alone, especially on night shift. You should also like working with people. A polite and friendly personality is helpful.

Porters need to be flexible and enjoy doing a variety of jobs. The ability to drive may be needed for some jobs.

Pay and Opportunities: Pay rates for porters/security attendants vary, depending on the employer and duties. The pay rates given below are approximate. Porters/security attendants earn in the range of £210-£230 a week, rising to £260-£270. Higher earners can make around £320 a week.

Security attendants work a basic 38-39 hour week, which may include shifts, nights, weekends and bank holidays.

Employers are local authorities, educational establishments, offices, private apartment blocks, housing associations and some firms in industry and commerce. Jobs exist in all areas throughout the UK. Vacancies may be advertised in local newspapers and Jobcentre Plus offices.

The following information is sourced from government statistics. The government's definition of types of job is slightly different to that used in this programme. For this type of job, the most relevant Government-defined occupation is 'Caretakers'.

In 2001 there were 8,200 people working as 'Caretakers' in Scotland. 38 in every 10,000 employees working in Scotland were employed as 'Caretakers'.

Entry Routes and Training: Training is on the job. A senior porter usually gives new entrants instruction and supervision. You will learn the range of duties and basic tasks, such as how to use cleaning equipment and maintain the heating plant. The Security Industry Authority (SIA) and the Security Industry Training Organisation (SITO) run short courses in security work.

As a porter you will be expected to learn fairly quickly and move on to work with minimum supervision.

Qualifications: No educational qualifications are usually required for entry to this job, although some employers prefer some Standard Grades including Maths and English.

A driving licence may be needed for some jobs.

Adult Opportunities: Maturity, reliability and life experience are considered important.

Experience of similar work, as a hotel porter, for example, can be an advantage.

Relevant work experience can be useful, for example, voluntary work in a hospital helping the portering and estates staff.

Some evidence of practical skills can also be useful.

- 26% of porters/security attendants work part-time.
- 3% have flexible hours.
- 1% of employees work on a temporary basis.

ADT Careers

Overview: As the leading electronic security services company in the U.S., ADT Security Services, Inc., looks for bright, assertive professionals to grow along with us. Larger than the next six largest security companies combined, ADT features a wide range of cutting-edge technology products and systems for home and business supported by round-the-clock monitoring at five Customer Monitoring Centers located strategically across the country. With annual revenues of $4 billion, ADT employs 20,800 associates at more than 180 sales and service offices.

Working at ADT Security Services means working as part of a team; you'll find the tools, resources and support to help you explore opportunities within ADT and realize your full potential. Our mission is to be the leading systems, services and solutions provider in the world by exceeding customers' expectations through superior service delivery, world-class talent and applied technological innovation, making ADT the most profitable business in the Tyco portfolio.

To support further growth, we are looking for highly motivated, technically skilled, customer-focused individuals who want to be part of a winning team. Local managers have great flexibility to grow their markets within broad guidelines. As a result, ADT associates enjoy a highly entrepreneurial, fast-paced culture. Generous incentive plans are in place to reward positive results. The corporate headquarters staff provides marketing and financial support, state-of-the-art human resource programmes and a sophisticated technology infrastructure.

Special Agents

Diplomatic Security special agents are federal law enforcement officers who serve worldwide. Overseas, our special agents advise ambassadors on all security issues and coordinate all of a mission's security programmes. In the United States, agents investigate passport and visa fraud and protect the Secretary of State and visiting foreign dignitaries.

Qualifications

- U.S. citizenship
- BA/BS degree at time of appointment

- 20 years of age to apply. Candidates must be at least 21 years old but must not have reached their 37th birth date at time of appointment.
- If required, registration under the Military Selective Service Act
- Successfully undergo written and oral assessment
- Successfully undergo a thorough background investigation and qualify for a Top Secret security clearance
- Pass a stringent medical exam, be available for worldwide assignment and qualify for a Department of State Class 01 medical clearance
- Pass physical fitness tests and be fit for strenuous physical exertion
- Possess a valid U.S. driver's license
- Be willing to carry and use firearms and qualify with firearms throughout career
- Be willing to travel and accept assignments throughout the world. Officers are required to live and work a substantial portion of their career overseas.
- Foreign language ability is desirable, but not mandatory
- Successfully complete all aspects of 6-month training

The men and women of Diplomatic Security are specially trained federal law enforcement professionals. Diplomatic Security special agents are Foreign Service security officers assigned domestically and overseas to ensure that American diplomacy is conducted in a safe and secure environment. Overseas, they advise ambassadors on all security matters and manage a complex range of security programmes designed to protect people, facilities and information. In the United States, agents investigate passport and visa fraud, conduct personnel security investigations and protect the Secretary of State and certain foreign dignitaries.

Training: Comprehensive and Specialized

A substantial training investment is made in each candidate selected for this programme. Six months of training begin with an orientation period in Washington DC, followed by basic and specialized training at the Federal Law Enforcement Training Centre in Brunswick, Georgia. Training continues at State Department facilities in the Washington area. Candidates must pass all required tests at FLETC.

Initially, candidates are trained in personal protection techniques, criminal law and investigation, background investigations, first aid, firearms and defensive driving. To prepare for specific overseas assignments, officers are trained in security management, post operations, counterintelligence, electronic security and languages. Other instruction includes advanced firearms techniques, explosive devices, ordnance detection, arson investigation and medical assistance.

First Assignment: Practical Application of the Basics

Special agents are most frequently assigned first to a domestic field office for 2 years. Here, they receive practical experience performing the variety of security functions for which the Bureau of Diplomatic Security is responsible in the United States, including background investigations on personnel, passport and visa fraud investigations, counterintelligence and other criminal investigations.

Domestic assignments also can include protection services for the Secretary of State and certain visiting foreign dignitaries or temporary assignment to an overseas post to perform a specific task.

Overseas Assignment: On to Greater Responsibility

Special agents spend a substantial portion of their careers abroad serving at diplomatic posts. While assigned abroad, special agents are often referred to as regional security officers (RSOs).

Overseas assignments offer great opportunity for career growth and usually occur immediately after the initial tour of duty in a domestic field office. Assignment abroad can, however, occur much earlier depending upon needs of the service.

At U.S. embassies and consulates abroad, RSOs develop and implement the various aspects of a comprehensive security programme designed to protect personnel, property and information against terrorists, foreign intelligence agents and criminals.

With proven aptitudes and on-the-job performance, a Diplomatic Security special agent may advance to the position of regional security officer, responsible for managing security operations for an embassy or for several diplomatic posts within an assigned area. RSOs work closely with top State Department officials and serve as operational supervisors of U.S. Marine Security Guard detachments.

Domestic assignments are equally challenging and rewarding. An officer can aspire to managing field office programmes or a Department headquarters office responsible for support operations.

Salary and Benefits

Starting salaries range from $37,413 to $51,788, depending on qualifications, location of assignment and related specialized experience. Upon successful completion of all training, special agents become eligible for Law Enforcement Availability Pay (LEAP), equal to a 25 percent increase of their base salary.

Satisfactory performance earns employees automatic grade and pay increases during the first 3 years. Thereafter, promotions are competitive based on the recommendations of annual selection panels.

An excellent benefits package includes:

- Health Benefits Plans
- Thrift Savings Plan (equivalents to 401(K) with Government matching)
- Life Insurance
- Law Enforcement Availability Pay (LEAP)
- Long Term Care Insurance
- Annual Leave
- Sick Leave
- Family Medical Leave
- Student Loan Repayment Programme
- Ten Paid Holidays Per Year

- Career Counseling and Development
- Child Care Centers (Domestic only)
- Child Care Subsidy (based on income)
- Credit Union, Fitness Facility and More
- Employee Assistance Programme
- Employee Consultation Service
- Employee Recognition through our Incentive Awards Programme
- Employee Recreation Association
- Extensive Training Opportunities through our Foreign Service Institute (FSI)
- Flexible Work Hours (alternative work schedules)
- Global Career Mobility Opportunities (if desired)
- IQ: INFORMATION QUEST
- Managerial and Leadership Development
- MetroChek Transit Subsidy
- Periodic Performance-Based Pay Adjustments (within grade/step increases)
- Shuttle Bus Service to State Annexes
- Voluntary Leave Transfer Programme
- Workers' Compensation Coverage for Work-Related Injuries/Conditions
- Salary Determination
- Government-provided quarters or housing allowance overseas
- Home leave to the United States between overseas assignments
- Rest and recuperation leave, with transportation partially paid, when employees and their dependents are assigned to designated hardship posts
- Cost of living allowance
- Educational allowance for dependents under certain circumstances
- Danger pay at designated posts
- Moving expenses for assignments

A high level of responsibility, good opportunities for promotion and an excellent benefits package await you. Make the most of your unique skills and abilities as a Diplomatic Security special agent.

Protective Services Careers

Oakland County is committed to providing a safe environment for its citizens-safety and security is a priority to us. It's why we're here-so there is someone to turn to for assistance in times of crisis. By focusing on finding the most qualified and capable individuals to fill these important roles, we are able to make a difference in someone's life-one step at a time.

Pursuit of Excellence

Outstanding protective services workers are critical members of the Oakland County team. Our approach to creating a world-class area to live, work and play-and be safe-allows for us to demand the best and provide the best, to our protective services team.

Building Your Career

Protective Services professionals have a wide range of options at Oakland County, including assignments in:

- Animal Control
- Court Services and Investigation
- Building Safety
- Fire Safety and Security
- Emergency Management
- Marine Safety and Mechanics
- Medical Examiner's Office
- Parks Deputy
- Tax Collection
- Prosecutor's Office

Protective Services positions can be an excellent career at Oakland County. You can begin with challenging assignments that match your skills and interests...and take your career practically anywhere you want to go.

Senior Protective Services Supervisor

The Victor Project of De Beers Canada Inc. offers an exciting and challenging opportunity for an individual to join its team as a Senior Protective Services Supervisor.

This is a unique opportunity in the sense that it exposes the successful candidate to "high risk" security practice in a professional environment. Due to the specific character of a diamond company the level of security is commensurate to the associated security risks.

This position will be based at the Victor mine site on a two week on/two week off rotation with frequent travel. The incumbent will be accountable for the day-to-day protective services at the mine site including acting in the absence of the Manager as required. Duties will include threat and vulnerability assessments, monitoring compliance to diamond control standards, interaction with people as our greatest asset to protection, onsite investigations, high-tech video surveillance, integrated access control and the general security of the mine site.

The successful candidate will develop and implement mitigation plans and research to prepare drafts of site specific procedures as required. Additional responsibilities include coordinating the training and development of Protective Services personnel and ensuring familiarity with documented procedures.

Interested candidates should have formal police/security training from an accredited institution/organization combined with a minimum of five years experience in security or police supervision and three years experience in major case management and/or intelligence operations.

Salary will be commensurate with qualifications and experience and is complemented with a comprehensive benefit package.

Private Protective Services

Nature of Work: Individuals with private security training work in occupations concerned with guarding property from illegal entry, fire or theft, as well as enforcing safety regulations.

Moraine Valley's programme recognizes the need to provide quality security education for many specialty areas, including:

- Health care institutions-hospitals
- Retail-shopping centers, malls, stores
- Industrial-public and private utilities
- Special events-civic centers, fairs, exhibits
- Government-government buildings, public housing
- Schools-elementary, secondary, college

Related Job Titles

Armoured-Car Guard, Airline Security Representative, Bodyguard, Security Guard, Merchant Patroller, Store Detective, Shopping Investigator, House Officer, Patroller

Employment Outlook

Job openings for persons seeking work in loss prevention and as security guards are expected to be plentiful through the year 2008. This is primarily due to high turnover. Many opportunities are expected for persons seeking full-time employment, as well as for those seeking part-time or second jobs at night or on weekends. Some competition, however, is expected for in-house security guard positions. Job growth is expected to be concentrated among contract security guard agencies because engaging the services of a security guard firm can be easier and less costly. Employment potential for Illinois is large and stable. Median annual earnings of guards who worked full time in 1998 were about $16,240. The middle 50 percent between $13,430 and $20,110. The lowest 10 percent earned less than $11,970 and the highest 10 percent earned more than $26,640. Guards generally earn slightly more in urban areas.

Health Protection

The concept of health protection has been around for many years. Back in the 1850s, John Snow's investigation of the London cholera outbreak led to the closure of the Broad Street water pump; and in 1950 the observation that a steep rise in the number of deaths coincided with the London smog led to the first Clean Air Act. Today, the details may be different, but the principles of health protection are just the same.

So what is health protection?

Health protection is an integral part of public health and is defined as "those public health activities intended to protect individuals, groups and populations from infectious diseases, environmental hazards such as chemical contamination and from radiation." Until recently, the Acheson Report of 19882 formed the framework for training in communicable disease control. Then, in 2002, the Department of Health described the wider scope of health protection in its strategy Getting Ahead of the Curve. As a result, the Health Protection Agency was created in England to provide an integrated approach to protecting public health. It aims to protect people's health and reduce the impact of infectious diseases, chemical hazards, poisons and radiation hazards. Similar modernisation programmes are being developed in all of the home nations.

What do health protection consultants do?

Health protection requires a wide range of expertise and consultants work at local, regional and national levels. Public health trained doctors work in specialist divisions of the Health Protection Agency such as the Communicable Disease Surveillance Centre, the Chemicals and Poisons Division and the Emergency Response Division. Consultants working at the Communicable Disease Surveillance Centre specialise in the surveillance of infectious and communicable diseases, new and emerging diseases and biological threats and they undertake policy development and research in these areas.

The Chemical and Poisons Division specialises in non-infectious disease hazards and consultants provide strategic and operational support and advice to colleagues dealing with these issues. The Emergency Response Division is responsible for emergency preparedness and consultants work at a national level to develop emergency plans and to test emergency arrangements through tabletop and field exercises.

Box 1: Key skills

- Good communication and interpersonal skills

- **Good problem solving skills**
- **Leadership**
- **Self motivation**
- **Effective interpersonal and influencing skills**
- **Commitment to team working**
- **Ability to prioritise work**
- **Ability to be adaptable to situations and to think both proactively and reactively**
- **Computer literate**
- **Numerate**

Box 2: Pros and cons

Pros

- **Challenging job with many different aspects**
- **Opportunity to influence positively the health of the population**
- **Flexible training possible**
- **Manageable on-call duties**
- **Work as part of a multidisciplinary team**
- **Good work-life balance**

Cons

- **Loss of clinical responsibilities and patient contact**
- **Impact of work on health not immediately apparent except in cases of outbreaks**
- **Public health protection may be regarded as a low profile specialty compared with clinical specialties**
- **Pay during training may be lower than clinical specialities owing to low banding of out of hours commitment**

The largest division of the Health Protection Agency is the Local and Regional Services. As the name suggests, consultants in this division work at both local and regional levels and are responsible for delivering services and support to the NHS and other organisations to protect people's health. There are nine regions in England, each having two regional epidemiologist posts. The key elements of the regional service are surveillance,

advice and support to regional public health teams, local Health Protection Agency teams and the NHS; advice to professionals on communicable disease control and outbreak support; and promotion of professional standards, including training, research and audit.

Health Protection Units

By far the largest number of consultants in health protection work at local level, based in health protection units. In England, they are known as consultants in communicable disease control, but their remit is much broader than the name suggests as they are responsible for providing advice and support in all areas of health protection, including radiation. Consultants in communicable disease control work with multiagency partners, so it is essential for them to have a thorough understanding of the role of all agencies concerned with health protection. Much of the day to day activity includes advice on communicable disease control in community institutions such as schools, nurseries and residential settings; advice on immunisations to the public and health professionals; and the follow up of notifications of infectious disease and chemical, radiological and other environmental hazards.

They also advise and liaise with NHS partners, environmental health departments and other agencies on communicable disease and environmental hazard issues, teaching and training, the investigation and control of outbreaks and incidents and health emergency planning and participation in emergency exercises.

Training

Developing a career in communicable disease control was described in a previous Career Focus article. The Faculty of Public Health has made recent recommendations for training in health protection in the United Kingdom reflecting the broader role. At present, there is no recognised subspecialty of health protection and most consultants come from a background of public health, infectious diseases, or microbiology.

If you want to take the public health route, you will be expected to have at least two years' postregistration experience before being considered for higher specialist training in public health. For specialist registrars, the higher specialist training programme will include a minimum of 12 months working in general public health before tailoring your own training to meet your chosen professional development in health protection.

Core training will include experience in communicable disease and environmental epidemiology, investigation and management of communicable disease and environmental incidents, microbiology, infectious diseases, environmental public health, disease prevention programmes and health emergency planning. Exams lead to membership of the Faculty of Public Health and the annual record of in-training assessment (RITA) leads to a certificate of the completion of specialist training (CCST) in public health medicine. Consultant posts

Consultant posts will continue to be open to individuals on the appropriate specialist register-at the moment it is not envisaged that consultant posts in health protection will be restricted to those who have had specialist training in health protection The appointments advisory committee will continue to decide on the suitability of each applicant for a given post.

Research Opportunities

All trainees with a national training number in public health medicine are expected to undertake a postgraduate degree (MPH, MSc, or DPH). In addition, a research degree can be undertaken by taking time out of the programme or by securing a clinical lecturer position. The options include either an MD or a PhD.

Why choose health protection?

Health protection has a wide variety of opportunities, ranging from a front line responder to an academic career, so jobs will suit a wide variety of individuals. The key attributes of a successful career in health protection are the ability to be flexible and persistent, to be self starting and highly motivated, to be an effective team player and to have effective communication skills.

A day in the life of a consultant in communicable disease control: It's Monday morning. Just before you have your first cup of coffee the phone rings. It is the headmistress of a local primary school asking whether the schoolchildren should be kept in at playtime. There was a fire in an adjacent shop the previous night and flakes of white fibres are scattered across the playground. She has been told that these look like asbestos.

Discussion: This type of incident can happen at any time and is likely to involve several agencies, usually coordinated by the consultant in communicable disease control. Your immediate actions are to keep the children safe and to prevent further exposure. The next action is to confirm that the substance is asbestos, to identify the people exposed to asbestos, to arrange with allied organisations remediation of the school playground and testing of neighbouring properties, to weigh up the possible risk to health following exposure and to arrange follow up as necessary and to broadcast information to the local community via the media.

What happened next?

The agencies concerned with dealing with this incident were numerous and included the local education authority, the county council, the local authority, the fire service, a local contractor, a consultant in communicable disease control, the chemicals and poisons division, the local primary care trust, the local vicar and the local press and radio. The risk of health consequences in people exposed to the large asbestos fibres that were present in the playground was deemed to be low and the children were all sent home safely at lunchtime by a non-contaminated route. The school was closed for a week while environmental cleaning of the site of the fire and surrounding area was undertaken.

However, this career will not suit everyone. You are likely to become disillusioned quickly if you have no particular interest in health protection issues, yearn for immediate outcomes, don't want to look for alternative solutions to problems, or are unable to deal with politics.

Firefighter

Firefighters work in teams to reduce deaths and losses from fire. They do this not only by providing a practical firefighting and rescue service but also by offering fire safety advice and education and ensuring that fire safety standards are complied with. When an emergency call is received, a controller decides how best to deal with the incident. A Watch or Station Commander takes charge of the operation and leads the fire crew(s). With a major incident, a more senior Commander coordinates the work.

Apart from fire, the emergency could involve rescuing people, animals or property from a disaster such as a flood, road, rail or air crash or releasing someone trapped in a dangerous or confined space. Equally, it could be a bomb alert, a spillage of chemicals or other hazardous substances. In dealing with the injured, firefighters use first aid techniques to administer immediate help before the arrival of emergency medical services.

In addition to some 41,000 full-time firefighters, there are around 17,900 'retained' or part-time firefighters, mainly in rural areas and small towns. About 1,400 people work as volunteer firefighters in Scotland.

Entry Level: Firefighters need a good general education. Some brigades may ask for specific GCSEs/S grades, while some entrants already have A levels/AH or H grades or a degree. You may have to pass a written entrance test and you would have to undergo a series of initiative and physical tests. These may be conducted over two days. Brigades may also test for practical aptitude and aerobic fitness and the ability to work well in a team.

There is no minimum or maximum height, but you must pass a test of fitness and strength. You need good eyesight without glasses or contact lenses and you must be at least 18.

Making the Grade: As a new full-time recruit in England and Wales, you would attend an induction course, lasting between 12 and 16 weeks, in a local fire training centre. In Scotland, you would attend a 16-week course at the Scottish Fire Training School.

Initial training includes using protective clothing and breathing apparatus, entering smoke-filled rooms, using foam and other fire extinguishing media, using ladders, hoses, knots, hydraulic and other equipment and administering first aid. There is also an emphasis on personal discipline and fitness.

After induction training, you would join a fire station and spend a probationary period of up to two years learning from experienced firefighters. In most brigades, you would be encouraged to work towards National/Scottish Vocational Qualifications (NVQ/SVQ) Levels 2 and 3 in Emergency Fire Services. You would be expected to continue to train throughout your career.

Induction training for retained firefighters is usually spread over a series of weekends. Throughout their service, retained firefighters attend weekly drill nights at which they practise the same practical skills as full-time firefighters.

Personal Qualities

Firefighters need courage, stamina and an advanced standard of physical fitness. You must be able to react quickly but to remain calm in hazardous situations. You would need a high level of personal discipline and must enjoy working as a member of a close-knit team.

You should have good practical skills to operate a variety of hand and power tools and equipment and the ability to write clear incident reports, which may be used by accident or insurance investigators as a basis for claims in a court of law.

Good communication skills and the ability to inspire confidence are necessary when dealing with members of the public who are frightened, injured or in a state of shock.

Looking Ahead

There is considerable competition for full-time firefighter positions and there are always many more applicants than vacancies. However, some rural areas find it difficult to fill all retained firefighter positions.

All new entrants start in the same grade, with promotion strictly on merit. If you can demonstrate competence in your current role and pass the necessary exams, you can progress from firefighter to crew commander, then to watch, station, area, group and finally brigade commander. It is usually necessary to move to different areas for promotion and most senior officers have worked in several brigades, at one of the training colleges or with the Fire Service Inspectorate.

A firefighter is trained and equipped to put out fires, rescue people, aid and assist during natural disasters and, increasingly, provide emergency medical services. The fire service, also known in some countries as the fire brigade or fire department, is one of the emergency services.

Firefighting is the process and profession of extinguishing fires. Firefighting and firefighters have become ubiquitous around the world, from urban areas to wildland areas and on board ships. Not all firefighters are paid for their services. In some countries, including the United States, Canada, Finland, Australia and New Zealand, there are often paid, or "career" ("professional" is falling out of popular usage due to the perception that non-paid volunteers would thus be termed "unprofessional") firefighters working. Additionally, there are volunteer and "call" or "retained" (firefighters who are paid for the specific time they are responding to emergencies) firefighters who are not employed full time as firefighters.

In the United Kingdom and Ireland, the use of retained firefighters (who are part-time, but are paid when on duty) rather than volunteers is standard. In Australia volunteer Brigades which are unpaid mostly rural services (although traditionally they are paid by their employers if called out during working hours) are separate from career Brigades and if arriving at a fire scene first can assume command over the local career Brigade as their training is similar to profesional firemen. These volunteers also man career firestations during emergencies.

In Germany, volunteer fire departments are established in every town: even the biggest German city, Berlin, with more than 3.4 million inhabitants, has volunteer fire fighters bedides a career fire service. In fact, only 101 German cities (most of them are towns with more than 100,000 citizens) have a career fire service, called "Berufsfeuerwehr" in German, but in every of these cities a volunteer fire service exist, too. In cities with a career fire service, volunteer fire brigades support the career fire service at big fires, accidents and desasters. Many of the so called volunteer departments (usually in towns with 30,000 till 100,000 inhabitants), except in very small towns and villages, are in fact a mixed service of a core of career firemen who are supported by true volunteer firefighters should need arise. However, the official title of those departments is nevertheless "volunteer fire service".

Goals of Firefighting

The three main goals in firefighting are (in order) life safety, incident stabilization, property conservation and environmental preservation. Firefighting is an inherently difficult occupation. As such, the skills required for safe operations are regularly practiced during training evolutions throughout a firefighter's career. In the United States, the preeminent fire training and standards organization is the National Fire Protection Association (NFPA). Often initial firefighting skills are taught during a local, regional, or state approved fire academy. Depending on the requirements of a department, additional skills and certifications such as technical rescue and Paramedicine may also be taught at this time.

Firefighters work closely with other emergency response agencies, most particularly local and state police departments. As every fire scene is technically a crime scene until deemed otherwise by a qualified investigator, there is often overlap between the responsibilities of responding firefighters and police officers such as evidence and scene protection, initial observations of first respondents and chain of evidence issues. The increasing role of firefighters in providing emergency medical services also brings firefighters into common overlap with law enforcement. One example of this is a common state law requiring all gunshot wounds to be reported to law enforcement agencies.

Most career (full time, paid) firefighters in North America are represented by the International Association of Fire Fighters

Fire fighting has several basic skills: prevention, self preservation, rescue, preservation of property and fire control. Firefighting is further broken down into skills which include size-up, extinguishment, ventilation and salvage and overhaul. Search and Rescue, which has already been mentioned, is performed early in any fire scenario and many times is in unison with extinguishment and ventilation.

Prevention

Prevention attempts to ensure that no place simultaneously has sufficient heat, fuel and air to allow ignition and combustion. Fernando Cardona, the leading researcher in fire prevention is accredited with much of the advancement and improvement to modern fire fighting technique. Most prevention programmes are directed at controlling the energy of activation (heat). Fire suppression systems have a proven record for controlling and extinguishing unwanted fires. Many fire officials recommend that every building, including residences, have fire sprinkler systems. Correctly working sprinklers in a residence greatly reduce the risk of death from a fire. With the small rooms typical of a residence, one or two sprinklers can cover most rooms.

In addition, a major duty of fire services is the regular inspection of buildings to ensure they are up to the current building fire codes, which are enforced so that a building can sufficiently resist fire spread, potential hazards are located and to ensure that occupants can be safely evacuated, commensurate with the risks involved.

Self-preservation: Self-preservation is critical. The basic technique firefighters use is to know where they are and to avoid hazards. Current standards in the United States recommend that firefighters work in teams, using a "two-in, two-out" rule whenever in an IDLH (Immediately Dangerous to Life or Health) environment.

Tools are generally carried at all times and are important for not only forcible entry but also for self rescue. A Self Contained Breathing Apparatus (SCBA) delivers air to the firefighter through a full face mask and is worn to protect against smoke inhalation, toxic fumes and super heated gasses. A special device called a Personal Alert Safety System (PASS) is commonly worn independently or as a part of the SCBA to alert others when a firefighter stops moving for a specified period of time or manually operates the device. The PASS device sounds an alarm that can assist another firefighter (Firefighter Assist and Search Team), in locating the firefighter in distress.

Firefighters often carry personal self rescue ropes. The ropes are generally 30 feet long and can provide a firefighter (that has enough time to deploy the rope) a partially controlled exit out an elevated window. Lack of a personal rescue rope is cited in the deaths of two New York City Firefighters, Lt. John Bellew and Lt. Curtis Meyran, who died after they jumped from a fourth floor of a burning apartment building in the Bronx. Of the four firefighters who jumped and survived only one of them had a self rescue rope. Since the incident the Fire Department of New York City has issued self rescue ropes to their firefighters.

In the United States, 25% of fatalities to firefighters are caused by vehicle accidents while responding or returning from an incident. Many firefighters are also injured or killed by vehicles while working at an incident (Paulison 2005). However, a large percentage of firefighters also succumb to heart disease, in the line of duty.

Occupational Health and Safety

Occupational cancer among firefighters is a major occupational health and safety concern. Every year, these lesions produce significant human and financial costs for workers and employers. However, it is difficult, in the absence of epidemiological studies, to establish a link between the appearance of a cancer and the characteristics of the job. Critical reviews of the epidemiological literature related to cancer risk in firefighters include:

- "Risk of Brain Tumours in Firemen"
- "Risk of Urinary Bladder Tumours in Firemen"
- "Risk of Kidney Tumours in Firemen"

Rescue

Rescue operations consist of searching for and removing trapped occupants of hazardous conditions. Animals may also be recovered, if resources and conditions permit. Generally triage and first aid are performed outside, as removal from the hazardous atmosphere is the primary goal in preserving life. Search patterns include movement against room walls (to prevent rescuers from becoming lost or disoriented) and methodical searches of specific areas by designated teams. Unlike a fire control team, a rescue team typically moves faster, but has no hose to follow out to safety through the smoky darkness. A rescue rope may be needed for tethering a team involved in exceptionally dangerous conditions.

Incident commanders also arrange for standby search and rescue teams to assist if firefighters become lost, trapped, or injured. Such teams are commonly and often interchangeably, known as Rapid Intervention Teams (RIT), or Firefighter Assist and Search Teams (FAST). According to "two-in, two-out", the only time it is permissible for a team of firefighters to enter a burning structure without backup in place outside is when they are operating in what is known as "Rescue Mode". Rescue Mode occurs when firefighters have arrived at the scene and it is readily apparent that there are occupants trapped inside who need immediate rescue. At such a time, properly equipped firefighters (exercising good judgment tempered by training and experience) may enter the structure and proceed directly to victims in need of rescue, RIT will then be put in place when resources permit.

The Worcester Cold Storage Warehouse fire provides a stark example of disoriented rescuers perishing when their air supply was exhausted during a fruitless primary search and subsequent RIT searches.

Searches for trapped victims are exhaustively detailed, often including searches of cupboards, closets and under beds. The search is divided into two stages, the primary and secondary. The primary search is conducted quickly and thoroughly, typically beginning in the area closest to the fire as it is subjected to the highest risk of exposure. The secondary search only begins once the fire is under control and is always (resources and personnel permitting) performed by a different team from that which did the primary search.

Rescue operations may also involve the extrication of victims of motor vehicle crashes (abbreviated MVC). Here firefighters use spreaders, cutters and hydraulic rams, collectively called hydraulic rescue tools--known better to the public as Jaws of Life--to remove metal from the patient, followed by actually removing the patient, usually on a backboard with collar and transferring to a waiting ambulance crew in the cold zone. More technical forms of rescue include subsets such as rope rescue, swiftwater rescue, confined space rescue and trench rescue. These types of rescue are often extremely hazardous and physically demanding. They also require extensive technical training. NFPA regulation 1006 and 1670 state that a "rescuer" must have medical training to perform any technical rescue operation. Accordingly, firefighters involved in rescue operations have some kind of medical training as first responders, emergency medical technicians, paramedics or nurses.

Communication and Command Structure

Firefighters are trained to use communications equipment to receive alarms, give and receive commands, request assistance and report on conditions. Since firefighters from different agencies routinely provide mutual aid to each other and routinely operate at incidents where other emergency services are present, it is essential to have structures in place to establish a unified chain of command and share information between agencies. The U.S. Federal Emergency Management Agency has established a National Incident Management System. One component of this system is the Incident Command System.

Property

Buildings that are made of flammable materials such as wood are different from so called "fire-resistant" buildings such as concrete high-rises. Generally, a "fire-resistant" building is designed to limit fire to a small area or floor. Other floors can be safe simply by preventing smoke inhalation and damage. All buildings suspected of being on fire must be evacuated, regardless of fire rating.

While sometimes fires can be limited to small areas of a structure, wider collateral damage due to smoke, water and burning embers is common. Utility shutoff (such as gas, electricity and water) is typically an early priority of arriving fire crews. Furthermore, fire prevention can take on a special meaning for property where hazardous materials are being used or stored.

Some fire fighting tactics may appear to be destructive, but often serve specific needs. For example, during "ventilation" firefighters are often forced to open holes in the roof or floors of a structure (called "vertical ventilation") or open windows or walls (called "horizontal ventilation") to remove smoke and heated gases from the interior of the structure.

Whenever possible, movable property is moved into the middle of a room and covered with a heavy cloth tarp (a "salvage cover"). Other steps may be taken to divert or remove fire flow runoff (thus salvaging property by avoiding unnecessary damage), retrieving/protecting valuables found during suppression or overhaul and boarding windows, roofs and doors against the elements and looters.

Fire Control

Fire control (or fire fighting) consists of depriving a fire of fuel, oxygen and/or heat that are necessary to sustain itself or re-kindle. Firefighters are equipped with a wide variety of equipment to accomplish this task. Some of their tools include ladder trucks, pumper trucks, tanker trucks, fire hose and fire extinguishers. Very frequent training and refresher training is required.

Structure fires may be attacked, generally, either by "interior" or "exterior" resources, or both. Interior crews, using the "two-in, two out" rule, may advance hose lines inside the building, find the fire and cool it with water. Exterior crews may direct water into windows or other openings, or against other nearby fuels exposed to the initial fire. A proper command structure will plan and coordinate the various teams and equipment to safely execute each tactic.

Equipment

A partial list of some standard equipment used by firefighters:

- flat-head axe
- halligan bar
- closet hook
- pike pole
- halligan hook
- bunker gear, including turnout jacket and pants
- fire-retardant and water-resistant boots with steel toe and a full length steel sole
- flashlight
- Nomex hood
- Self-Contained Breathing Apparatus (SCBA)
- helmet, face mask and/or visor
- NFPA-compliant, fire-resistant work gloves
- PASS device (Personal Alert Safety System)
- handheld radio
- hydraulic rescue tools
- Duck-bill lock breaker
- Spanner wrench
- Circular saw ("K-12")

History of Fire Brigades

The history of organized combating of structural fires dates back at least to ancient Egypt. Today, fire and rescue remains a mix of paid, call and volunteer responders. The UK have the retained fire service, whereby fire fighters are on call with pagers from their homes and/or place of work. The most notable is Malpas retained in Cheshire.

Firefighting Worldwide

Traditions, protocol and trends in firefighting vary from country to country. For more information on national firefighting procedures.

Miscellaneous

In popular literature, firefighters are usually depicted with Dalmatian dogs. This breed originated in southern Europe to assist with herding livestock and run along with horses and in the days of horse-drawn fire vehicles, the horses were usually released on arrival at the fire and the Dalmatians would lead the horses through traffic and to a safe place to wait until the fire was out. Dalmatians also filled the role of protecting the horses' feet from other dogs as equipment was being transported to the fire scene.

In reality, most fire dogs were mutts pulled from the street (and thus cheaper to acquire). In addition, Dalmatians have a reputation for skittishness and congenital defects, such as deafness due to inbreeding.

Fire hydrants are referred to in some regions as "fire plugs". This term originated with the advent of the first municipal water systems, in which the "pipes" were often actually hollowed out logs. For firefighting purposes, cobblestones were removed from the street or sidewalk to access the wooden water main. A hole was drilled into the log and then "plugged" with a wooden plug or stake. In the event of a fire, firefighters would locate the "fire plug" and unplug it to obtain water.

Many fire companies around the world, especially in the United States develop annual beefcake calendars. In these calendars handsome and muscular firemen appear scantily clad and sometimes cavorting. These calendars proceeds function as fundraisers for their fire department and for charities.

Social Workers

Significant Points: About 9 out of 10 jobs were in health care and social assistance industries, as well as State and local government agencies.

While a bachelor's degree is the minimum requirement, a master's degree in social work or a related field has become the standard for many positions.

Employment is projected to grow faster than average.

Competition for jobs is expected in cities, but opportunities should be good in rural areas.

Nature of the Work: Social work is a profession for those with a strong desire to help improve people's lives. Social workers help people function the best way they can in their environment, deal with their relationships and solve personal and family problems. Social workers often see clients who face a life-threatening disease or a social problem, such as inadequate housing, unemployment, a serious illness, a disability, or substance abuse. Social workers also assist families that have serious domestic conflicts, sometimes involving child or spousal abuse.

Social workers often provide social services in health-related settings that now are governed by managed care organizations. To contain costs, these organizations emphasize short-term intervention, ambulatory and community-based care and greater decentralization of services.

Most social workers specialize. Although some conduct research or are involved in planning or policy development, most social workers prefer an area of practice in which they interact with clients.

Child, family and school social workers provide social services and assistance to improve the social and psychological functioning of children and their families and to maximize the family well-being and academic functioning of children. Some social workers assist single parents, arrange adoptions, or help find foster homes for neglected, abandoned, or abused children. In schools, they address such problems as teenage pregnancy, misbehaviour and truancy and advise teachers on how to cope with problem students.

Increasingly, school social workers are teaching workshops to an entire class. Some social workers specialize in services for senior citizens, running support groups for family caregivers or for the adult children of aging parents, advising elderly people or family members about choices in areas such as housing, transportation and long-term care and coordinating and monitoring these services.

Through employee assistance programmes, they may help workers cope with job-related pressures or with personal problems that affect the quality of their work. Child, family and school social workers typically work for individual and family services agencies, schools, or State or local governments. These social workers may be known as child welfare social workers, family services social workers, child protective services social workers, occupational social workers, or gerontology social workers.

Medical and public health social workers provide persons, families, or vulnerable populations with the psychosocial support needed to cope with chronic, acute, or terminal illnesses, such as Alzheimer's disease, cancer, or AIDS. They also advise family caregivers, counsel patients and help plan for patients' needs after discharge by arranging for at-home services, from meals-on-wheels to oxygen equipment. Some work on interdisciplinary teams that evaluate certain kinds of patients-geriatric or organ transplant patients, for example. Medical and public health social workers may work for hospitals, nursing and personal care facilities, individual and family services agencies, or local governments.

Mental health and substance abuse social workers assess and treat individuals with mental illness or substance abuse problems, including abuse of alcohol, tobacco, or other drugs. Such services include individual and group therapy, outreach, crisis intervention, social rehabilitation and training in skills of everyday living. They also may help plan for supportive services to ease patients' return to the community. Mental health and substance abuse social workers are likely to work in hospitals, substance abuse treatment centers, individual and family services agencies, or local governments. These social workers may be known as clinical social workers. (Counselors and psychologists, who may provide similar services, are discussed elsewhere in the Handbook.)

Other types of social workers include social work planners and policymakers, who develop programmes to address such issues as child abuse, homelessness, substance abuse, poverty and violence. These workers research and analyze policies, programmes and regulations. They identify social problems and suggest legislative and other solutions. They may help raise funds or write grants to support these programmes.

Working Conditions: Full-time social workers usually work a standard 40-hour week; however, some occasionally work evenings and weekends to meet with clients, attend community meetings and handle emergencies. Some, particularly in voluntary nonprofit agencies, work part time. Social workers usually spend most of their time in an office or residential facility, but also may travel locally to visit clients, meet with service providers, or attend meetings. Some may use one of several offices within a local area in which to meet with clients. The work, while satisfying, can be emotionally draining. Understaffing and large caseloads add to the pressure in some agencies. To tend to patient care or client needs, many hospitals and long-term care facilities are employing social workers on teams with a broad mix of occupations, including clinical specialists, registered nurses and health aides.

Training, Other Qualifications and Advancement: A bachelor's degree in social work (BSW) degree is the most common minimum requirement to qualify for a job as a social worker; however, majors in psychology, sociology and related fields may qualify for some entry-level jobs, especially in small community agencies. Although a bachelor's degree is sufficient for entry into the field, an advanced degree has become the standard for many positions. A master's degree in social work (MSW) is typically required for positions in health settings and is required for clinical work as well. Some jobs in public and private agencies also may require an advanced degree, such as a master's degree in social services policy or administration. Supervisory, administrative and staff training positions usually require an advanced degree. College and university teaching positions and most research appointments normally require a doctorate in social work (DSW or Ph.D.).

As of 2004, the Council on Social Work Education (CSWE) accredited 442 BSW programmes and 168 MSW programmes. The Group for the Advancement of Doctoral Education (GADE) listed 80 doctoral programmes in social work (DSW or Ph.D.). BSW programmes prepare graduates for direct service positions, such as caseworker and include courses in social work values and ethics, dealing with a culturally diverse clientele, at-risk populations, promotion of social and economic justice, human behaviour and the social environment, social welfare policy and services, social work practice, social research methods and field education. Accredited BSW programmes require a minimum of 400 hours of supervised field experience.

Master's degree programmes prepare graduates for work in their chosen field of concentration and continue to develop the skills required to perform clinical assessments, manage large caseloads, take on supervisory roles and explore new ways of drawing upon social services to meet the needs of clients. Master's programmes last 2 years and include a minimum of 900 hours of supervised field instruction, or internship.

A part-time programme may take 4 years. Entry into a master's programme does not require a bachelor's degree in social work, but courses in psychology, biology, sociology, economics, political science and social work are recommended. In addition, a second language can be very helpful. Most master's programmes offer advanced standing for those with a bachelor's degree from an accredited social work programme.

All States and the District of Columbia have licensing, certification, or registration requirements regarding social work practice and the use of professional titles. Although standards for licensing vary by State, a growing number of States are placing greater emphasis on communications skills, professional ethics and sensitivity to cultural diversity issues. Most States require two years (3,000 hours) of supervised clinical experience for licensure of clinical social workers.

In addition, the National Association of Social Workers (NASW) offers voluntary credentials. Social workers with an MSW may be eligible for the Academy of Certified Social Workers (ACSW), the Qualified Clinical Social Worker (QCSW), or the Diplomate in Clinical Social Work (DCSW) credential, based on their professional experience. Credentials are particularly important for those in private practice; some health insurance providers require social workers to have them in order to be reimbursed for services.

Social workers should be emotionally mature, objective and sensitive to people and their problems. They must be able to handle responsibility, work independently and maintain good working relationships with clients and coworkers. Volunteer or paid jobs as a social work aide offer ways of testing one's interest in this field.

Advancement to supervisor, programme manager, assistant director, or executive director of a social service agency or department is possible, but usually requires an advanced degree and related work experience. Other career options for social workers include teaching, research and consulting. Some of these workers also help formulate government policies by analyzing and advocating policy positions in government agencies, in research institutions and on legislators' staffs.

Some social workers go into private practice. Most private practitioners are clinical social workers who provide psychotherapy, usually paid for through health insurance or by the client themselves. Private practitioners must have at least a master's degree and a period of supervised work experience. A network of contacts for referrals also is essential. Many private practitioners split their time between working for an agency or hospital and working in their private practice. They may continue to hold a position at a hospital or agency in order to receive health and life insurance.

Employment: Social workers held about 562,000 jobs in 2004. About 9 out of 10 jobs were in health care and social assistance industries, as well as State and local government agencies, primarily in departments of health and human services. Although most social workers are employed in cities or suburbs, some work in rural areas. The following tabulation shows 2004 employment by type of social worker:

Child, family and school social workers	272,000
Mental health and substance abuse social workers	116,000
Medical and public health social workers	110,000
Social workers, all other	64,000

Job Outlook: Competition for social worker jobs is expected in cities, where demand for services often is highest and training programmes for social workers are prevalent. However, opportunities should be good in rural areas, which often find it difficult to attract and retain qualified staff. By specialty, job prospects may be best for those social workers with a background in gerontology and substance abuse treatment. Employment of social workers is expected to increase faster than the average for all occupations through 2014.

The rapidly growing elderly population and the aging baby boom generation will create greater demand for health and social services, resulting in particularly rapid job growth among gerontology social workers. Many job openings also will stem from the need to replace social workers who leave the occupation.

As hospitals continue to limit the length of patient stays, the demand for social workers in hospitals will grow more slowly than in other areas. Because hospitals are releasing patients earlier than in the past, social worker employment in home health care services is growing.

However, the expanding senior population is an even larger factor. Employment opportunities for social workers with backgrounds in gerontology should be good in the growing numbers of assisted-living and senior-living communities. The expanding senior population also will spur demand for social workers in nursing homes, long-term care facilities and hospices.

Strong demand is expected for substance abuse social workers over the 2004-14 projection period. Substance abusers are increasingly being placed into treatment programmes instead of being sentenced to prison.

Because of the increasing numbers of individuals sentenced to prison or probation who are substance abusers, correctional systems are increasingly requiring substance abuse treatment as a condition added to their sentencing or probation. As this trend grows, demand will increase for treatment programmes and social workers to assist abusers on the road to recovery.

Employment of social workers in private social service agencies also will increase. However, agencies increasingly will restructure services and hire more lower paid social and human service assistants instead of social workers. Employment in State and local government agencies may grow somewhat in response to increasing needs for public welfare, family services and child protection services; however, many of these services will be contracted out to private agencies. Employment levels in public and private social services agencies may fluctuate, depending on need and government funding levels.

Employment of school social workers also is expected to grow as expanded efforts to respond to rising student enrollments and continued emphasis on integrating disabled children into the general school population lead to more jobs.

There could be competition for school social work jobs in some areas because of the limited number of openings. The availability of Federal, State and local funding will be a major factor in determining the actual job growth in schools.

Opportunities for social workers in private practice will expand, but growth may be somewhat hindered by restrictions that managed care organizations put on mental health services. The growing popularity of employee assistance programmes is expected to spur demand for private practitioners, some of whom provide social work services to corporations on a contractual basis.

However, the popularity of employee assistance programmes will fluctuate with the business cycle, because businesses are not likely to offer these services during recessions.

Earnings: Median annual earnings of child, family and school social workers were $34,820 in May 2004. The middle 50 percent earned between $27,840 and $45,140. The lowest 10 percent earned less than $23,130 and the top 10 percent earned more than $57,860. Median annual earnings in the industries employing the largest numbers of child, family and school social workers in May 2004 were:

Elementary and secondary schools	$44,300
Local government	40,620
State government	35,070
Individual and family services	30,680
Other residential care facilities	30,550

Median annual earnings of medical and public health social workers were $40,080 in May 2004. The middle 50 percent earned between $31,620 and $50,080. The lowest 10 percent earned less than $25,390 and the top 10 percent earned more than $58,740. Median annual earnings in the industries employing the largest numbers of medical and public health social workers in May 2004 were:

General medical and surgical hospitals	$44,920
Home health care services	42,710
Local government	39,390
Nursing care facilities	35,680
Individual and family services	32,100

Median annual earnings of mental health and substance abuse social workers were $33,920 in May 2004. The middle 50 percent earned between $26,730 and $43,430. The lowest 10 percent earned less than $21,590 and the top 10 percent earned more than $54,180. Median annual earnings in the industries employing the largest numbers of mental health and substance abuse social workers in May 2004 were:

Psychiatric and substance abuse hospitals	$36,170
Local government	35,720
Outpatient care centers	33,220
Individual and family services	32,810
Residential mental retardation, mental health and substance abuse facilities	29,110

Median annual earnings of social workers, all other were $39,440 in May 2004. The middle 50 percent earned between $30,350 and $51,530. The lowest 10 percent earned less than $24,080 and the top 10 percent earned more than $62,720. Median annual earnings in the industries employing the largest numbers of social workers, all other in May 2004 were:

Local government	$42,570
State government	40,940
Individual and family services	32,280

About 1 out of 5 social workers is a member of a union. Many belong to the union associated with their place of employment.

A Career in Child Protection

Child Protection Practitioner—CPW

Most children and young people are adequately cared for and nurtured by their families. It is only when parents or caregivers are unable or unwilling to protect children against significant harm that the child protection network must take up this responsibility. The Child Protection Service is specifically targeted to those children and young people who are at risk of significant harm and whose parents are unable or unwilling to protect them.

The Child Protection Service is part of a broader child and family welfare network of community professionals and organisations that share the responsibility for working with vulnerable families and for promoting and ensuring the health and wellbeing of children and young people. Child protection practitioners also work with the courts, police and other government agencies to keep children safe from harm.

The Child Protection Service in Victoria employs around 1,000 people in regional offices around the state. Child protection is a specialist field of social welfare practice. It often involves work with families struggling to parent children in a context of issues such as poverty, addiction and violence. Many of these families do not welcome our involvement and the work requires patience, sensitivity and an ability to think clearly and analytically.

A Career in Radiation Protection

What Is Radiation Protection?: Radiation protection, often called health physics, is a specialised multidisciplinary part of health and safety. Radiation Protection Practitioners (RPPs) give advice and guidance on work with ionising and non-ionising radiations and with radioactive materials. This advice and guidance can be provided for people at work or for protection of the public and the environment.

All aspects of radiation protection are covered by Government Regulations and enforced by Regulators some of whom are experienced in radiation protection.

Radiation Protection Practice: **The practice of radiation protection includes:**

operational radiation protection;
radiation dosimetry;
radiation measurement techniques;
design and safety assessments;
research;
emergency planning;
the control and safety aspects of radioactive waste management;
the safe transport of radioactive materials;
environmental monitoring and protection.

Operational radiation protection covers the day to day safety of workers and the public via the application of basic principles and by ensuring compliance with regulations. A RPP requires strong interpersonal skills, particularly in the areas of communication and industrial relations and the job will usually include training people.

Radiation dosimetry and radiation measurement techniques are often specialisms within radiation protection and require a higher level of specific technical competence.

Design and safety assessment covers all types of plant and equipment, both large and small and includes learning from operational experience. Research takes place to support the operational practice and covers, for example, radiobiology, epidemiology, measurement techniques and assessment of environmental impact.

Radiation Protection requires people working at every level of competence? from routine measurements using simple hand held instruments to highly sophisticated laboratory equipment and from simple instruction to advice that has a very high political, social or economic impact.

Qualifications and Training

The initial qualification required is very dependent upon the area of radiation protection in which you choose to work and the level of responsibility associated with your duties.

You can commence a career in radiation protection with GCSE and A-level qualifications in numerate subjects (sciences generally). However, in all cases, you will require additional specialist training. Courses are run at some Further Education Colleges, usually in association with The City and Guilds of London Institute.

At the full professional level you will normally require a degree in a science subject, most commonly physics, chemistry or biology. A higher degree, such as a Masters Degree or Doctorate, will normally be required if you are seeking a career in research. The IPEM provides a structured four year training programme for graduate trainees entering the radiation protection profession in the medical field.

Several MSc courses include radiation protection in their syllabus. The Radiation Protection Division of the Health Protection Agency runs training courses and also provides short courses on particular aspects of radiation protection. Similarly, other professional societies provide training courses usually focused on their own specialism.

The Ionising Radiations Regulations 1999 require an employer using ionising radiations to seek advice from and if necessary appoint, a suitable Radiation Protection Adviser (RPA). An RPA is an experienced RPP who has been legally required, by HSE, to demonstrate competence by being the current holder of either:

- A Certificate of RPA Core Competence from an Assessing Body. (RPA2000 is such an awarding body); or
- A National Vocational Qualification in Radiation Protection Practice, at Level 4.

In addition, an employer has to be satisfied that the RPA is suitable to give advice in relation to that employer's particular uses of ionising radiations. This means that the RPA must have relevant experience prior to the appointment or must be suitably trained by the employer before appointment.

Most employers provide extensive on the job training to supplement formal education and qualifications. This training is clearly oriented to the employer's particular area of work.

At all levels of Radiation Protection, you will need to keep up to date with developments and continue to maintain your expertise. You will be able to do this through a Continuing Professional Development (CPD) Scheme, such as the SRPs own scheme.

Potential Employers: Employment opportunities exist in:

general industry (radiography, source manufacture, transport, instrumentation);

the nuclear power industry;

hospitals;

universities and research establishments;

government departments;

specialist contractors, agencies and consultancies serving radiation protection.

The nuclear industry is probably the largest employer of full time RPPs, often known as Health Physicists, covering all aspects of radiation protection. Nuclear Power Stations are operated by British Energy and by the British Nuclear Group. The British Nuclear Group also manufactures and reprocesses nuclear fuel. Many nuclear sites are owned by the Nuclear Decommissioning Authority and operated under contract by a variety of companies.

The Ministry of Defence and its contractors operate dockyards for nuclear vessels at Devonport in Southern England and at Rosyth and Faslane in Scotland. There are nuclear weapons establishments at Aldermaston and Burghfield and at other locations.

GE Healthcare manufactures radioisotopes for medicine and research at establishments in Amersham and Cardiff.

The Radiation Protection Division of the Health Protection Agency, with premises at Chilton near Oxford, Leeds and Glasgow, is a national centre of expertise and not only advises the UK government on radiation protection standards but provides advice to radiation users on a commercial basis.

There are research establishments run by the Medical Research Council and the Science and Engineering Research

Council at Chilton and by the Centre for Environment, Fisheries & Aquaculture Science at Lowestoft.

Hospitals require full time RPPs and information can be obtained from the Institute of Physics and Engineering in Medicine (IPEM).

Universities and colleges may employ a RPP (often known as a Radiation Protection Officer) and information can be obtained from the Association of University Radiation Protection Officers (AURPO).

Government Regulators also employ RPPs but do not normally recruit candidates direct from university since they are usually seeking staff with prior work experience.

Career Structure: All of the major employers have a good career structure with promotion based upon merit including, in some cases, progression across the graduate interface. Particularly on the operational side, responsibility comes at an early stage, with consequent promotion opportunities. There is a fair degree of interchange between major employers. In some cases promotion from radiation protection managerial posts to higher general managerial posts is also possible. Formal appointment as a Radiation Protection Adviser, as required by the Ionising Radiations Regulations, is a likely target for those involved in operational radiation protection.

Bursaries and Studentships: Bursaries and Studentships are available from a number of sources for both undergraduate and postgraduate courses. The SRP offers a number of annual bursaries for postgraduate study. Some organisations offer graduate sponsorships to appropriate students.

Professional Societies

The SRP is exclusively concerned with radiation protection. Its membership exceeds 1400, comprising Fellows, Members, Graduates, Associates, Students and Affiliates. Its objectives are to aid the development of scientific, technical, medical and legal aspects of radiation protection in the manner of a learned society and to promote and improve radiation protection as a profession. The SRP achieves its objectives by means of meetings, conferences, lectures and publications, with emphasis on those subjects which contribute to the knowledge and practice of radiation protection. The Society has an official publication, The Journal of Radiological Protection, which is published quarterly and supplied free to members. The SRP is the UK Associate Society of the International Radiation Protection Association. Details of membership of the SRP and further information about any of the matters in this leaflet may be obtained from the SRP Administrative Office. In summary, the SRPs activities include:

Scientific Meetings

E-mail discussion groups

Journal

Continuing Professional Development Scheme

Newsletter

Information about job vacancies

Networking

Representation on Management Board of RPA 2000

Bursaries

Other Professional Societies include

Association of University Radiation Protection Officers (AURPO)

Institute of Physics and Engineering in Medicine (IPEM)

Human Services Caseworker

Job Description: Human Services Caseworkers in the Office of Elder Services perform professional social work in the areas of adult protective services and public guardianship and/or conservatorship. Caseworkers provide services that promote client self-determination and enhance welfare with the least restrictive alternatives consistent with the client's need for services.

This position requires teamwork and flexibility within the work environment to meet client needs. Work includes assessing danger and/or risk of abuse, neglect, or exploitation; client's mental capacity and dependency; support systems; developing a case plan; providing ongoing case management; and petitioning for guardianship and/or conservatorship. Case management activities for adults under guardianship/conservatorship include medical, psychiatric, placement and financial decision-making.

Minimum Requirements: In order to qualify, you must have a Bachelors Degree in Social Work/Social Welfare, or a Bachelors Degree in a field related to social work/social welfare* as determined by the Maine State Board of Social Worker Licensure.

Necessary Special Requirement: Applicants must have or be eligible for conditional or full licensure at the Licensed Social Worker (LSW) level as issued by the Maine State Board of Social Worker Licensure. An LSW requires an earned BA/BS in social work/social welfare. An LSW-Conditional requires an earned BA/BS in a field related to social work/social welfare.

Maine State Board of Social Worker Licensure regulations defines a field related to social work or social welfare as including but not limited to: "behavioral science, social and behavioural sciences, childhood development, education and human development, mental health and human services, psychology, psychology/educational psychology, rehabilitation services and sociology."

General Information:

- The Department of Health and Human Services has vacancies on a regular basis throughout the State. These positions require extensive travel in an assigned geographic area and work requires regular after-hours (overtime) work. We are seeking individuals who reflect the cultural, ethnic and linguistic diversity of our clients.
- Qualified applicants will be added to the existing Employment Register which will be used to fill future vacancies throughout the state as they occur.
- Please include one self-addressed, stamped envelope with your application for notification of your Training & Experience Evaluation results.

Typical duties in this job classification include:

- Solicits and evaluates information concerning indicators of mental functioning, dependency, immediate danger and substantial risk of danger.

- Interviews clients, family, collateral contacts and professionals.
- Assesses client mental capacity, including ability to give informed consent.
- Assesses client support systems.
- Visits client regularly for ongoing assessment of client needs and safety.
- Makes findings, based on facts, regarding incapacitation, dependency and danger or substantial risk of danger.
- Develops, implements and monitors case plans to eliminate or reduce danger or substantial risk of danger.
- Responds to crisis situations to protect client.
- Refers clients to appropriate services, negotiates for and coordinates services on behalf of the client.
- Advocates for service provision.
- Locates resources and effects placement in alternative living arrangements.
- Facilitates and attends treatment team meetings and case conferences.
- Collects and compiles social case history.
- Provides related court activities such as preparing and filing petitions, testifying and preparing clients and witnesses for hearings.
- Develops budget plans and monitors client expenses and assets.
- Maintains accurate case records of assessment, activities and plans; writes summaries, reports, letters and memos.

Testing Procedure: The information you provide with your application will be compared to criteria developed by experts who are familiar with this job and its requirements and converted to a numerical score. You should highlight experience which demonstrates a commitment to the elderly and/or adults with disabilities-AND-an understanding of issues important to these groups. The Bureau of Human Resources reserves the right to use any other selection devices necessary in order to identify those candidates who are most qualified.

Warden

Traffic wardens keep traffic moving smoothly through towns and cities. They patrol the streets looking out for illegally parked vehicles. They check that vehicles display valid 'pay and display' tickets and so on. Wardens write parking tickets (fixed penalty notices) when there are infringements of regulations.

Work Activities: Traffic wardens aim to keep traffic moving smoothly through towns and cities. They patrol the streets, deal with illegally parked vehicles and issue parking tickets (fixed penalty notices). They also advise motorists and the general public. For instance, they may tell motorists where they can park and give directions to nearby places. Increasingly, wardens are employed to support operational policing tasks.

Wardens take responsibility for directing traffic when there is an accident or when traffic lights fail at a major junction. They help the police to direct traffic at big events such as pop concerts or demonstrations.

Traffic wardens look out for and report out-of-date tax discs. This can involve liaising with DVLA (Driver and Vehicle Licensing Agency) clamping teams. Wardens also look out for stolen cars and unroadworthy vehicles. It may be necessary to appear in court to give evidence. Occasionally, wardens write reports on traffic incidents.

Other duties include assisting with the removal of illegally parked vehicles, receiving vehicles that have been towed away and enforcing night-time lorry bans.

At the beginning and end of each day, wardens report to the traffic wardens' office. The rest of the time is normally spent on the streets. While a lot of time is spent on foot patrol, wardens also patrol in cars, vans and on motorcycles.

A uniform and protective/wet weather clothing are provided.

Personal Qualities and Skills: Traffic wardens need to be observant, alert and able to think and act quickly. Common sense and initiative are required. Experience of working with the general public is useful. You need to be capable of dealing calmly with motorists who are upset or aggressive. Tact and patience are needed and a sense of humour helps. The ability to work alone, without close supervision, is important.

To be a warden you need to be physically fit, as you will spend a lot of time on your feet, working outdoors in all weathers. A full driving licence is usually required.

Pay and Opportunities: Pay rates for traffic wardens vary. The pay rates given below are approximate. Traffic wardens earn in the range of £13,500-£15,500 a year. Earnings may increase with shift allowance.

Hours of work for traffic wardens vary according to local parking conditions; there may be early starts (7.30 or 8 am) and late finishes (up to 10pm), worked in shifts. Wardens usually work some Saturdays, with a day off during the week. In some areas, traffic wardens have duties on Sundays.

In most parts of Scotland traffic wardens are civilians employed by the local Police Authority. They work under the direction of the Police. However in Aberdeen, Edinburgh, Glasgow and Perth and Kinross they are employees of the local council.

The following information is sourced from government statistics. The government's definition of types of job is slightly different to that used in this programme. For this type of job, the most relevant Government-defined occupation is 'Traffic wardens'.

In 2001 there were 300 people working as 'Traffic wardens' in Scotland. 1 in every 10,000 employees working in Scotland was employed as 'Traffic wardens'.

Entry Routes and Training: Entry requirements vary from area to area. The minimum age for traffic wardens is normally 18; in some areas it may be 20 or even older. Good health and eyesight (with glasses if worn) are necessary and applicants may have to pass a medical. Some areas set entrance tests.

Training is on the job, with new recruits learning from experienced wardens. Short courses may also be available from time to time. Trainees learn about traffic laws and regulations, procedures for issuing parking tickets and how to direct traffic.

Qualifications: Basic literacy and numeracy are required—some employers set entrance tests in these subjects.

Adult Opportunities: While some employers have basic entrance requirements, work experience is also acceptable for entry. This could be three years' relevant work experience involving dealing with the public, for example, as a parking attendant.

13% of traffic wardens work part-time.

Car Park Attendant

Car park attendants organise the parking of cars in car parks. They may also collect parking fees, direct drivers to free spaces and be responsible for the security of the cars.

Work Activities: Car park attendants' work largely depends on the type of car park they work in. Some work in only one car park and others drive to different ones during the day.

Some attendants supervise outdoor car parks, working from a small hut at the entrance. When customers arrive they pay the attendant, who then gives them a ticket. An attendant also often directs drivers to free spaces in the car park.

Some car parks are 'pay and display', where the driver parks their car and puts money in a machine to get a ticket; they then display the ticket in their car. Here, attendants might have to check a group of car parks, such as those located in a town centre. They might have to empty cash from pay and display machines and make sure that the machines are stocked with tickets.

In some car parks, including multi-storey and some supermarket car parks, attendants work from a small booth at the exit and take payments from drivers as they leave. They find out how much to charge by taking the driver's entrance ticket and putting it into a machine; this reads the ticket and shows the price to charge.

In some car parks there are reserved places for regular users. Attendants may deal with bookings for these and set out cones. There may also be a security role for attendants in some car parks—patrolling the car park and using closed-circuit televisions. A lot of the work takes place outside in all weather conditions.

Personal Qualities and Skills: Some car park attendants spend a lot of time on their feet so stamina is needed, but others may spend most of the time sitting down—it depends on the kind of car park it is.

You may need number skills to work out the length of time that customers have spent in the car park, how much they owe and how much change to give them when they pay.

As a car park attendant you should be reliable and trustworthy. You should have a responsible attitude towards security and safety. You should be self-reliant and able to work on your own. You also need to be polite and friendly when dealing with the public.

Pay and Opportunities: Pay rates for car park attendants vary with employer. The pay rates given below are approximate. Car park attendants earn in the range of £190-£220 a week, rising to £270-£340. Higher earners can make around £370 a week.

Hours of work vary depending on employer. Some car park attendants work a 39-hour week and others work part time. Shift work, early starts and weekend work may be required. Overtime may be available. Car park attendants work in all areas of the UK. Employers are large car parking companies, small individually owned parking site operators, some large hotels and local authorities.

The following information is sourced from government statistics. The government's definition of types of job is slightly different to that used in this programme. For this type of job, the most relevant Government-defined occupation is 'Car park attendants'.

In 2001 there were 700 people working as 'Car park attendants' in Scotland. 3 in every 10,000 employees working in Scotland were employed as 'Car park attendants'.

Entry Routes and Training: This is the kind of job that you would go straight into and get your training on the job.

Some large employers might run induction courses for new people. And there may be short courses to train you in new procedures, such as security work.

Qualifications: You don't need formal qualifications for this job.

Adult Opportunities: A previous background in security attendant work is helpful.

- 27% of car park and lift attendants work part-time.
- 6% work on a temporary basis.

Scenes of Crime Officer

Scenes of crime officers work for the police. They collect and record evidence for use in criminal investigations. Their work includes taking fingerprints, photographs and forensic evidence.

Work Activities: Scenes of crime officers (SOCOs) collect forensic evidence at the scene of a crime and sometimes at accidents. They make sure that the evidence is preserved and recorded for future reference.

One of their main roles is to collect impressions of fingerprints and palm prints. They usually do this by brushing surfaces with powder and transferring the impression, via adhesive tape, to a sheet of acetate.

These examinations can be carried out at the scene of a crime or items may be taken away and examined elsewhere. For example, a car that's been used for criminal activity may be taken to a police garage.

SOCOs may also take impressions of fingerprints from people. They fingerprint anyone who may have had access to the scene of crime. This eliminates innocent people from an enquiry, as well as providing incriminating evidence that could lead to a conviction.

Another element of the SOCOs work is taking fingerprints of people who have died. This is done when the dead person's identity is unknown. At the post-mortem an accurate record is made of anything arising from the examination, including information passed on by the pathologist.

Photography plays a vital role in the work of a SOCO. Photographed evidence is put together in albums for use in court. Video equipment may be used at the scene of some major incidents such as rapes and murders.

SOCOs are responsible for the maintenance of any equipment they use. They also have administrative tasks such as preparing and writing reports, statements and other necessary documentation. They need to keep accurate records, so that colleagues can refer to them when necessary. Evidence has to be labelled and packaged, then stored away for safe keeping or for use as exhibits. SOCOs sometimes have to attend court hearings to give evidence.

New technology is playing a bigger part in crime detection. For instance, special equipment may be used to:

- identify and photograph fingerprints on documents such as cheques
- record shoe marks
- take DNA swabs
- collect fibres from clothes and furniture.

SOCOs work closely with both uniformed and plain clothes police officers. Other people you will work with are:

- pathologists
- forensic scientists
- medical personnel
- court officials
- the general public
- other members of the emergency services.

Personal Qualities and Skills: SOCOs need to be patient, understanding and sympathetic when dealing with the victims of crime. You'll have to be prepared to attend incidents that could be very distressing and work in unpleasant or dirty conditions.

SOCOs have to be methodical enough to follow set procedures and flexible enough to cope with unusual work patterns. You will also need good communication skills.

Pay and Opportunities: Salaries for scenes of crime officers (SOCOs) vary depending on the employing force and responsibilities.

Salaries are generally in the range of £18,000 a year, rising to around £24,500 a year, including shift allowances and benefits. In some forces, there are also positions of assistant senior SOCO and senior SOCO, which pay more, around £28,000-£32,000 a year depending on the force structure and responsibilities.

Some forces employ Assistant SOCOs or Volume Crime Examiners, who undertake routine duties. These positions attract a lower pay rate than full SOCOs.

SOCOs work shifts. Some forces work shift patterns that allow SOCOs to work 37 hours a week spread over a five-day period (including weekends). The majority of forces have shift rotas that provide 24-hour cover from approximately 7am/8am until 11pm/midnight. For the remaining hours, SOCOs normally take part in an on call rota.

About 1,800 people work as SOCOs in the UK. All UK police forces employ SOCOs. Posts are usually advertised in the local press, Jobcentre Plus offices, official police magazines and on many regional police force websites. Competition for posts is fierce.

The following information is sourced from government statistics. The government's definition of types of job is slightly different to that used in this programme. For this type of job, the most relevant Government-defined occupation is 'Protective service associate professionals not classified elsewhere'.

In 2001 there were 1,100 people working as 'Protective service associate professionals not classified elsewhere' in Scotland. 5 in every 10,000 employees working in Scotland were employed as 'Protective service associate professionals not classified elsewhere'.

Entry Routes and Training: As a new SOCO you will attend a nine week residential training course and spend time working with an experienced SOCO. You will learn about fingerprinting and photographic techniques, technical aids and forensic science. The skills you learn are tested by a series of written and practical exams.

You will have to take a short driving course that can qualify you as a police-approved driver.

Further practical experience and training leads to the Diploma in Scientific Support Skills. Teesside University offers a BSc degree course in Crime Scene Science.

Qualifications: Qualifications required for this job vary enormously between Forces. They can range from a few Standard Grades (1-3) to Highers and degrees. Subjects testing the use of English and science subjects are normally preferred.

Other qualifications are usually accepted in place of traditional academic subject passes, for example National Certificate, Higher National Certificate or or Higher National Diploma qualifications.

Photographic qualifications and/or experience are also considered, as are applicants with scientific backgrounds and/ or qualifications. A driving licence is essential.

Adult Opportunities: Emotional maturity and life experience are viewed as essential requirements.

Contact your local police headquarters for details of age policy and entry requirements.

Entrants with relevant skills and experience, for example, gained in laboratory work, have an advantage.

3% of people who work in occupations such as scenes of crime officer work part-time.

Prison Officer

Prison officers keep inmates in secure custody. They also aim to help with rehabilitation. Officers work in a variety of institutions. They all undertake security work, which can include escort duties. Trades officers also teach a skill or trade to prisoners. The minimum age for recruitment is 20 years.

Work Activities: Prison officers have three main priorities: the secure detention of offenders, their rehabilitation and eventual integration with the community. Officers work in a variety of institutions, ranging from detention centres for young offenders to high security closed prisons for long-term criminals.

Male and female inmates are usually housed in separate prisons. It is possible for female officers to serve in male prisons and vice versa. In private prisons, prison officers are known as custody officers.

Whatever the type of prison, officers have security duties, including:

- surveillance of inmates' work or recreation activities
- cell searches
- patrolling buildings and grounds
- supervising inmates.

Certain officers may have special training in dog handling or electronic security techniques. Others are concerned with the reception of new inmates, issuing clothing, completing paperwork and liaising with medical and welfare staff.

In prisons and remand centres where offenders are awaiting sentence, prison officers may be involved in the assessment of prisoners. This helps to determine the type of prison to which they should be sent. In some prisons, officers also have escort duties, taking prisoners to and from court or transferring them to another prison. However, in certain areas of the country these duties are being taken over by private security companies.

There are opportunities for prison officers who are trained in a practical skill or trade. Trades officers are fully trained prison officers and have security duties, but they also practise their skill and teach it to prisoners. Specialisms include building trades, catering, laundering, physical education, metalwork, needlework, engineering, rugmaking, market gardening, hairdressing and household management.

Personal Qualities and Skills: You need to be able to get on with people. You will also need to be firm and able to act with authority when necessary. You should be able to demonstrate understanding and commitment to helping with the rehabilitation of offenders.

As a prison officer you may need to act quickly and must keep calm during a crisis. Good judgement is important, as are decision-making skills and initiative. Teamworking skills are useful.

Good communication skills are essential. Trades officers require teaching skills and should be able to explain things clearly. You need to be fit and active to do this job. A sense of humour can be useful.

Pay and Opportunities: Prison officers in Scotland are paid on a rising scale. The general entry minimum salary on 1st November 2006 was £14,373 a year, rising to £19,130 a year.

Prison officers work 39 hours a week, which usually includes shifts on a rota basis, including evenings and weekends.

The following information is sourced from government statistics. The government's definition of types of job is slightly different to that used in this programme. For this type of job, the most relevant Government-defined occupation is 'Prison service officers (below principal officer)'.

There are over 3000 prison officers in Scotland. In 2006 there were 15 prisons and 2 Young Offenders Institutions in Scotland accommodating around 7,000 prisoners (including around 300 women). Officers may be posted to different areas and therefore must be prepared to move if necessary.

Entry Routes and Training: The selection process covers 5 stages, from application through to final medical assessment.

If you match the selection criterion you will be invited to an assessment session. If you pass short multiple choice tests in English and Arithmetic you will be asked to take a fitness test.

Fitness is essential for the modern prisoner officer, to ensure you can meet minimum standards. The fitness test takes about 20 minutes. Candidates who pass the fitness test will be given a date to attend an interview.

To further test your suitability you will be interviewed by a panel of three Scottish Prisoner Service assessors who will ask you why you want to work for the Scottish Prison Service and about how you might react in certain situations. There are no right and wrong answers and you should feel free to answer the questions openly and honestly.

Candidates have to produce a certificate from Disclosure Scotland to show they have no criminal convictions.

Candidates will have a medical examination lasting approximately 30 minutes. (travelling expenses will be paid for this examination only).

Their height and weight ratio will be checked at this stage. If they are passed as fit to be a modern prison officer, they then go onto the final stage where they are matched with a vacancy.

Qualifications: Entry to the Scottish Prison Service requires 5 Standard Grades (1-3), or equivalent, including English and Maths or 3 years experience of managing people. This could be gained in a wide range of work contexts including skilled trades, retail, administration and the caring professions.

All entrants have to take an aptitude test and a medical examination.

Adult Opportunities: All entrants go through the normal selection procedure of aptitude and medical tests. The normal entry requirements apply to all ages.

Work experience in a related occupation can be useful, for example, as a security guard or a detention officer.

2% of prison officers (below Principal Officer) work part-time.

Prison Governor

Prison governors manage prisons and other units, such as young offender institutions. They deal with staff including training and discipline. Governors are responsible for security and the overall care and progress of prisoners.

Work Activities: Prison governors are the managers of the prison service and are responsible for the administration and smooth running of a prison unit. They work at different levels of responsibility according to their management grade. These range from Governor 5 to Governor 1 grade.

Governor 5 grade is the initial management grade. This role is largely made up of training and supervising staff, as well as arranging work and leisure activities for inmates. A Governor 5 may work in all parts of the prison and have frequent contact with prisoners. Governor 4 staff have additional responsibilities to those above, while those at Governor 3 grade may have overall responsibility for a small prison. Governors working in the larger establishments are graded 2 or 1.

All prison governors need to have a good knowledge and understanding of what is going on in their prison or centre. As well as carrying out inspections, governors liaise with probation officers, social workers, medical staff and prison psychologists. They also attend meetings, courses and conferences that may take them outside the prison from time to time.

Personal Qualities and Skills: You need to have leadership qualities and the ability to motivate both staff and inmates. You should be able to build-up teams and work in them effectively. Sensitivity to the needs of staff and inmates is important. You must also be able to deal with any unrest or difficult situations. The job requires you to make responsible decisions and take disciplinary action. The ability to remain calm under pressure is vital. You need to be able to get on with people. A sense of humour is useful. Listening and general communications skills are a must.

You should be physically fit and will need to meet a specified height to weight ratio.

Pay and Opportunities: Prison governors are paid on a rising scale from grade F to grade A. Salaries start at £25,506 a year (grade F), rising to £76,793 a year (grade A).

Prison governors work an average 39 hours a week, which usually includes evenings and weekends on a rota basis.

The Prison Service employs about 1,400 prison governors who work in 128 prisons throughout the country. These include:

Young Offender Institutions—dispersal prisons where high security offenders are kept—open prisons that keep a cross-section of prisoners—local prisons, which keep prisoners awaiting court and assess prisoners after sentencing.

Prison Governors in Scotland are employed by the Scottish Prison Service. Governors may be posted to different areas and therefore must be prepared to move if necessary. There are also opportunities with the growing number of 'contracted out' prisons run by private companies. Entry to the governor grades is fiercely competitive.

The following information is sourced from government statistics. The government's definition of types of job is slightly different to that used in this programme. For this type of job, the most relevant Government-defined occupation is 'Senior officers in fire, ambulance, prison and related services'.

In 2001 5 in every 10,000 employees working in Scotland were employed as 'Senior officers in fire, ambulance, prison and related services'.

Entry Routes and Training: The traditional route to becoming a prison governor is to join the service as a prison officer and work your way up. However this can take at least 10-15 years.

It is possible to enter directly at Governor level with a degree and at least 3 years management experience. Training is on the job and is for 12 months. This is also the probationary period. You will begin as a Unit Manager. Promotion is then possible through the 5 grades of Prison Governor. Candidates for the Scottish Prison Service have to produce a certificate from Disclosure Scotland to show they have no criminal convictions.

Qualifications: Many prison governors are officers who have worked their way through the ranks. This requires 5 Standard Grades (1-3) including English and Maths or 3 years experience of managing people. This could be gained in a wide range of work contexts including skilled trades, retail, administration and the caring professions.

Adult Opportunities: All entrants are required to take the standard entry tests including medical examinations.

The maximum age of entry for application to the open competition Accelerated Promotion Service (APS) to become a governor is 57 years.

The opportunities for adults are improved by three entry schemes, for:

- existing prison staff

- those with relevant management experience
- those already in the Civil Service.

Graduates entering the Fast Track Scheme can have an honours degree in any subject.

An interest or background in human resources or institutional management, law, psychology or social sciences is helpful but not essential.

Contracted-out prisons have their own recruitment and selection procedures.

10% of prison governors (Principal Officer and above) have flexible hours.

2

Career in Defence Services

Defence Services

Armed Forces in India: Indian Armed Forces have a reputation of being one of the finest in the world and offer a very challenging and Attractive career for Indian youth (both men and women). Indian armed forces, after induction, impart required training to ensure that individual becomes fully capable of handling difficult and complex situation arising in operational and administrative spheres. The services environment offers:-

- A very healthy work culture. It offers challenging and result-oriented environment and is best suited for honest and upright person to serve and as such holds the promise of bringing high social standing and honour to an individual joining the same.
- Individual becomes true nationalist and stops distinguishing individuals based on religion, cast and regional basis. It is the only career which demands and teaches supreme sacrifice for the country.
- Armed forces is a major setup, which provide reasonably good and fast career growth. Career growth in armed forces depends on performance and your skill. Certain courses entitle you to additional pay and allowances.
- Life in armed forces is regimented and it takes priority over normal life and builds up Esprit-de-Corps.

Indian armed forces render invaluable service to the nation, both in times of war and peace. Though there prime task is defending our nation against external aggression, many times it is called to restore internal strife and help in natural calamities.

Work: Service in Armed Forces demand spirit of adventure as well as unflinching loyalty and integrity for nation and readiness to lay down ones life for the nation when required. Work involves defending territorial, coastal and air space integrity of our country against all external and internal threats.

It also involves man management of highest order, continuous development of leadership qualities of highest order and on job training to achieve required perfection for these jobs.

Nature of work in armed forces is diverse and also demands serving in most difficult terrain and weather conditions obtaining through out the country and hence there is a need of constant physical fitness of highest order.

Service in Armed forces requires training for war in peace time in trying conditions and sacrifice and bravery of highest order to save the pride and integrity of the nation at the time of war. A brief description of works of all three branches of the Armed Forces is as follows:-

The Indian Army: The Indian Army is responsible for defending the territorial integrity of the country against all external aggression and internal disturbances. During war army is responsible to protect the nation against external aggression, whereas, during peace time also it provides aid to the civil authorities during natural calamities and helps in maintenance of law and order when required.

The army is mainly divided into combat arms and services. The combat arms are the infantry, the artillery and the armoured corps, The Corps of Engineers and Corps of Signals. Whereas, services includes Army Service Corps, Army Ordnance Corps, Army Postal services, Army Medical Corps, Army education corps, Intelligence Corps and So on.

Combat arms are responsible for actual combat, whereas, services are responsible to ensure continuous flow of required ordnance including food for men and animal, Fuel for vehicles and tanks and ammunition.

The Indian Navy: The Indian Navy is responsible for defending the extensive coastline of the country in times of war and peace. The navy also responsible to safeguard our maritime interests including defence of off-shore oil and gas installations, coastal shipping and fisheries rights and to protect the vital trade links.

The Navy has three main branches.

- The Executive Branch which manages the navy's warships and submarines as instruments of tactical warfare. and
- The Engineering Branch which is responsible for the maintenance and service of engineering equipment and the propulsion systems on board the ships including electrical and electronic systems, weapon systems, missiles, radar and radio communication systems.
- The Education Branch ensures that the officers and men are update in their technical knowledge and tactical.

The Indian Air Force: The Indian Air Force is responsible for the air defence of the country, ensuring both offensive and defensive roles. It is also responsible for the air defence of vital installations of strategic importance to country.

The Air force is divided into three main branches.

- The Flying branch includes fighter pilots who fly combat or fighter planes carrying ammunition and missiles; transport pilots who fly planes which carry men and materials and helicopter pilots who provide air support to a moving army, or are used for para-dropping men and supplies.
- The technical branch which includes engineering sections and is responsible for the engineering equipment and weapons systems of the air force.
- The Administrative Branch includes all the departments that provide logistical, meteorological, educational and administrative support to the flying and technical branches.

Entry: There are number of types of entries in the Armed Forces in India, basic Entry for all the three forces is through National Defence Academy (NDA). Entries are at 10+2 Level, after graduation and after professional courses (graduate /post graduate level).

There are following entries to armed Forces:-

- Entry through NDA in all three wings, permanent commission, after 10+2 level through prescribed competitive examination known as National defence Academy / naval Academy Examination.
- Entry after graduation through Combined Defence Services Examination, through Indian Military Academy (IMA) Dehradun for Army, the Naval Academy, Goa for Indian Navy and the Air Force Academy, Hyderabad for Air Force as permanent Commission officer. Through Officers Training School as Short Service Commission officer.
- All three services can be joined after completion of technical education *i.e.* Engineering Degree, requirement of each service is different.
- Army Medical Corps, which serves all three services can be joined after completion of MBBS degree, either through Armed Forces Medical college or from any other medical College.

Eligibility: General eligibility conditions demand that a candidate must be—a citizen of India (subjects of Bhutan, Nepal, Tibetan refugees or migrants from the rest of the Indian subcontinent with the intention of settling permanently in India can also apply). In addition, candidates must be physically fit in accordance with the prescribed physical standards. They should be unmarried males or female. There is a Women's Special Entry Scheme (officers) for women graduates in specified subjects between 19-27 years of age.

Selection Process for the National Defence Academy:

- If you are between the age of 16½-19 and have completed the junior year of high school, you can write the Union Public Service Commission (UPSC) exam which is meant for entry into the National Defence Academy (NDA). The exam is held every six months at various centers in India. Out of the 50,000 to 60,000 candidates who write the UPSC exam, only around one-third pass.

Individual faring well in this exam you be called in for a Services Selection Board (SSB) interview which lasts for three to four days. In this interview they conduct medical & written tests, outdoor activity contests, personal interviews, etc. Candidates who want to join the Indian Air Force, have to take a Pilot Aptitude Test which once failed, can never be taken again. All candidates have to undergo extensive psychological examinations and meet exhaustive physical parameters to appear on the SSB merit list, from which 300 join the NDA as cadets for three years.

NDA takes in new cadets every January & June. There are no fees to join NDA, but an individual wish to opt out, as a small percentage do, it is very expensive. An NDA drop-out has to pay the government, costs incurred in training, which are calculated by the number of weeks that have been spent at NDA.

NDA Courses: While in the NDA, a cadet earns a Bachelor Degree in Arts, Science or Computer Science, which is affiliated to the Jawaharlal Nehru University in New Delhi. The three years in the NDA are divided into 6 semesters. Five are general semesters, which every candidate has to take and in the sixth and final semester, each candidate specialises for either the Army, Navy or Air Force.

Academics constitute around 57% of thc programme comprising 12 disciplines, which are 8 languages, three pure sciences, two applied sciences and four social sciences. There are also Common Service Subjects like military history, area study, service writing, leadership, paramilitary forces, weapons training and situational instruction.

Also a part of the curriculum are Special Services Subjects like training in battlefield and peace-time skills and operations specific to individual streams of the Army, Navy or Air Force. There is also outdoor training which includes physical training, drill and equitation.

After three years in the NDA, Army cadets join the Indian Military Academy at Dehradun, Navy cadets join the INS Tir or INS Krishna at Cochin and Air Force cadets move on to the Air Force Training Academy at Hyderabad. These courses are of 18 months duration after which, individual gets a commissioned rank.

Graduate/Direct Entry: Individuals between the age of 19 and 22 and having a three year Bachelor degree, can appear for the Combined Defense Services Exam (CDSC), which is held every 6 months at various centers in India. Again like the NDA process, there will be a SSB interview and a medical examination. On clearing these, individual is straight away enlisted into the Indian Military Academy (if he opts for the Army), without entering NDA and get trained there for 18 months after which, get a commissioned rank.

Technical Entry: Individuals having an engineering degree, can apply for direct commission. He can directly appear for the SSB interview and medical exam. If cleared them, he will be paid a stipend by the Indian Government during his senior years. After completing the degree, you are straight away enlisted into the Air Force Training Academy in Hyderabad (if you opt for the Air Force), without entering NDA, with a commissioned rank or in Army, ie., through IMA.

Personal Attributes Required

A good communication skills—officers need to deal with soldiers. Love for one's country; commitment; dedication; perception; the will to fight and face hardships in order to protect the nation; an alert mind; integrity; flavour for discipline and adventure.

Job Prospects: Training for the defence services automatically qualifies students to become full-fledged officers of the service to which they are appointed. They are guaranteed a job, along with all the perks and allowances, many of which continue even after retirement. Jobs in the Defence Services involve a great deal of power and authority, though there are frequent transfers. Competent officers always have a chance of being promoted to senior positions over the years.

Aerospace and Defence

Frost & Sullivan, a global growth consulting company, has been partnering with clients to support the development of innovative strategies for more than 40 years. The company's industry expertise integrates growth consulting, growth partnership services and corporate management training to identify and develop opportunities. Frost & Sullivan serves an extensive clientele that includes Global 1000 companies, emerging companies and the investment community by providing comprehensive industry coverage that reflects a unique global perspective and combines ongoing analysis of markets, technologies, econometrics and demographics.

Research

- Establish a plan of client focused and industry relevant research service titles with timelines and deliver the same punctually
- To monitor the quality and quantity of research services being produced within the programme area
- Develop mechanisms to ensure constant client feedback that reflect appropriately on research content
- Ensure the development and fulfilment of high quality, high value offerings
- Contribute to the development and fulfilment of key deliverables in subscription services

Sales/BD

- Pursue opportunities for additional product offerings and revenue generation
- Meeting with clients to develop strong business relationships within the sector
- Supporting in business development activities of the IRG along with the sales team
- To drive the marketing and PR strategy of the sector by working closely with relevant Frost & Sullivan departments
- Attend and present at conferences relevant to research group and build a strong network of clients

People Management

- Mentor/Manage a team of client focused analysts

- Provide regular internal training to develop a wide range of analyst skill set
- Identify skills being offered by team members/analysts and utilise the same as and when required
- Conduct regular IRG meetings and one-to-one line management meetings with analysts
- Maintain a constant sense of positive environment within the team/CBU and be a motivator as a leader

Client Engagement / Project Management

- Fulfil consulting engagements as either a lead analyst or as a project manager as required by the specific engagement
- Develop client engagement skills by working closely with senior consulting team members of Frost & Sullivan
- Develop and implement constant improvisation processes that could be applied in consulting projects to enhance client satisfaction
- Define the project milestones and communicate the same to the project team
- Focus on punctuality and quality of consulting delivery by regularly monitoring the performance and contribution of the project team assigned to the consulting engagement

Strategic Contribution

- Play an active role in the contributing to the overall business unit' s sales and product/service strategies
- Identify new areas with business potential for the IRG and the business unit and be able to communicate the same to the entire business unit

Targets: You will have targets based around the following:

1. Programme area revenue generation target for research, consulting and best practices
2. Personal revenue generation target to reflect contributions to consulting projects
3. Business development target

4. Business Unit /Global projects as agreed with your Manager
5. Team management and development
6. Fulfilment of research content plan for the Research Group

Knowledge, Skills and Abilities

- A thorough understanding of market research methodologies and/or strategic marketing
- Strong client relationship skills
- Excellent people skills (internal relationship building abilities)
- Excellent verbal and written skills
- Ability to present key findings to senior level executives both internally and externally
- Excellent project management skills
- Proactive approach to business development and sales

Qualifications and Experience

- Masters degree or MBA in related technical or business discipline
- At least 2-3 years of experience in consultancy or market research within industry focus area
- Experience of having successfully worked in a team environment
- Client engagement experience
- Project management experience
- Leadership skills
- Strategic planning skills

Not Just a Job-A Career!

If you are a highly driven and self-motivated individual, Frost & Sullivan will afford you an exciting and lucrative career opportunity. We offer a fast-paced and dynamic work environment, with a focus on exceeding both individual and team expectations. We encourage you to take risks and develop creative, outside-the-box solutions to impact the value of the products and services you will offer our clients. You'll be encouraged to maintain your individual style while adopting a consultative partnership approach. Most importantly, you will be provided the training, support and environment to excel and succeed with a leading-edge company. If you are enthusiastic, highly motivated and looking for a great career opportunity, we encourage you to apply today!

Defence Services

Looking for a Career Option in the Field of Defence Services? This section features Defence Services as a career option, elaborated with reference to the job profile, personality traits required, the courses and training involved, premier institutions and future prospects.

The defense services offer dignified, disciplined and prestigious placements. The chosen officer could serve in the Indian Air Force or Indian Navy on combat duty, on administrative assignments, in the medical services, in the engineering services, in the Judge Advocate-General's Department (JAG's Dept.), the Education Corps; in short, in any one of the various departments.

Personality Traits: Effective intelligence, courage, sense of responsibility, ability to reason, determination, ability to organize group activity, take the initiative, self-confidence, alacrity in making balanced decisions, social adaptability; and excellent powers of expression are useful traits for an aspiring defence officer.

Eligibility: General eligibility conditions demand that a candidate must be—a citizen of India (subjects of Bhutan, Nepal, Tibetan refugees or migrants from the rest of the Indian subcontinent with the intention of settling permanently in India can also apply). In addition, candidates must be physically fit in accordance with the prescribed physical standards. They should be unmarried males or female. There is a Women's Special Entry Scheme (officers) for women graduates in specified subjects between 19-27 years of age.

Entry Scheme—NDA/ Naval Academy Examination: There is one common written examination for entry into Army,

Air Force and Naval Wings of NDA and 10+2 (Executive Branch) of Naval Academy on the following pattern

Mathematics-2 1/2 hours-300 marks

General Ability-2 1/2 hours-600 marks

The syllabus is given in the Employment News Weekly announcement of the examination.

Candidates who are declared qualified in the written examination have to appear before a Services Selection Board (SSB) for intelligence and personality test to assess the candidates' for their officers' potentiality and those for the Air Force in Pilot Aptitude Test and officer potentiality.

While in the NDA, a cadet earns a Bachelor Degree in Arts, Science or Computer Science, which is affiliated to the Jawaharlal Nehru University in New Delhi. The three years in the NDA are divided into 6 semesters. Five are general semesters, which every candidate has to take and in the sixth and final semester, each candidate specialises for either the Army, Navy or Air Force.

Academics constitute around 57% of the programme comprising 12 disciplines, which are 8 languages, three pure sciences, two applied sciences and four social sciences. There are also Common Service Subjects like military history, area study, service writing, leadership, paramilitary forces, weapons training and situational instruction.

Also a part of the curriculum are Special Services Subjects like training in battlefield and peace-time skills and operations specific to individual streams of the Army, Navy or Air Force. There is also outdoor training which includes physical training, drill and equitation.

After three years in the NDA, Army cadets join the Indian Military Academy at Dehra Dun, Navy cadets join the INS Tir or INS Krishna at Cochin and Air Force cadets move on to the Air Force Training Academy at Hyderabad. These courses are of 18 months duration after which, individual gets a commissioned rank.

Graduate/Direct Entry: Individuals between the age of 19 and 22 and having a three year Bachelor degree, can appear for the Combined Defense Services Exam (CDSC), which is held every 6 months at various centers in India. Again like the NDA process, there will be a SSB interview and a medical examination. On clearing these, individual is straight away enlisted into the Indian Military Academy (if he opts for the Army), without entering NDA and get trained there for 18 months after which, get a commissioned rank.

Technical Entry

Individuals having an engineering degree, can apply for direct commission. He can directly appear for the SSB interview and medical exam. If cleared them, he will be paid a stipend by the Indian Government during his senior years. After completing the degree, you are straight away enlisted into the Air Force Training Academy in Hyderabad (if you opt for the Air Force), without entering NDA, with a commissioned rank or in Army, ie., through IMA.

Naval College of Engineering, Lonavala prepares officers to make a career in Marine/ Electrical/ Electronics/ Aeronautical Engineering and Naval Architecture cadres of the Indian Navy. The college is one of the best engineering colleges in the country and the only one of its kind in Asia.

Unmarried male Indian citizens approx. between 16 1/2 years to 19 years of age, passed Senior Secondary Examination (10+2) pattern or ots equivalent with at least 75% aggregate marks in Physics, Chemistry and Mathematics and at least 50% marks in English either in Class X or Class XII may apply. Minimum 157 height with correlated weight and proportionate chest with minimum 5 cm expansion; uncorrected eyesight without glasses 6/12, 6/12 corrected with glasses 6/6, 6/6 are other requirements.

Short listed candidates on the basis of the marks obtained in the academic examination are called for the SSB interview. Candidates recommended by the board and declared medically fit will be appointed for training in order of merit. On successful completion of the course they are awarded a B. Tech. Degree by the JNU (Jawaharlal Nehru University). The entire cost of training including books and reading material, is borne by the Navy.

MBBS at Armed Forces Medical College

Those who are interested in joining the Armed Forces Medical Services as permanent commissioned officers after graduation (MBBS) may join the Armed Forces Medical College (AFMC), Pune. Admission is through an entrance examination in physics, chemistry, biology, intelligence, logic and reasoning, English language and comprehension. After the written examination successful candidates are called for an interview.

Admission is open to unmarried candidates (boys and girls), passed XII Std/ pre-professional/ premedical exam or equivalent exam as a regular student in the first attempt in English, Physics, Chemistry and Biology securing not less than 60% of aggregate marks in three science subjects taken together, not less than 50% marks in English; Must have attained 17 years but not attained 22 years as on 31st December of the year of joining.

B.Sc. (Nursing) at College of Nursing

AFMC, Pune and Diploma in General Nursing and Midwifery (GNM) Course at various Armed Forces Hospitals.

4-year B.Sc. (Nursing) at College of Nursing, AFMC, Pune and 3-year Diploma in General Nursing and Midwifery (GNM) Course at various Armed Forces Hospitals is open to Indian Females who are unmarried or divorced or legally separated or widows without encumbrances. The candidate should have passed in the first attempt 10+2 exam with Physics, Chemistry and Biology with minimum 50% aggregate marks as a regular student, minimum height 142 cms. Age group should be between 16 and 24 years approx. Medical fitness should be as per military stds.

Those selected to the course have to execute a bond to serve in the Military Nursing Service (MNS) for 5/4 years.

Entry Schemes Combined Defence Services Examination (After Graduation)

CDSE (Combined Defence Services Examination) is held twice every year for the entry into the defence forces. The examination is announced about 5-6 months prior to the date of the examination. Through CDSE unmarried male candidates can get into the Indian Military Academy-Dehradun or the Naval Academy—Goa or Air Force Station-Hyderabad or the Officers' Training Academy (OTA), Chennai.

SSB Interview

Candidates qualifying in the written examinations for entry into the defence services (NDA)/ ‵Naval Academy, CDSE) as well as for the other schemes of entry based on application scrutiny are called for tests by the SSB. Most of the tests require an average intelligence. The testing is spread over a period of 3-4 days at least and is a through as well as an elaborate process. A three-pronged approach is followed by the SSB.

1. Personal interview
2. Outdoor test or group task officer tests
3. Psychological testing apparatus

Ay this stage the purely spontaneous and natural responses of the candidate are sought to be accessed by the SSB. The tests are administered on an individual basis and also in groups. During the course of this subtle testing pattern, candidates are under observation throughout.

SSB's primary aim is to select individuals with the potential to be groomed into and trained as, officers for the defence services finally. Motivation for joining the defence forces is an important question to be prepared for the interview. Everything is assessed while the interview is on—verbal answers as well as non-verbal attitude, gestures, stance, power of expression, self confidence, self assurance etc.

The SSB pattern includes a number of physical tests to evaluate the candidate' s stamina, physical fitness, aptitude for physical activity, flexibility of the body, agility as well as courage for making daring attempts.

The psychological testing apparatus comprises verbal and non—verbal exercise, word association exercise, thematic apperception, situation reaction, self appraisal, aptitude for logical reasoning and objectivity.

Placements a Prospects

Defense personnel are liable to be transferred anywhere in the country. Upto a certain level of seniority promotions are bound by a time scale, after which they are gone on selection basis depending on vacancies arising at the top level.

They are guaranteed a job, along with all the perks and allowances, many of which continue even after retirement. Jobs in the Defence Services involve a great deal of power and authority, though there are frequent transfers. Competent officers always have a chance of being promoted to senior positions over the years.

Army Officer

The exact expertise and work of an army officer depends on the arm or service chosen. This could be, for example, a combat arm, such as the Infantry, Air Corps, Household Cavalry, Special Air Service Regiment or Royal Armoured Corps. It could be a combat support arm, such as the Royal Artillery, Royal Engineers, Royal Signals or Intelligence Corps. It could be one of the services corps, such as the Royal Electrical and Mechanical Engineers, Royal Logistics or one of the branches of the Adjutant General's Corps (staff and personnel support, education and training, legal services, military police). It could be a specialism in medicine, music or religion.

Whichever corps or regiment they serve in, officers lead and manage a group of soldiers as well as developing their own expertise in their arm or service. They fit into a highly structured system of management of resources and personnel. They would have to make decisions about the welfare, training and deployment of the soldiers under their command and would be expected to maintain the morale of their soldiers, often in extreme conditions. A typical first command would be a platoon of around 30 soldiers of different ages and ranks.

All officers are trained in the handling of weapons and are expected to go into areas of combat.

Entry Level: Around 80% of army officers are graduates, although the minimum educational qualifications to join as an officer are five GCSEs/S grades (A-C/1-3) and two A levels/ Advanced Highers or three H grades, or equivalent. You must normally have English language, maths and either a science subject or a foreign language.

Entry is possible between 17 years 9 months and 29 years. You must pass a medical entrance test and meet the army's nationality requirements. Selection involves a series of interviews and practical and written tests.

Making the Grade: If selected for officer training, you would start with the commissioning course at the Royal Military Academy Sandhurst. This 44-week course is uniquely demanding, with many physical, mental and emotional challenges alongside leadership and management training.

Following the Passing Out parade at Sandhurst, you would join your regiment or corps and undertake specialist training relevant to your chosen role, occupation or profession. There would be many opportunities for you to gain further academic and vocational qualifications as you progress.

The length of specialist training can vary according to your qualifications before you join. Individuals with professional qualifications in law, medicine, dentistry and veterinary studies, for example, train for just four weeks instead of the usual 44.

You would normally be awarded a three-year (six-year in the Army Air Corps) Short Service Commission (SSC) from the date you leave Sandhurst. This may be extended to a maximum of eight years. After two years' service an SSC officer, you may apply to convert to an Intermediate Regular Commission (IRC).

The IRC offers a mid-length career, with service for up to 16 years. After two years as an IRC officer, you may apply to convert to a full career Regular Commission. This offers a full career, potentially for 34 years, or to the age of 60 if that is earlier. There are also two short, gap year commissions available for pre-university students or for current undergraduates.

Personal Qualities: As an army officer, you need to be a decisive, effective leader, ablc to inspire and motivate others. You must be adaptable, physically fit and prepared to operate in combat situations.

You need to be highly motivated and able to think and react quickly in any situation, capable of using your own initiative while fitting into a highly organised structure. Good teamworking skills are essential. You must be able to communicate with people at all levels, often in stressful situations.

Looking Ahead: There are about 12,500 officers in the army. Around 700 are recruited each year and promotion prospects are good. Promotion follows a clearly structured system, from second lieutenant to lieutenant, captain, major, lieutenant colonel and beyond. Up to the rank of major, you have to pass promotion exams but for higher ranks promotion is on selection and merit.

All non-graduate officers start as second lieutenants; graduates also start as second lieutenants but on lieutenants' pay. Professionally qualified officers are commissioned as lieutenants or captains, depending on their qualifications and experience.

Military Careers: Protective Service Officers

Military men and women actively serve all over the world. Maintaining a strong national defense encompasses a great range of activities such as running a hospital, programming computers and many others. Are you looking for a military occupation? If you relish the chance of making a military career, you should know that the military offers excellent 'learn-and-earn opportunities.

The military is a large organization that carries out many activities and operations offering a vast array of career opportunities. The military is thus a huge employer offering competitive positions. Your chances for a rewarding career will improve if it matches your interests, values and skills. Have your choice of careers in the military! Becoming an officer in one of the branches of the military can provide you with career skills you need to get on in life.

Why choosing to become a protective service officer?

Protective service personnel encompasses officers who enforce military laws and regulations and provide emergency response to natural and human-made disasters. They are thus responsible for the safety and protection of lots of people. Helping individuals on military bases and vessels is a worthwhile cause, but it requires special skills. Protective service occupations require expert competences that can be acquired only in a military school. Protective service officers provide emergency response teams to disaster situation, while other teams work at maintaining food quality and proper handling. They also develop warning, control and evacuation plans which are to be used in the event of disaster.

Law enforcement and security officers strictly enforce all applicable laws on military bases and investigate crimes committed on military property. They act as a law enforcement agency regulating and putting into force military laws and regulations. Military police control traffic, prevent crime and guard inmates in military correctional facilities. Firefighters control and help prevent fires in buildings, on aircraft and aboard ships.

Royal Air Force Airman/Woman

In the Royal Air Force (RAF) the title airman/woman covers around 45 different jobs, all aimed at keeping the RAF running efficiently. Some of these, such as weapons systems operator or air loadmaster, involve flying as non-commissioned aircrew; others, including chef, nurse and technician are ground-based and come under the general heading of ground support staff. Given that the main role of the RAF is to defend the UK and its interests, airmen/women have military duties too, such as guarding RAF stations and taking part in military exercises and training.

As a weapons systems operator (acoustic and electronic warfare), you would fly in surveillance aircraft, using radar and sonar to search for ships above and below the oceans. As a weapons systems operator (linguist), you would monitor and operate the sophisticated electronic observation equipment. As an air loadmaster, you would be responsible for whatever the aircraft is carrying, from troops and fuel to heavy weaponry and explosives.

Ground support staff occupations include aerospace systems operators, air cartographers, aircraft engineering technicians, assistant air traffic controllers, chefs and mess managers/ stewards, firefighters, flight operations assistants, intelligence analysts, medical assistants, musicians, nurses (in the Princess Mary's Royal Air Force Nursing Service), personnel administrators, physical training instructors and the RAF police.

RAF Regiment gunners defend RAF airfields and other installations from ground and low-level air attack.

All trades, except RAF Regiment gunner, are open to women.

Entry Level: No formal qualifications are needed for most jobs but you must pass the RAF aptitude tests. Some trades require GCSE/S grade passes (A-C/1-3) or equivalent. Entry is between 16 and 29 years.

You must also pass medical and eyesight tests and meet RAF nationality and residence requirements. Aircrew have to pass a swimming test before they can start flying training.

Making the Grade: Most new entrants complete a seven-week training course at RAF Halton in Buckinghamshire, followed by specialist trade training lasting from three weeks to three years, depending on the trade. Training usually involves working towards nationally recognised qualifications.

Different training arrangements are made for aircrew and RAF Regiment gunners. Weapons systems operators and air loadmasters, for example, take a 12-week basic training course at the RAF College Cranwell in Lincolnshire, followed by a seven-week leadership training programme. After that comes training specific to their specialisation.

Personal Qualities: As an airman/woman, you must be able to work as part of a team, living and working closely with other people. You will have to follow orders much of the time but you must also be capable of using your initiative to make decisions and react quickly while remaining calm under pressure. You must be willing to accept responsibility and able to supervise others.

You must have good practical and technical skills, together with a high level of physical fitness.

Each specialism then has its own particular requirements. You would need, for example, good diagnostic and problem-solving skills to work as a technician; on the other hand, a methodical approach to analysing information would be essential if you train as an intelligence analyst.

Looking Ahead: The usual terms of service mean a regular engagement for nine years. You may be able to re-engage to complete 22 years' service, or continue up to the age of 55. If you enlist before the age of 17 years 6 months, you can leave on a free discharge during the first six months of service, but only after completing at least 28 days' training.

You can also give notice to leave following the completion of three years' service after training. Non-commissioned aircrew enlist for 12 years in the first instance.

Promotion above the rank of senior aircraftman/aircraftwoman is based on merit. Airmen/women who are eligible can apply to become commissioned officers.

Royal Marines Commando

The Royal Marines regularly carry out some of the most physically demanding tasks of any armed force in the world. Royal Marines commandos are therefore trained to exceptionally high standards for front-line combat duties, often in hostile environmental conditions. Once you have passed your initial training, there are 25 specialisations for you to choose from, all offering a wide variety of qualifications. Whichever one you choose, your primary role will always be as a Royal Marines commando. Most newly trained recruits join the General Duties specialisation but you can volunteer for any of the other 24. These range from aircrew, armourer or assault engineer to mountain leader, platoon weapons instructor, swimmer canoeist or telecommunication technician.

All trained marines are regarded as specialists except musicians or buglers, who are not commando-trained and serve only with the Royal Marines Band Service.

Entry Level: You can apply from the age of 16 up to your 28th birthday. No academic qualifications are required, although you would have to pass the Royal Navy selection test involving

English language, numeracy, reasoning and mechanical understanding, together with an interview and medical. You would also have to meet nationality and residence requirements and—except for musicians and buglers—pass the Potential Royal Marine Course (PRMC), which consists of three days of aptitude tests, physical exercises and a personal interview.

You must be at least 151.5 centimetres tall (approximately five feet) and your weight must be in proportion to your height, although you must weigh at least 60 kilograms (approximately nine and a half stones). Currently, only men can join the Royal Marine commandos.

To enter as a musician or bugler (open to men and women), you would have to pass a medical, including a dental and fitness check, plus an audition and musical aptitude test.

Making the Grade: After the PRMC, your initial commando training would last 30 weeks, based at the Commando Training Centre, Royal Marines, at Lympstone in Devon. The syllabus includes military drill, survival skills, weapons training and care of equipment, often focused on small groups to consolidate your team-working skills. You would experience endurance tests, heavy weapons training and the use of live ammunition.

The training culminates in a final exercise replicating the conditions of war. If you successfully complete this, you become a full commando, entitled to wear the green beret and to participate in the Pass Out parade.

You can then choose to train further for a specialist trade and you would be encouraged to take nationally recognised qualifications appropriate to your trade and existing qualifications.

Musicians and buglers train at the Royal Marines School of Music in Portsmouth. The first 15 weeks of service would involve military training, before you go on to professional musician training, lasting from two terms to nearly three years, depending on your entry level.

Personal Qualities: The right to wear the green beret does not come easily and is one that has to be earned by completion of the most demanding training course in the British armed forces. There are no exceptions to this requirement, a 'no compromise' approach reflecting the corps' fierce pride and important in maintaining its standards and commitment to excellence.

The essential qualities required of a commando include fitness, commitment, discipline and self-confidence. Some of this can be instilled during the training programme, but fitness, initiative and determination must be displayed from the start and you will find that most successful recruits have always been keen on sports or outdoor pursuits. All Royal Marines must be able to work as part of a team, living and working closely with other people. You must to be able to follow orders and use your initiative to make decisions and react quickly. Practical and technical skills are important, as a wide range of equipment and advanced weaponry is used in all areas of the work. Each specialism has its own requirements. For example, marines specialising in the swimmer canoeist role must be particularly strong swimmers and have passed the UK Special Forces Selection Course.

Looking Ahead: You would normally serve on what is known as an 'Open Engagement' lasting 22 years. On completion of this, you would immediately qualify for a pension. If you decide soon after joining that you are not suited to life in the Marines, you can apply to leave during your first six months of service provided you have completed at least four weeks' training.

People who do well in training and exercises have good prospects for promotion. It is possible to reach the rank of corporal after four years and sergeant after nine years.

You can also gain a commission from the ranks to become an officer.

Many Royal Marines gain qualifications and experience as part of their work that are acceptable to civilian employers.

Royal Navy Officer

Royal Navy Officers are responsible for managing and leading operations that may be undertaken on ships, submarines, aircraft, naval air stations and shore establishments. Their particular role may include such duties as commanding a warship in the Atlantic, flying a Lynx helicopter, supervising the safe operation of a submarine nuclear propulsion plant or providing emergency medical care. They also take responsibility for the management and leadership of non-commissioned personnel.

Officer specialisms include warfare, aviation, diving, Royal Marines, hydrographic and meteorology, engineering, supply and training management. You could also serve as a medical, dental or nursing officer or as a chaplain.

Entry Level: The minimum qualifications for Royal Navy officers are two A levels/AH grades or three H grades and three GCSEs/S grades (A-C/1-3), including English language and maths at either level. Alternative qualifications may also be considered. There are about 7,500 officers in the Royal Navy and, apart from submarines and clearance diving, all jobs are open to men and women.

You can join the Royal Navy as an officer from the age of 17. The minimum height is 151.5 centimetres and your weight must be in proportion to your height. There are strict eyesight standards and you must pass a medical. You must also meet the Royal Navy nationality and residence requirements.

You would normally start through Naval College Entry (NCE) or, if you have a degree, through Direct Graduate Entry (DGE). Your rank on joining would be either midshipman or sub-lieutenant, depending on your age. There are separate entry and training routes for medical, dental and nursing officers and chaplains.

You would have to pass a series of selection tests held at the Admiralty Interview Board at HMS Sultan, Gosport. These last two days and include aptitude tests, practical initiative tests, gym tests and interviews.

Making the Grade: All new officers begin with Naval General Training at the Britannia Royal Naval College at Dartmouth. This varies from two to five terms, depending on your qualifications and entry route. It includes six weeks on an operational warship. Specialist training for your chosen branch begins at the end of this course.

Warfare officers, for example, follow their Naval General Training with up to 12 months at sea, before moving on to further professional training such as the 16-week Officer of the Watch course. If they wish to specialise, they can progress to further training in areas such as air traffic control or fighter control, aircrew trainee pilot or observer, mine warfare and clearance diver, submariner or hydrographic surveyor. They may also take a Principal Warfare Officer course.

Personal Qualities: Outstanding leadership and teamworking skills are essential. You must be able to think and react quickly and be ready to accept responsibility, make decisions and manage other people. You should be able to communicate with people of all abilities, explain ideas, give spoken and written instructions and motivate others. You must take a keen interest in the people you lead, given your responsibility to inspire, guide and discipline them. You must be physically fit and prepared to work in combat. An interest in science and technology would be important in many of the jobs.

Each specialisation has its own requirements. For example, air traffic control and fighter control officers must be able to stay calm, think quickly and concentrate for long periods; supply officers must be methodical and have a flair for organisation; engineer officers need technological ability and must be good at finding solutions to problems.

Looking Ahead: You would join on an initial commission of 12 years as a Royal Navy officer or eight years as a Royal Marines officer. Regardless of your entry route, you would have an equal opportunity to demonstrate your potential and progress to longer commissions. Selection for further commissions begins around two to three years after finishing initial training.

You should be able to expect a new appointment every two or three years. Promotion is through a structured system from midshipman (aged 17-26), through sub-lieutenant (aged 20 plus), lieutenant (aged 22-34) and lieutenant commander (aged

30-37). Beyond that, there are more limited opportunities to progress to commander (aged 38-44), captain (aged 45-48) and admiral (at around 52). Promotion depends on a number of factors, including your ability, experience, qualifications and training.

You may leave before the end of your commission, generally within five years of finishing training.

Airlines Operations

Airlines Operations is, one of the most charming & high status carrier, let us know something about this. There are numbers of jobs available with aviation industry in India. In India, it is the Airport Authority of India (AAI) that is responsible for the management and development of international airports, domestic terminal, civil air terminals and civil enclaves at Defense aerodromes. The AAI manages and the entire Indian airspace. It is responsible for constructing runways, aircraft movement, cargo complexes and warehouses, ground help, air traffic and safety services. The AAI has to ensure efficient functioning of these services and equip the airports with the latest facilities available. To achieve this, the AAI has several centers for training personnel such as fighting squads, communication personnel and aerodrome personnel. It naturally goes without saying that job opportunities with the AAI are aplenty and remunerative too.

Eligibility: A basic graduate degree. Command over the English language and Hindi are mandatory. Knowledge of a foreign language is considered an asset. Foreign airlines too recruit ground staff and reservation staff from India to work in the different air terminals from where they operate their flights. Here too, fluency in English is mandatory and knowledge of a foreign language is an asset.

Job Prospects

Irlines Ground Staff: The commercial operations divisions of airline offices require staff at the airport to take care of passenger facilities such as checking in passengers, issuing and checking boarding passes, directing passengers, answering queries, preparing passenger lists, completing luggage formalities, attending to cargo documentation etc. They are the first members of the airlines office to receive the passengers at the airport and guide them through formalities such as immigration clearance, customs, security clearance, etc.; till the passenger enters the aircraft and similarly guide and direct passengers when they arrive at the end of the journey. They also employ traffic assistants to oversee loading and unloading of passengers' luggage.

Several departments at the terminals and the AAI employ managers who are placed in charge of each of the departments. There are cargo managers, personnel managers, legal managers, economic planning managers, commercial managers, housekeeping managers, stores and purchase managers, airport managers and managers in charge of electronics and technical matters. Every post is self-explanatory and the responsibilities are implicit. Broadly speaking the respective manager looks after the functioning of each of the department.

The requirements for the post of managers are as follows:

Economic Planning Manager: The post is generally open to post graduates in economics, statistics or mathematics, with a background of transport economics. Previous experience is considered an asset.

Commercial Manager: Graduates with experience in handling commercial or revenue matters are considered for this post.

Cargo Manager: A degree holder or an MBA with experience in cargo at supervisory level in airlines, seaports, Air Force or IATA approved cargo agencies, supplemented with a knowledge of computers and EDP systems is considered for the cargo manager's post.

Housekeeping Manager: This is open to graduates with a diploma in hotel management and three years' experience in executive capacity at a hotel.

Stores and Purchase Manager: Graduates trained in materials management, with five years' experience in managing stores.

Personnel Manager: A degree or diploma in personnel management or labour welfare or law or social science is a must. He should also have minimum five years' experience in personnel management.

Law Manager: A degree in law.

Career in Indian Army

Officer in the Indian Army: As an officer in the Indian Army, you will be heir to a glorious heritage. Blended perfectly with the latest in hi-technology, training techniques and strategic doctrines. You will be part of one of the world's finest Armies. Trained not just to be an officer, but a Soldier's Soldier.

You are a Special Person: Every year, thousands apply to become officers. Only a handful get through. You could be one of the chosen few. Do you have it in you? The time has come. To tighten your belt. To brace yourself for the road ahead. To choose the right path. The path that will decide where your life goes from here. Are you ready for the decision that will change your life forever? The Indian Army is looking for a few good men & women. A few of the best and the brightest. A few with fire in their belly. A few with intellect, idealism and courage. If you have it in you, we're looking for you.

We Build Men and Women of Character: An Indian Army Officer is the hallmark of what every human being aspires to be..... a pillar of strength and courage, whose mettle has been put through the acid test time and again. A career in the Army. It will teach you to face the toughest of situations in life with panache you have never known before. It will help you become a multidimensional personality who will be a force to reckon with. Interested? Unlimited Opportunities While the Indian Army trains you in the art of war the curriculum consists of academic subjects too. Besides it also gives you ample scope to acquire new skills constantly. You can participate in activities like river rafting, para jumping, rock climbing, trekking, mountaineering or even desert safaris. When it comes to adventure and sports, there's no place like the army.

Unparalleled Education

The Indian Army is a place where you'll never stop learning. Nowhere else can you get such phenomenal opportunities to constantly hone and upgrade your skills. NDA awards you a Bachelor's degree in Arts, Science or Computer Science on completion of your training. If you join the technical stream, you will be offered a Graduate and Post Graduate degree in Engineering from one of the finest institutes of technology in the country.

If you are selected for the prestigious Defence Services Staff College course. You'll be awarded a Master of Science degree in Defence and Strategic Studies. The Indian Army also runs some of the country's most prestigious academies and institutes. This covers a wide range of subjects from engineering to medicine, administration to strategy and armament technology to management. The choice is indeed limitless. In fact, you can even get into Research & Development, if you desire. That's not all. You can also take a study leave amidst your tenure for an added educational qualification.

Unmatched Lifestyle: As an Indian Army Officer at 21, you'd be looking at a lifestyle that one cannot imagine in any other profession, so early in life. For all those of you who want to take the plunge, here's how you can get into the Indian Army. You have several options. You can join right after school or after graduating. Read on to find out more.

Permanent Commission: A Permanent Commission means a career in the Army till you retire. For a Permanent Commission you have to join the National Defence Academy (NDA) or the Indian Military Academy (IMA)).

Other Rank

Indian Army: A Unique and Dignified Career

Recruitment in Army for Other Ranks is broad based. Every male citizen, irrespective of caste, class, religion and domicile, is eligible for recruitment in the Army, provided the person meets the laid down age, educational, physical and medical standards.

For a career in other Ranks, what you need to do is:

Visit the nearest Branch Recruiting Offices (BRO) HQ Recruiting Zones and find out dates of recruitment rallies. These are also published in all local news papers.

You must carry a certified copy of your educational qualification certificate and six copies of your recent passport size photographs alongwith all original certificates on the day of the rally. Details of documents required should be ascertained from the BRO/ZRO office.

Children of servicemen, ex-servicemen and war widows can also report directly to the nearest Training Centre on the day of screening alongwith required documents in original. They will however be screened only if they fulfill laid down standards for recruitment.

Indian Air Force

Working in the Air Force is about being in the middle of supersonic jets, state-of-the-art technology and best of the people. You are where the action is. Air Force provides you with the most modern facilities, gives you an unparalleled way of life and creates an environment, where the best in you comes out.

Whether you are a graduate or you have finished your schooling or you have passed your class tenth, Air Force has an exciting career opportunity for you. Click on the link below, to know how you can join the Indian Air force to jumpstart a secure future for you and your family. However we will focus solely on the prospects for graduates.

Air Force invites young, enthusiastic and committed, men and women, to lead and manage as officers. Candidates short-listed after the initial selection procedure go through a rigorous training regimen at one of the Air Force training establishments. Thereafter, they are commissioned as officers and posted at any of the Air Force Stations.

Eligibility: Age 20 to 23 years

Marital Status Single

Nationality Indian

Gender This is applicable to both men and women.

Educational Qualifications

You can apply if you are a graduate with a minimum score of 60%.

Job Prospects: **Unlike other career options Air Force is replete with risks, obstacles and thrills galore. Hence the aspiring youth need to do some serious thinking about adopting this profession.**

If you happen to possess any or most of the following qualities, consider yourself eligible

You must be bold, dashing and daring.

Must have a sense of adventure.

Must be willing to risk your life for the nation

Must be philosophical and realise the ephemeral quality of life

Must be hardworking, able to withstand strain

Must be fond of travelling

Must be able to fly for long hours

Must have a calm temperament and strong nerves

Where to Apply?

The recruitment for all kinds of course in the Indian Air force are carried out by the Ministry of defence with its headquarters in Newdelhi. The ministry of defense brings out notification in various leading dailies as well as Employment News.

Indian Army

The Army is the largest and the oldest branch of the Indian armed forces. It is trained to fight on land and consists of various divisions including the infantry, the artillery, the armoured corps etc. Besides, these combat divisions the support division in the army include the supply corps, the engineers, the ordinance supply corps, military intelligence and medical staff. The primary responsibility of the army is to safeguard the geographical boundaries of the country and to capture enemy territory in the event of a war. The army training includes both offence and defensive operations. In addition to the primary responsibility, the army is also called upon in peace time to aid in relief and rescue operations during natural calamities and for counter insurgency. The army is divided into various divisions. A brief description of the division and nature of duties is as listed below:

Candidates who have completed 12 years of education, *i.e.* have cleared the class XII examination, or its equivalent. Graduates and postgraduates in subjects like law, veterinary sciences and medicine and between the ages of 21-25 years are also recruited into the army.

Job Prospects

Infantry: The infantry consists of troops who fight the enemy on foot using equipment including from self loading rifles, automatic rifles, machine guns, grenades, mines, anti tank weapons, shoulder fired missiles and rocket launchers. Infantry troops capture and hold on to enemy positions or defend their own positions. For high mobility, troops make use of transport including personnel carriers and jeeps. Elite commando units and paratroopers are also part of the infantry. Infantry officers and troops have to undergo intensive training in arms handling.

Artillery: The artillery uses long range field guns, multi barrel rocket launchers and missile for their manoeuvres. The role of the artillery is twofold. In civilian areas the artillery uses weapons such as anti aircraft guns and surface to air missiles to protect sensitive locations such as dams, airfields, oil rigs, power generating stations, ports etc. from attack. On the warfront the artillery uses long range field guns, multi barrel rocket launchers and missiles for their attacking and defensive operations.

Armoured Corps: The armoured corps consists of battalions of tanks and other armoured vehicles. The armoured corps can advance swiftly and are used to capture enemy territory along with the infantry. They can also defend positions by engaging enemy tanks in battle. Armoured corps are considered to be one of the most prestigious divisions of the army.

Engineers: The primary responsibility of the army engineers is to quickly construct roads, bridges, airfields, helipads etc. so the all the three sections of defence forces can advance rapidly. Engineers also destroy enemy bases and cause obstacles for the advancement of enemy troops. Besides these they also lay minefields and clear enemy minefields, defuse explosives and construct other infrastructure for the combat troops.

Signals: The officers and men in the signals regiment are responsible for the quick implementation and maintenance of communication links between the army headquarters and the forward positions during war time. Besides this they are also responsible for electronic warfare.

Army Service Corps (ASC): ASC personnel are responsible for the movement of troops, vehicles, rations, petrol/diesel, arms and ammunition etc. The personnel of the ASC use road, train as well as water transportation in the movement. They are also responsible for safe storage of rations, arms and ammunition, clothing and special equipment.

Electrical and Mechanical Engineers: The armed forces have a large number of equipment ranging from simple rifles to sophisticated missiles. Electrical and mechanical engineers are responsible for the maintenance of all the equipment of the armed forces and ensure that it is always in peak condition. The officers in this service include engineers from the field of mechanical, aeronautical, electrical, electronics and communication engineering.

Intelligence Corps: The officers of this branch are involved in the collection, analysis and interpretation of information about the enemy troops including their movements and plans. Officers in the intelligence corps specialise in encoding and decoding messages, analysis of pictures taken by aircraft and satellite, data collection and analysis.

Ordinance Corps: The ordinance corps are responsible for procurement, storage and maintenance and issue of types of military equipment including ammunition and spares.

Army Medical Corps: The army medical corps includes

doctors who provide medical care for the families of troops and officers of the armed forces. During a conflict they provide emergency medical care to the wounded officers and troops on the battlefront.

The armed forces train their own doctors and nurses at the Armed Forces Medical College and College of Nursing respectively. They also induct doctors from other medical colleges.

Nursing officers: The nursing officers nurse the officers, troops and their families in the hospitals and clinics of the armed forces.

Dental Officers: The responsibility of the dental officers is to provide dental care to the personnel of the armed forces and their families.

Education Corps: Education officers provide continuing education to the armed forces personnel especially with respect to the latest development in weapon systems, new techniques of warfare, computerisation, communication systems etc.

Postal Services: The personnel in this service are responsible for looking after the postal requirement of the army. All money orders, personal letters and general mail is handled by the postal services.

Military Police: Personnel of the military police are responsible for maintaining discipline and order among the troops of the armed forces.

Judge Advocate General: This branch inducts law graduates to provide legal help to the army for handling various civil cases as well as disciplinary action against armed forces personnel.

Veterinary Corps: Some regiments of the army use animals such as horses, mules and dogs. The officers of the veterinary corps ensure the well being of these animals.

Graduate and Post Graduate Entry into the Army

Combined Defence Services Exam (CDSE): Those over the age of nineteen years and want to join the defence services can opt for the Combined Defence Services Exam. Union Public

Service Commission through its notification in leading newspapers and Employment news, in the months of April and October, conducts an entrance examination for entry into the officer cadre of the Army, Navy and Air force.

After qualifying the written test, candidates have to appear for an interview before the Service Selection Board. After the selection in the interview, the candidate has to undergo the medical examination. On clearing the medical examination the candidates are sent the following training establishments according to choice given by the candidates and their merit list ranking.

- Indian Military Academy, Dehradun (IMA)
- Naval Academy, Goa
- Air Force Academy, Begumpet, Hyderabad
- Officers Training Academy (OTA), Chennai

Those joining in any of the first three establishments get permanent commission. Candidates selected for OTA Madras are given short service commission. The applicant is required to clearly give his preferences for the services which he desires to join. If an applicant is competing for OTA as well as for any other course *i.e.* Indian Military Academy, Naval Academy and Air Force Academy, the OTA will always be his last choice. In such cases, the applicant must, therefore, give OTA as his last choice as otherwise OTA will be deemed to be the last choice even if it is given a higher preference by the applicant.

Incentives to NCC Cadets: In every course of the Indian Military Academy (IMA), 50 seats are reserved for National Cadet Corps 'C' certificate holders, who have passed the UPSC exam and have also been cleared by the Service Selection Board. Graduates with 50% marks, NCC 'C' certificate with B grade and serving for two years, can directly appear for the Service Selection Board interview, for the Staff Selection Commission (SSC) at OTA, Chennai.

Training

Indian Military Academy, Dehradun: Army cadets undergo rigorous military training for a period of 18 months, with the aim of turning out capable officers to take on the responsibility of leading infantry sub-units. On the successful completion of their training, the cadets are granted permanent commission in the rank of 2nd Lieutenant.

Officers Training Academy, Madras: Candidates, once selected undergo a training course of approximately nine months duration at the Academy. At the end of this period the Cadets are granted a short service commission in the rank of 2nd Lieutenant from the date of completion of training. Officers are kept on probation for six months from the time they receive their commission. Any officer reported on during this period, as being unsuited to retain his commission, may at any time during or after expiry of probation, have his commission terminated.

Entry for Women

Over the last few years women have made their presence felt in almost every male dominated profession and the armed forces is also one of them. Although women have always been a part of the armed forces, by participating in various welfare and social activities and have also been an integral part of the Medical and Nursing Services, the armed forces always remained a male dominated area.

From the year 1992 the Indian Army has allowed women to join as regular officers. Women are now found in most of the ground jobs in the army, such as, Army Service Corps, Ordnance Corps, Education Corps, Signals, Army Intelligence Corps, Electrical and Mechanical Engineers and the Judge Advocate General's Branch. The women candidates are normally selected for short service commissions which is of about 5 to 10 years duration.

Physical Standards for Women

There should be no signs of excess weight, weak constitution or physical handicap. The minimum acceptable height and weight for women is 142 cms and 36 kg respectively. The candidate must be in good shape, both mentally and physically. The candidate should not have any disease or disability, which is likely to cause a hindrance in the discharge of his duties.

Indian Navy

The Indian Navy is the seventh largest in the world and is a well knit, cohesive fighting force with tri dimensional capabilities. These include the navies' ability to engage in undersea, surface and aerial operations. The Indian Navy boasts of modern air carriers, destroyers, frigates, gunships, missile boats, submarines and naval aircraft. Supply ships provide them with rations, fuel, armaments, repair and other services extending their range of operations. Behind the well equipped and modern fleet are the well trained and dedicated naval officers andrew who are doing yeoman's service in safeguarding India's interests and playing a vital role in the country's defence preparedness.

Eligibility

Nationality: A candidate must be either

1. a citizen of India, or
2. a subject of Bhutan, or
3. a subject of Nepal, or
4. a Tibetan refugee who came over to India before the 1st January, 1962 with the intention of permanently settling in India, or
5. a person of Indian origin who has migrated from Pakistan, Burma, Sri Lanka, the East African countries of Kenya, Uganda, United Republic of Tanzania (formerly Tanganyika and Zanzibar), Zambia, Malawi, Zaire and Eth

Candidates belonging to categories (2), (3), (4) and (5) above must possess a certificate of eligibility, issued by the Government of India. Certificate of eligibility is not, however, necessary in the case of candidates who are Gorkha subjects of Nepal.

Age limits and marital status: Unmarried male candidates in between the age of 18 and 22 years are only eligible for training at Naval Academy.

Educational Qualifications: Candidates are required to have a B.Sc with Physics and Mathematics or a Bachelor in Engineering for Naval Academy.

Candidates who are still studying in their final year degree course and have yet to pass the final year examination can also apply, but will be required to submit proof of passing the degree examination.

Job Prospects: The primary duty of the Navy is to safeguard the exclusive economic zone of the country, it vital offshore installations and important trade links. Besides the navy has to escort friendly merchant ships and ensure safe passage on the country's ships. On the offensive side, the navy has to attack and blockade enemy harbours, prevent supply ships from reaching them, attack vital installations and coastal defences and engage enemy warships and submarines in battle.

The life of a naval officer is a tough and challenging. What is required to succeed is a sense of professionalism, adventure, camaraderie and a total commitment to the nation. A Naval officer may be required to spend long periods of time at sea, away from the family.

On the other hand it offers opportunities to visit new destinations and interact with a variety of people. At sea, Naval officers hold important positions commanding battleships, submarines and other vessels or flying naval aircraft. On shore they are required to offer technical support, coordinate fleet movements, plan strategies and train junior officers.

Where to Apply

National Defence Academy (NDA): In order to get admission to the NDA, which trains cadets for all the three branches of the armed forces (including the navy) the candidate has to appear for a competitive exam conducted by the UPSC, which is held in February and also in September. The course of training is for 3 three years and there are two courses starting every year in the months of January and July.

The candidate is required to give his preference for the service he wishes to join, however the final decision also depends on the rank he secures in the merit list. The candidate should first decide their preference for the two academies *i.e.* National Defence Academy and Naval Academy (Executive Branch).

Examination Centers: Agartala, Ahmedabad, Aizawl, Allahabad, Bangalore, Bareilly, Bhopal, Kolkata, Chandigarh, Chennai, Cochin, Cuttack, Delhi, Dharwar, Dispur (Guwahati), Gangtok, Hyderabad, Imphal, Itanagar, Jaipur, Jammu, Jorhat, Kavaratti (Lakshadweep), Kohima, Lucknow, Madurai, Mumbai, Nagpur, Panaji (Goa), Patna, Port Blair, Raipur, Sambalpur, Shillong, Shimla, Srinagar, Tirupati, Trivandrum, Udaipur and Vishakhapatnam. The centres and the date of holding the examination are liable to be changed at the discretion of the Commission.

Written Examination: All applicants are required to take a written examination to gain admission to the NDA. The examination consists of two papers, each of about 2 to 2.5 hours duration.

1. Mathematics-120 questions, Max. marks 300.

This paper covers arithmetic, algebra, geometry, trignometry, set theory and statistics, as per the secondary school curriculum of classes VII to X.

2. General Ability-150 questions, Max. marks 600.

This has two parts:

Part A: 50 questions, English language and comprehension

Part B: 100 questions, physics, chemistry, biology, history, geography, civics, economics, current affairs and general knowledge.

The papers in all the subjects consist of objective type questions only.

Interview and Special Tests

After the UPSC written examination, all candidates are required to appear for an interview and take some special tests, designed by the Service Selection Board. These are verbal and non-verbal intelligence tests, designed to test not only their intelligence but also their social traits and interest in current affairs. The candidate can get a maximum of 900 marks in these tests.

Personality tests—These tests are as follows:

- Situation Reaction Test (SRT)—Sixty situations are given

and the candidate is required to answer the reactions within 30 minutes.

- Thematic Apperception Test (TAT)—A set of 12 pictures are shown and the candidate is required to write a story in 3 minute for each picture.
- Word Association Test (WAT)—Sixty words are projected and the candidate is required to make a sentence, in 15 seconds for each word.

Group Test—Group Test is conducted in batches of 8-10 candidates. The test consists of group planning, group discussion, outdoor group tasks. The candidates are asked to take lectures on certain topics.

Interview—This is to test the personality of the candidate. This includes general awareness.

Intelligence test-Engineers and other ground duty applicants go through the officers intelligence rating test. This test is designed to find out the basic intelligence level of the candidates. Only those who achieve a minimum acceptable level and grade are required to undergo the Personality Test which is common to all candidates. Engineering Knowledge Test-Engineers take this test to asses their basic knowledge of engineering in various fields. This test has to be cleared before taking the personality test.

Physical Standards: Candidates recommended by the Services Selection Board must undergo a medical examination by the Board of Service Medical Officers and are allowed to go for the training programmes only after being declared fit by the medical board.

The candidate must be in good shape, both mentally and physically. The candidate should not have any disease or disability, which is likely to cause a hindrance in the discharge of his duties. There should be no signs of excess weight, weak constitution or physical handicap. The minimum acceptable height is 157.5 cms.

Coast Guards

The defence services of the country are responsible for the guarding our national boundaries from external aggression.

However for internal security, as also for providing additional support to the defence forces in guarding the national frontiers, paramilitary services *viz.*, CRPF, BSF, ITBP and CISF had been constituted many decades ago. Each of these units plays a well-defined role besides coming to the nation's rescue at times of national calamities.

Eligibility: Graduates from any stream, who can pass the written test as well as the physical fitness criteria, are all welcome to join in. The forces take in candidates at the Sub-Inspector level, wherein the academic eligibility is not very high, but the physical fitness is given more emphasis. Similarly, there are vacancies for technical graduates, education officers, medical officers and other specialists.

Job Prospects: Assistant Commandants/Company Commanders who are recruited directly are given rigorous training in the respective police academies. They are taught various skills like shooting, driving, controlling riots, mountaineering etc.

After successful completion of the training these officers are put on 'general duty', which apart from normal field duties also involves administrative responsibilities. Managerial and administrative responsibilities increase with seniority and promotions.

Where to Apply?

Since the job of a coastguard involves the country's security and a lot many technical things, all-round, on-the-job training is provided by the ministry of defence.

Paramilitary Services

The defence services of the country are responsible for the guarding our national boundaries from external aggression. However for internal security, as also for providing additional support to the defence forces in guarding the national frontiers, paramilitary services *viz.*, CRPF, BSF, ITBP and CISF had been constituted many decades ago. Each of these units plays a well-defined role besides coming to the nation's rescue at times of national calamities.

Eligibility: Graduates from any stream, who can pass the written test as well as the physical fitness criteria, are all welcome to join in. The forces take in candidates at the Sub-Inspector level, wherein the academic eligibility is not very high, but the physical fitness is given more emphasis. Similarly, there are vacancies for technical graduates, education officers, medical officers and other specialists.

Job Prospects: Assistant Commandants/Company Commanders who are recruited directly are given rigorous training in the respective police academies. They are taught various skills like shooting, driving, controlling riots, mountaineering etc. After successful completion of the training these officers are put on 'general duty', which apart from normal field duties also involves administrative responsibilities. Managerial and administrative responsibilities increase with seniority and promotions

Since the job of personnel in paramilitary forces involves the country's security and a lot many technical things, all-round, on-the-job training is provided by the department itself.

3

Career in Detective Services

The Detective and Protective Services

Threats to life, escalating public violence, mushrooming mafia strongholds and political and domestic violence have heightened the need for the services of security providers and private investigators. An alternative career that is as interesting as it is challenging.

FOR years now, safeguarding our homes and workplaces meant employing the famous warrior people from Nepal, the Ghorkas. The Ghorkas and Sherpa clans often migrated to India in search of employment and gradually created a niche for themselves as domestic security providers who kept vigil at night. However, all that is in the past now. With the burgeoning community of organised business houses, it has become a norm to seek the services of professional agencies specialising in offering security services. You now find uniformed security personnel adorning the entrances and exits of every apartment building, restaurant, bank, corporate house or even a cinema hall. These security guards are often employed on a contractual basis from agencies offering such services.

An established and flourishing business abroad, the novel business proposition is just breaking ground in India. Retired armed personnel find it an apt post retirement profession to dabble in. Detective services are also available for the asking. Not a very common choice for a profession, but definitely an unusual and adventurous proposition for those with enough imagination to solve murky mysteries. It is as demanding as it sounds exciting. Sleuthing is a high-powered business. Private sleuths are employed for various under cover activities, from tracking an errant husband to corporate or business associates, unearthing murky secrets of organisations, tracing missing people, solving political imbroglios and even verifying the credentials of prospective marriage partners.

These services have begun to emerge as support services to the law and order enforcement agencies of the country. They not only lighten the burden of these agencies but also strive to address the issue of civilian security adequately.

Professional Security Services

Work at the management level in a security agency primarily revolves around managing the regular administrative duties of the establishment. Public relations is an important aspect of the job. As a manager of the establishment, you would be required to acquire clients, manage them and run the business on profit. Since security personnel are hired on a contractual basis, building a loyal clientele is important for the health of the business. Awareness of the latest security systems and good man-management skills are necessary to run the business smoothly.

As a manager of the outfit, you must be able to recruit the right type of people high on integrity, honesty, courteousness, problem solving capabilities and a vigilant nature.

Crisis management is a vital function in this profession. Security personnel have to be able to face up to confrontations and at the same time be able to resolve misunderstandings as well as be able to deal with demanding clients. Physical well-being is also an important factor as the security personnel have to be robust, capable of working long hours and be resourceful in times of sudden attack or an emergency.

Professional security providers provide security and protection to business establishments, institutions, residential complexes, stores, retail outlets, restaurants, star hotels, etc. However, certain high security duties or assignments may require trained personnel, especially in case of threat to life or while safeguarding highly sensitive areas. These purposes require the agency to possess a licence permitting them to use firearms for defence.

What you Need to Know?

Mental alertness, ability to cope with stress, good reflexes and good observation skills, with physical and mental courage are necessary to extricate yourself out of difficult situations. Hence most organisations prefer personnel who are assertive and who adhere to the company's security policy.

You need to spot the right talent and check for the following criteria-Literacy, commonsense, manual dexterity, good communication skills and an ability to tackle hazards, which are some of the useful qualities of a security guard. Coordination and teamwork is essential among security personnel.

They also have to be able to control their temper. Good character references are necessary. Presence of mind and good interrogation skills are important for security personnel who are in constant and frequent contact with the public.

Private Investigators

Though it may appear to be an exciting career proposition, sleuthing is not an easy task. It involves odd hours and can mean erratic travel schedules.

As a private investigator, there are various options to specialise in. Clients may require an investigator to look into the credentials of a potential employee, investigate cases of fraud and espionage or credit reports, birth and death records, tax filings, press reports and others.

However, private investigators do not have any authority under law to detain or interrogate anyone. They, therefore have to adopt ingenious methods to gather the necessary information to investigate the case. At the end of the assignment, the investigator usually submits a detailed report to the client.

What Makes for a Sleuth?

To be a detective, you need to have an analytical bent of mind and an inquisitive nature. You must be adventurous and be able to take risks, be extremely observant and patient. A background in forensic sciences, though not essential would help the private investigator in his work.

The Indore Christian College is only institution in India that offers a one-year diploma course in the art of private investigation. However, no specific educational qualifications are necessary.

The Specialist

People higher up the hierarchical order in a private detective's firm usually have a background in the defence forces and the armed services or possess professional qualifications like a degree in law, etc.

Security is an important issue and investigators specialising in a particular field can put to good use their services. Technical experts can help quell cyber crimes and hacking, while financial wizards can aid in nabbing embezzlers and investigate bank frauds. Legal experts can aid law firms in investigating their cases, locating witnesses and gathering evidence.

The Routine

A lot of paper work is usually involved in detective work, which requires secretarial services and a number of administrative staff. Well-established detective service providers can have in-house experts such as forensic scientists and chemists.

Personnel working in security agencies need to be adept at handling firearms, alarms and filling-in inquiry reports.

Money, Money, Money

At the entry level, investigators working with established agencies can expect to earn approximately Rs. 5,000 per month.

However, those operating on their own can charge anywhere from Rs. 1,000 and more depending on the nature of the case.

Future Prospects

In the present scenario, there seems to be no sign of an abating crime rate, thereby increasing the dependency on security services.

Threats to life, escalating public violence, mushrooming mafia strongholds and political and domestic violence has heightened the need for the services of these security providers, further emphasised by the presence of multinationals and international business houses in India.

Detective Service

The Detective Service of the SAPS is responsible for the investigation of crime. It consists of six components, namely General Investigation, Criminal Record Centre, Forensic Science Laboratory and Serious and Violent Crime, Organised Crime and Commercial Branch.

General Investigation is made up of operational detectives who investigate a broad category or crime. They normally work from police stations. The detectives at police stations carry out duties such as-

- gathering evidence;
- executing warrants of arrest or search warrants;
- using investigative techniques;
- preparing case dockets for court proceedings;
- attending crime scenes;
- tracking and arresting suspects;
- searching premises and seizing evidence;
- investigating reported crime; and
- serving summonses and subpoenas.

Detectives and personnel of the Criminal Record Centre (CRC) carry out the following duties:

- Collecting, processing and providing information on arrested and convicted criminals in support of investigations and court proceedings.
- Providing information on persons, vehicles, firearms and stolen goods for investigation and clearance purposes. This information is obtained from various databases.
- Applying a scientific approach and skills during crime investigations.

The CRC head office is situated in Pretoria. There are Local Criminal Record Centres (LCRC) in al nine provinces.

The Forensic Science Laboratory (FSL) provides a support service to investigating officers. Forensic scientists who work at the FSL analyse physical evidence that is collected at crime scenes. Forensic science is the use of scientific methods in the investigation of crime. All relevant physical evidence and clues are studied and interpreted according to acceptable scientific principles. During investigations, forensic science is used to bring criminals to justice and to protect innocent people against prosecution.

Minimum requirements for appointment at the FSL:

- Three years' relevant experience and a Senior Certificate (Grade 12) with Mathematics and Science.
- One or more of the following: A BSc honours degree, diploma or degree in chemistry; a BSc degree in Chemistry; a degree or diploma in photography, graphic design or fine art with photography as a subject; a diploma or degree in Police Science or Criminology.
- A relevant degree or diploma in one of the following: Zoology; Soil Science; Botany; Physics; Inorganic, Analytical and Physical Chemistry and Electron Microscopy; Anthropology; Criminology; Armourer; Medical Technology; Medicine; Medical Science; Statistics; Geology; Geochemistry; Mineralogy; Electronic Engineering; and Molecular Biology; or an LLB degree.

Members of the FSL work in the following six units: The Ballistics Unit examines firearms and tool marks. Ballistics is the science of projectiles and firearms. The duties of a ballistics analyst include-

- analysing crime scenes for ballistic-related evidence;
- examining ballistic objects;
- attending post-mortem examinations;
- presenting expert evidence in court; and
- doing research.

The Questioned Document Unit is responsible for the forensic examination of any aspect regarding documents that is questioned, for example, handwriting.

The Scientific Analysis Unit provides a forensic service regarding:

- the analysis or investigation of primer residue
- the analysis of material;
- the analysis of trace evidence, electronics and images.

These tasks are performed by forensic science analysts. The Unit also carries out polygraph tests during crime investigations and takes photographs as part of forensic processes.

The Biology Unit studies exhibits of a biological origin by means of DNA analysis and microscopic comparison. A forensic biological analyst analyses crime scenes and attends post-mortem examinations to gather biological evidence. The preparation and examination of objects include trigonometry, DNA analysis, facial reconstruction and individualization. A forensic biological analyst also has to give expert evidence in court and do research.

The Chemistry Unit carries out a variety of chemical analyses. A forensic chemical analyst processes or reconstructs crime scenes to gather chemical evidence. He or she prepares and examines objects for chemical analysis in investigations relating to fires, poisons and narcotics (drugs). He or she also has to present expert evidence in court and do research.

The Explosives Unit manages and maintains a bomb-disposal service in the SAPS. Bomb technicians enforce the Explosives Act, 1956 (Act No 26 of 1956). They use computer systems to carry out this task. Vacancies in the Explosives Unit are filled by selecting trained members of the SAPS. Members who join the Explosives Unit undergo extensive in-service training.

Detectives working at Serious and Violent Crime (SVC) carry out the following duties:

- Investigate crimes against the State.
- Investigate murders involving important persons, the judiciary, politicians and members of the SAPS.
- Investigate actual or attempted armed robberies of financial institutions such as commercial banks.

- Investigate actual or attempted cash-in-transit heists.
- Investigate vehicle highjackings in which victims were shot.
- Investigate specific robberies and the theft of firearms.
- Investigate specific series of crimes of a serious and violent nature such as serial murders and rapes.
- Investigate intergroup violence, for example, political violence, taxi violence, train violence, gang violence and faction fighting.
- Investigate actual or attempted attacks on residents of farms and smallholdings.

The Commercial Branch investigates and prevents commercial crime. Therefore, it promotes the economic growth and prosperity of the country. The Commercial Branch investigates offences in terms of statutes (acts) and regulations regarding, for example, accountants and auditors, agriculture, banking and currency, companies, courts, debtors and creditors.

Under the common law, the Commercial Branch is also responsible for investigating fraud and theft committed under the following circumstances:

Fraud

- Fraud originating from inter-company or close corporation transactions only.
- Fraud by means of the double discounting of instalment sale agreements.
- Fraud originating from transactions on the stock exchange.
- Fraud by means of 'factoring' (the manufacture of one's own cheques to commit fraud).
- Fraud committed by means of stolen bank cards, debit cards, petrol cards and credit cards.

Theft

- Theft of trust money by any person who is legally bound to keep a separate trust account.
- Theft of the funds or assets of deceased estates by executors.

- Theft of the funds or assets of insolvent estates or estates under curatorship by trustees or liquidators.

Other responsibilities of the Commercial Branch are to investigate-

- white plastic (modified plastic cards used for fraud);
- clone cheques; and
- forgery and uttering (falsification and circulation) of credit cards, debit cards and petrol cards.

Detectives of the Organized Crime Component investigate offences relating to-

- diamonds and gold;
- narcotics;
- endangered species;
- high-flyers; and
- illegal alliances such as syndicates.

The component also investigates-

- stock theft;
- human trafficking related crimes;
- cash-in-transit robberies;
- corruption;
- vehicle crime; and
- cross-border crime.

Organized crime projects include-

- projects that are targeted at individuals nationally and internationally;
- projects of the Southern African Regional Police Chiefs Cooperation Organization (SARPCCO);
- projects that target pharmaceutical crimes; and
- projects of the National Crime Combating Forum.

Detective

Detectives investigate crimes and arrest suspected criminals.

Alternative Titles:

- CIB member

- Detective
- Detective Constable
- Detective Sergeant
- Senior Sergeant

Tasks and Duties

Detectives:

- examine the scene of the crime to find evidence
- interview suspects, witnesses and victims
- search for and identify offenders
- execute search warrants to recover property and evidence
- prepare and give evidence in court
- obtain and record information about criminals
- analyse crime data and information
- train and mentor new detectives.

Entry Requirements: To become a detective you need to have spent time as a police officer. You must then complete two and a half years detective training (which is mainly on the job) and pass the Criminal Investigation Branch (CIB) selection and induction and the Detective Qualifying course to become a fully qualified detective.

Secondary Education: There are no specific secondary education requirements to enter training to become a police officer. However, Sixth Form Certificate or NCEA equivalent English and maths may be useful as the police entrance exams test English and maths to this level.

Training on the Job: Detectives gain skills on the job and on police training courses.

Useful Experience: All detectives first gain experience as police officers. Experience in dealing with people or being part of a team environment (such as a sports team) is also helpful, as is a reasonable amount of life experience.

Skills & Knowledge: "People skills are important. You have to be able to deal with a wide range of people in a wide range of situations-from victim's and their families to interviewing offenders."

Richard Chambers, Detective Sergeant

Detectives need to have:

- knowledge of police procedures, including how to investigate crimes
- knowledge of police policies and the laws relating to police work
- knowledge of how the court system works
- knowledge and understanding of a range of cultures
- problem-solving skills
- record-keeping skills
- skill in analysing information and preparing written and verbal reports
- communication and people skills, including interviewing skills
- conflict resolution and negotiation skills.

Personal Qualities: Detectives need to be:

- honest and able to keep information private
- mature and responsible
- firm and fair
- able to remain calm in emergencies
- good at listening
- motivated, determined and disciplined
- able to relate to people from a range of cultures and backgrounds.

They also need to have an eye for detail and must be able to work as part of a team.

Physical Requirements: Detectives need to be fit, healthy and strong. They also need to have good hearing, good eyesight and normal colour vision.

Working Conditions: Detectives work in a variety of settings and conditions, including offices in police stations, city or country areas, courts and cars. They may also travel to different sites around the country and overseas to help investigate crimes and to attend conferences.

Some situations where detectives are present may be distressing or dangerous.

Equipment: Equipment detectives use includes:

- computers, including criminal investigation databases and tools
- phones, fax machines and other office equipment
- notebooks and pens
- handcuffs, batons, firearms and pepper spray
- radiotelephone
- cars and other vehicles.

Hours: Detectives work long and irregular hours during some investigations. Their hours include working nights, weekends and public holidays and they may need to be on call at times.

Contact with People: Detectives usually work independently and as part of a team. They interact with a wide variety of people including:

- police officers and officers from specialist sections, such as the finger print and dog sections
- social workers
- lawyers and court staff
- people from government agencies such as the New Zealand Customs Service and Corrections Department
- the public.

They may supervise small groups of staff, or groups working on criminal investigations.

Salaries: Salaries vary, but detectives usually earn between $50,000 and $90,000 per year depending on rank and experience.

Career Progression: Detectives may move into operations units such as forensics or search and rescue.

They can also move into management positions, which follow a specific management structure.

The Police Commissioner is responsible for the general running of the police and delegates powers to two deputy commissioners (one responsible for operations and one in charge of resource management). New Zealand is divided up into 12 policing districts with a district commander responsible for each. These are administered by the Wellington district commander.

Outlook

Outlook: Good

The outlook for detectives is good and the number of people employed in this occupation is expected to remain stable or increase moderately over the next two to three years.

General Prospects: The outlook for detectives is good and the number of people employed in this occupation is expected to remain stable or increase moderately over the next two to three years.

There are approximately 7,000 sworn police officers and around 12% of those are detectives. Urban areas have the biggest number of detectives and most work within a police district, although some work in units with a nationwide or international focus.

The number of detectives is determined by police decisions about where to allocate their resources. It can change in response to factors such as increased crime and population. Where detectives work and the type of work they carry out also changes as New Zealand's crime patterns change.

Ongoing Training Required: In line with changing crime patterns, police resources and training are constantly being reviewed. For example, units have been set up to deal with increases in methamphetamine, electronic and computer based crime and money laundering activities.

As training for detectives evolves to better match contemporary crime patterns, formal tertiary training may also be added in the near future to complement the existing methods.

Use of Technology Increasing: Like many police and law enforcement agencies, New Zealand's police are increasingly using advanced intelligence gathering methods in criminal investigations. This has meant that computer technology skills and intelligence analysis have become more important to most areas of detective work. Detectives are also beginning to receive training in procedures related to collecting DNA and other forensic materials as evidence. More traditional investigation and analysis skills are also still of great importance in this job.

Turnover: Turnover among sworn police officers is less than 5% each year. Detectives leave mainly for health reasons, retirement or to move to other areas of the police force. Detectives work in an area of high accountability and pressure, which may contribute to some turnover.

A Career as a Detective

Homicide Detectives are plainclothes investigators who specialize in gathering facts and collecting evidence for criminal cases involving murder.

Most of the work involves conducting interviews, examining records, monitoring the activities of suspects and participating in raids or arrests.

Cases are assigned on a rotating basis and homicide detectives work on them until they result in an arrest or conviction, or until the case is dropped. They may be assigned to interagency task forces, when, for instance, a murder incident involves other areas of crime investigation, such as narcotics.

Career Description for a Homicide Detective

While contributing to an investigation to solve a case, the homicide detective may carry out the following duties:

- Examining the scene of crime to obtain clues and gather evidence.
- Questioning witnesses.
- Questioning individuals linked to homicide victims or to suspects.
- Investigating and interviewing suspects.
- Investigating known or suspected criminals to detect criminal activity or clues.
- Investigating particular facts of the case to identify salient leads.

- Visiting known haunts and mixing with criminals to obtain information relevant to the case.
- Writing reports for submission to the officer in charge.
- Conducting arrests or assisting in the arrests of criminals and suspects.
- Preparing cases for court, in line with formal procedures.
- Testifying before courts or juries.

Would a Homicide Detective Career Suit You?

A police detectice career can be very dangerous and stressful. Officers need to be constantly alert and ready to deal with a range of threatening situations, including violence from suspected criminals. The experience of being present at murder scenes can be acutely stressful.

This kind of career can have a strong impact on the individual's personal life. Hours can be unpredictable and irregular, with paid overtime being common. Shift work is necessary. Junior officers frequently work weekends, holidays and nights. Detectives are required to work at any time, with especially long hours during investigations. Officers are frequently expected to be armed and to exercise their arrest authority whenever necessary, including outside working hours.

Outstanding personal characteristics required are honesty, good judgement, integrity and a sense of responsibility. An interest in people is essential, together with the ability to relate at all levels. The ability to withstand pressure and make sound, objective judgements and decisions in difficult circumstances is critical. Credibility as a witness is vital, as are good communication skills. The willingness to confront and resolve problems, coupled with good observational skills, is also important. Good physical health is a requirement.

Salary and Prospects for a Detective Career

Police officers usually become eligible for promotion after a probationary period ranging from six months to three years. In a large department, officers are promoted to detective and are assigned to investigative work after completing the appropriate selection and training. As they gain experience, they may gain further promotion and become responsible for controlling, planning and organizing the work of others.

Competition is keen for higher paying jobs in affluent areas. Career opportunities for a homicide detective are more widespread both in local and special police departments that offer relatively low salaries and in urban communities with relatively high crime rates. College training in police science or military police experience gives an applicant a distinct advantage.

Further career promotion to higher ranks usually depends on the detective's position on a promotion list, which is determined by scores on a written examination and on-the-job performance.

The Work and Career of a Detective

Previous it was argued that a police service in a democracy plays three distinctive roles: (i) public reassurance, visibility and patrol; (ii) crowd management; and (iii) criminal investigation. While the distinctions between these categories are by no means clear or consistent, almost all (legitimate) policing activities fall into one or more of them.

Furthermore, given the organisational dictum that structure follows strategy, functional police officers tend to be deployed in units or components whose activities are structured around one or other of these principal functions. Thus police officers can be crudely divided into those who provide services in the realm of public reassurance and crime prevention (uniformed officers at station level), those who police crowds (public order police service) and those who investigate criminal cases (detectives).

Naturally, these structures do not solely perform their primary tasks. For example, uniformed members can and do play a crucial role in investigating crime and policing collective action or public events and detectives do help the public in ways unrelated to their investigative work. Nevertheless, the distinction between the various functional structures in the SAPS does broadly reflect the distinctions between the various roles the police are expected to play.

This division of labour is not uncontroversial. Indeed, criminologists have sharply criticised the degree of organisational separation between these elements—not just in South Africa, but in other democracies as well. In essence, they argue that hermetically sealed units specialising in some or other aspect of a broader problem creates an artificial impression that the underlying problems are themselves fragmented. This leads to a fragmentation of effort, with the effect that policing problems are not tackled holistically.

This is further aggravated by the tendency of organisational components to start competing with one another, leading to the perverse effect that, rather than dealing with the problem, internal police dynamics can generate problems of their own. It has also been argued that, in creating a specialisation in investigation and career paths for specialist investigators, the development of distinct and relatively autonomous investigative components within police services undermines the organisation's unity of purpose.

The analysis that condemns the internal division of labour between investigation, visibility and crowd management reflects a relatively plausible assessment of police work, which includes the view that the various aspects of policing are (a) interrelated and mutually reinforcing; and (b) that the delivery of the relevant services are not so different that it could not be handled holistically and comprehensively. In terms of this view, not only is the functional division between different elements of policing unnecessary, it is also perverse in that it undermines a society's capacity to resolve crime problems by creating an organisational division between those who are to provide various aspects of the solution. Further, it is this seemingly artificial division of labour and management which is deemed to be behind the competitive and destructive relationship between uniformed members and detectives in South Africa.

It is, of course, important not to overstate the case for integrating the various aspects of policing. It is clear, for example, that even if all policing functions were integrated into a single command, with each member both capable of and actually performing, all tasks, the most important social functions in relation to the prevention of crime would still be outside the control of the police.

This seems desirable both from a managerial point of view as well as that of the maintenance of the rights of citizens and the protection of civilian rule. Police officers are typically neither trained nor interested in the delivery or management of other social programmes. As regards the latter, the expansion of the police into social crime prevention must, at some point, begin to mean that the role of the 'coercive arm of the state' has exceeded the bounds of acceptability.

If these arguments are correct, there are limits to the extent to which the management, control and delivery of various components of a society's crime prevention project can be integrated. Thus, before examining the division of labour within policing, it is important to recognise that policing is itself part of a larger division of labour in managing crime.

The division of labour between uniformed members and detectives is based both on differences in the nature of their work as well as the historical separation of members fulfilling different duties. This has contributed to very different experiences of policing, thereby creating and sustaining distinct and competitive police cultures. In South Africa, this division has been heightened by the existence and separateness of the security branch and the internal stability unit/public order police service (ISU/POPS) within the police service.

A Detective's Career

Unlike the security branch, which did its own 'head-hunting', the criminal investigation division (CID) accepted applicants as well as actively recruited members during the 1970s and 1980s. However, detectives recruited in that period maintain that standards of entry were high. Thus only members of the police who had demonstrated the potential to become solid detectives were allowed to join. They were then put on probation as 'student detectives' for six to 12 months, during which time three or four probation reports were written on their progress. Older detectives consistently argue that this process was not merely ritualistic and was used to ensure that only people with real potential were allowed to join. Furthermore, because of the nature of probation and the militaristic nature of the rank system, the process served to ensure that members interested in becoming detectives tended to join quite early in their careers, thus avoiding a situation where a student detective was more senior than the commanding officer or other senior detectives in a unit.

Joining the detectives was not always easy. One interviewee recounted that, when a CID commander approached him with a recruitment offer, he had to wage a war of attrition within the police bureaucracy because his station commander was loath to let him go.

Typically, recruitment was into a local branch of the CID. Depending on the size of the station and the establishment in the CID, the branch would be commanded by a warrant officer or officer. Usually, student detectives were given a light workload of relatively minor cases—such as theft from washing lines, theft of bicycles and the like. The performance of the detective in completing these cases—taking the statements, visiting the scene, following up evidence, etc.—was monitored, as was his or her general aptitude for the job.

Assuming that the prospective detective showed sufficient potential, s/he would be accepted into the CID as a detective—with a rank change to detective constable or detective sergeant—and would receive progressively more difficult cases. Throughout this developmental process, more senior detectives would review the trainee's work, instructing (as opposed to 'advising') on the steps to follow to complete a case. This would include what sorts of evidence to look for, the sorts of statements to take and the sorts of people to look for as potential witnesses.

Recruitment into the investigative function was facilitated by the extent to which the uniformed members of the SAP participated in criminal investigations. Unlike the present situation, in the 1970s and 1980s the uniformed branch was responsible for certain kinds of investigations. This depended on local practice, crime levels and resource constraints and could include minor assault cases, vehicle accidents and the like. This meant that the CID commander had a basis for assessing the potential of a prospective recruit prior to him/her joining the CID. Furthermore, the organisational culture of the time meant that the CID was able to attract members because of a relative freedom from personal supervision compared to the uniformed branch; improved access to vehicles; working in civilian clothes; etc.

These institutional incentives, together with the perceived status of the detectives and investigative work, meant that the CID was generally able to recruit whomever it wanted. These differences also fuelled internal animosity between detectives and uniformed members, with the former perceived as relatively overresourced and undisciplined and the latter as less skilled, less productive and more rule-bound.

Having been recruited into a branch of the CID, a detective would typically have one of two basic career paths: remaining in the basic CID structure and progressing within it, or joining a specialised unit and progressing there. In both instances, however, the detective was likely to be transferred a number of times.

Thus, after being recruited to a CID branch on the East Rand in 1965, an interviewee called K for these purposes spent a year on probation before being appointed as a detective. He then spent a few years working on minor crimes before being given more complex and important cases. He notes that the nature of the cases handed to a detective became a reflection of seniority and status.

With a bit of luck and a lot of hard work, he was placed in the elite group at his station, responsible for housebreaking and violent crimes. Apart from the status of such an appointment, detectives in those groups were better resourced, had access to better vehicles and had better offices. After two or three years K became the head of this group and stayed in this position before moving to a murder and robbery unit in another part of the Transvaal.

Until then, only the Brixton murder and robbery unit took its own dockets to court, while other 'field units' just gathered evidence and made arrests before handing the cases back to the local CID. K's recruitment was part of a process designed to give the unit in question the capacity to take its own dockets to court.

Then, as now, murder and robbery units did not investigate every murder; they were used only for complex murders involving firearms, or where the victims were white and the suspects either black or unknown. Because other murder and robbery units regarded Brixton as 'the best of the best', members of other units competed to receive the same recognition for successful convictions—hence they worked long, hard hours.

In 1976 K was working in the Soweto murder and robbery unit and was recruited by the security branch which, after the events on 16 June of that year, required experienced investigators to help investigate and prosecute activists involved in the uprising. This culminated in a terrorism trial of 12 people, one of whom was sentenced to death but whose sentence was later commuted. But K wanted to go back to fighting crime, so he returned to the CID; he first became a branch commander in a rural town in the Cape Province and was then transferred to an urban station in the Transvaal. After leaving the police for a period in the 1980s, K returned to the SAPS to resume his career as a branch commander in a major city.

While this story is unique to K, it is typical of the careers of many detectives—especially white detectives recruited into the CID in the 1960s, 1970s and 1980s. Black detectives, on the other and, had a variety of additional obstacles to overcome in the course of their careers. For instance, the fact that many black police officers had fewer scholastic and academic qualifications tended to prejudice them in the promotions system, which placed a high premium on qualifications.

Internal policies which prevented black officers of any rank from commanding white officers of a lower rank also meant that room for advancement was limited. This, combined with the common South African experience of black workers receiving less recognition for their achievements than their white colleagues, meant that black police officers were less likely to gain managerial and command experience. Besides these environmental constraints on advancement, black police officers who challenged racism, no matter how 'diplomatically', ran the risk of being perceived as 'politicians'.

Furthermore, the fact that detectives regarded themselves as an elite means that black police officers would have been less likely candidates than white officers. At the same time, however, all detectives recognise that white detectives, no matter how skilled, are often ill-suited to dealing with black victims, witnesses and perpetrators.

What Does a Detective Do?

Real detective work is very different from the popular accounts in films, fiction or on TV. Generally, cases are not solved with deductive logic applied to complex clues. Nor do they involve undercover work, shoot-outs with gangsters, or dramatic last-minute testimony by witnesses who are either hard to find or require active protection. Most detective work is relatively routine and repetitive. At the same time, different units and groups, working on different kinds of crimes, will use different methods to complete their cases. So while what follows reflects the kind of work typically done by detectives, it is by no means a comprehensive account.

To understand basic detective work it is important to bear in mind that, in terms of South African criminal law, an accused must be linked to a crime beyond reasonable doubt in order to be convicted and that a crime is deemed to have certain elements which, while they will differ in various instances, deal with the intention and actions of the alleged criminal. Therefore, in order to show that accused X committed crime Y, the state must show that X performed all the required actions and had the requisite intention. In doing this, there are three basic forms of proof: physical evidence, witnesses and confessions. Different crimes will tend to involve a different mix, but these are the basic ways in which guilt is established and all detectives use them.

Physical evidence is used both to show the nature of the crime—for example, that the accused is in possession of cocaine, not baby powder—and to link an accused to the commission of the crime. For the latter, although fingerprints are the most common form of evidence, DNA, fibre analysis and other scientific techniques are also used. In many crimes—particularly cases in which the possession of an item is itself a crime—physical evidence is frequently sufficient to obtain a conviction. Witnesses (including, where appropriate, police officers on the scene or making the arrest) and confessions are used to establish both the intention and actions of an accused.

Not unsurprisingly, the degree to which witnesses co-operate with the police depends on the nature of the crime—for instance, witnesses to murders related to taxi conflict are less likely to cooperate for fear of reprisals than some other witnesses. Other factors which can affect the level of co-operation are said to include the relationship of the witness to victim and perpetrator and the race of detective and witness. In this regard, for instance, white detectives in a major city acknowledged some difficulties in getting black witnesses to cooperate and reflected that black witnesses usually preferred to make their statements at a police station (out of sight of their neighbours) and in their mother tongue. On the other hand, a black branch commander in a township argued that he needed white detectives because, in some cases, this would help to ensure that the community regarded the investigator as neutral.

One further strategy used fairly commonly are so-called 'traps' in which the police, posing as civilians or criminals, buy contraband such as endangered species, stolen and 'grey' goods, drugs, unlicensed firearms, etc. Because, as sole witnesses, the police are extremely powerful in such cases, a number of checks and balances have been prescribed to protect the integrity of such operations. These controls are intended to ensure that the accused does not commit the crime solely because s/he is being enticed and that the police do not act as agents provocateurs in the process. Whether these checks and balances work or not is something that cannot be dealt with here.

Basic Detective Work

The precise treatment given to any particular crime will depend on its nature, mode of discovery, whether the crime is part of a local crime pattern and the resources available at station level. In general, however, no matter what the crime, no matter who discovers it and no matter what the resource constraint, all crimes reported to the police must be investigated and today all investigations are undertaken by detectives.

Detectives work two different sorts of week, although some stations use shorter or longer periods. One week the detective is on stand-by, meaning that it is his or her job to wait for cases to come in and conduct the initial investigations. Their primary duty, however, is to be available for the next case.

Each case they receive while on stand-by will be booked out to them and they will have to work on it the following week. This is the period in which detectives follow up leads from the initial investigations and complete their dockets. Within the stand-by system, detectives are often divided into groups dealing with different types of crime—a procedure which, depending on the type of crime, grassroots detectives both like and dislike.

The bulk of investigative work is done at station level and the bulk of that is property crime and different forms of interpersonal violence. For instance, in 1997 the SAPS opened more than 2 million cases of which murder, attempted murder, rape, attempted rape and assault made up about 25 per cent and robbery, burglary, stock theft and various other forms of theft another 60 per cent. These crimes come to the attention of the police in two basic ways: complaints by the public, or arrests performed in the course of police operations or standard crime prevention work. Of course, these latter operations may often be in response to information obtained from informers and other members of the public, whether anonymous or otherwise.

Arrests made by police officers in the course of their duty are generally related to 'open and shut' cases of possession, trespassing or the like, or of criminals caught in the act of committing a crime such as car theft, housebreaking, assault, etc. In such cases the arresting officer will make a statement as to the reasons for the arrest. That, together with other statements and relevant evidence—such as stolen property or contraband—will form the basis for the charge against the accused. Here the role of the detective is to put the docket together, ensure that there is evidence to prove all the elements of the crime and send the docket to the prosecutor. In the course of doing this, the detective will usually interview the accused, advise him of his rights and, if possible, obtain a statement as part of the formal charge laid against him.

When a docket is opened as a result of a complaint laid at a police station by a member of the public, the process is somewhat different and varies in relation to the nature of the complaint and the information it conveys.

A surprisingly large number of dockets is opened with the identity of the suspect already known. The complainant will, for instance, identify his or her assailant, or the person who allegedly stole property or committed fraud. In such a case the docket, after being registered on the computerised crime administration system (CAS), will be handed to a detective on stand-by duty. He will do some basic work on the docket and perhaps even make the arrest if the information in the docket is clear enough. Indeed, the arrest may be made by a detective on stand-by and only then handed over to another officer assigned to investigate the matter.

In such cases in particular, though it is true of all investigations, the detective's role is not merely to pursue the conviction of a person alleged to have committed a crime; he is also responsible for finding evidence that the crime has in fact been committed. Frequently, charges will be laid against people who have not in fact committed a crime. In such cases it is the duty of the detective to make sure that charges are well-founded and that there is prima facie evidence against the alleged perpetrator.

Further, especially in simple fraud cases involving dishonoured cheques and incidents of interpersonal violence, the complainants will sometimes withdraw the charges after resolving the matter or 'cooling off'. In any event, the investigation will be aimed at accumulating evidence which either supports or undermines the charge against the suspect and will be completed only when a docket is handed to the prosecutor or the case is closed for lack of evidence or because it was unfounded.

None of the above processes bear any resemblance to the portrayal of detectives in popular fiction, because the docket is opened with a clear indication of the identity of the suspect. Obviously, this is not the only manner in which crimes are reported. Many crimes are committed by people who are strangers to the victim. Even when the victim and perpetrator know each other, this may only be established after the crime is reported to the police.

In such cases the role of the investigator is similar to that portrayed in popular fiction: it is the detective's responsibility to establish what crime was committed and by whom and to put together sufficient evidence to prove this in court. To this end, the primary sources of evidence are statements by the victims and witnesses, physical evidence and confessions, as described earlier.

Where a crime has been committed by a stranger—including most property crime and some violent crime—obtaining a conviction is, for obvious reasons, much more complicated. Generally, convictions will only be obtained if there is a description of the perpetrator which links him or her to other crimes (in which he may be more directly identified); physical evidence (fingerprints or bodily fluid) which can be used to tie the perpetrator to the crime; or information from an informer. Frequently a combination of these is required, because a fingerprint is not helpful unless the suspect has a criminal record. It is because these cases are more complicated and require a higher application of intelligence, that murders committed by unknown perpetrators (especially if they are committed in the course of a robbery) are more likely to be dealt with by a murder and robbery unit with specialised training and information-gathering networks.

Obtaining a conviction for property crime—especially street crime—will typically require either catching the perpetrator in the course of the crime, or finding the perpetrator in possession of stolen property and then getting the victim to identify him or her, or using some piece of physical evidence to tie the perpetrator to the crime. Because the perpetrator of a housebreaking or theft is often unknown, catching him or her, in the absence of luck, requires information. This will usually occur after:

- checking pawn shops and receiving information about the person or persons who handed in stolen goods;
- an arrest made after seeing something suspicious;
- information from an informer or a member of the public; or
- an intelligence-gathering operation aimed at certain targets (such as cash-in-transit robbers).

While all these methods may be used, detectives acknowledge that a low-level thief/robber who neither steals too much nor too frequently will often be able to get away with his or her crimes and that the number of suspects taken to court reflects the number of criminals rather than the success of policing strategies.

It is for this reason that many cases of property crime are closed with only the most perfunctory of investigations: because there is little real prospect of tracing the suspect on the basis of the crime, all the police will do is enter the details of the stolen property into a computer system and close the docket. This reduces the pressure of open dockets on an investigator's desk, but allows the docket to be reopened if the stolen property is recovered.

Having put the case together, the investigating officer sends the docket to the prosecutor who may or may not require further evidence to be gathered, including taking additional statements or retaking existing statements. In some cases, investigating officers will also assist the prosecutors in court because they will often be more familiar with the facts—particularly when the cases are relatively complex or important (and where the investigating officers are unlikely to appear as witnesses). However, detectives say they tend to assist prosecutors less than they used to in the past, arguing that it is usually not necessary for a conviction.

Intelligence, Undercover Work and Organised Crime

Much has been said about the need for improved crime intelligence, as well as increasing the efficacy of the SAPS in the fight against organised crime. While these two elements of policing do need to be improved, they are not identical. After all, the need for intelligence is not confined to the fight against organised crime. At the same time, however, intelligence work and the investigation of individuals and structures involved in organised crime do overlap in some fields—notably in undercover work.

Undercover work has a long tradition in South African policing, though for much of that time its greatest successes were related to the maintenance of state security. But undercover work is an essential part of investigations into two kinds of crime:

- So-called 'victimless crimes', in which there is likely to be no complainant, such as prostitution, drug-related crimes and corruption; and
- Investigations into organised crime, in which some of the criminals are not directly involved in the criminal act itself (*e.g.* the actual theft of a vehicle).

In many instances investigations focusing on the former are quite simple processes culminating in a trap. In the latter cases, however, it may be necessary to obtain evidence over a long period against the 'subjects', either because there is a need to prove complicity in a number of crimes or to ensure that sufficient information is acquired so that 'when the net closes, it closes with the big fish inside it'.

Thus, in order to capture important figures in organised crime, it may be necessary to time the final arrest to coincide with a major transaction, so that evidence of the subject's involvement (and the scale of that involvement) is available. In order to do this, it is essential to have adequate information on the plans and operations of the subjects—a task made more difficult by the fact that major transactions do not occur all that often.

Thus, in order to move against the 'big fish', it is necessary to have information and evidence. Information can be obtained in three ways: via electronic interceptions of communication; from informers; and from agents. If recordings of conversations or intercepted mail are to be used as evidence, permission must be obtained for these procedures and information supplied by an informer or agent can only be used in court if that person is prepared to testify. For that reason the police tend to prefer using agents because, as paid police officers, they are certain to testify. Informers, on the other hand, who are associates of the subjects, usually refuse to testify, or may be discredited when they do.

However, the use of agents is difficult, time-intensive and has a limited life span, because once they testify their identities are revealed. Thus imaginative processes need to be designed to lengthen the productive life span of agents. Agents are an organisational response to the need for evidence in the fight against crime—they are primarily tasked with obtaining evidence against certain individuals.

However, this process need not be very direct. An officer who has infiltrated some syndicates in a South African city says he was so deeply under cover that he and his handler were able to manipulate police operations run against him into producing evidence in court cases without his having to testify. To this day, he says, the other investigating officers think that their operations against him failed because he was not arrested, but that they achieved their secondary objectives against some of his 'associates'.

Despite the potential for this approach, there seems to be a resource constraint on these sorts of operations: they are costly, require high levels of commitment and skill and, most importantly, require visionary and innovative managers. For this reason, other forms of intelligence work are usually used to help guide investigations into organised crime. The difficulty, however, is ensuring that the intelligence gathered can eventually be used as evidence in court.

These different approaches are often characterised as intelligence work versus investigative work. In South Africa, this distinction is a source of some differences on strategy within the detective service. Essentially, these differences revolve around the manner in which the service should organise the production of both intelligence and evidence, because these categories do not collapse into each other.

Because of the history of the SAPS and its component parts, there are historical differences between individuals who were members of the Security Branch and those who have spent their careers performing the 'normal' functions of a police service. In earlier years, the security branch was regarded with suspicion by other members of the police.

Indeed, a former member of the security branch related that they were known as the 'earthworm squad' because of their reputation for surfacing only to collect their pay. This suspicion was founded on the political and organisational strength of the Security Branch, its better resourcing and the increased freedom from supervision and control of its members. When, in the 1990s, the policing mandate was transformed, these members—the only ones trained in intelligence work—were deployed in units tasked with policing organised crime.

Detectives, with whom these members began to work, complain that the training, experience and methods of the security branch did not adequately prepare them for their new tasks. This is because the intelligence gathered by the branch was either never intended to be used in court, or was used in political trials using security legislation—in which due process considerations were often excluded by statute, facilitating the conviction of the accused.

Thus the intelligence generated by the deployment of former members of the branch was not 'court-related', either because of problems of method or because the sources used were of only limited use in combating organised crime.

While the passage of time and the process of acquiring skills and experience has apparently done much to alleviate this problem, old animosities and suspicions still seem to exist. This feature of internal politics is exacerbated by widespread concern about the integrity of individual officers and structures, making the sharing of information between units (and government departments) more difficult and less commonplace. In general, however, organised crime investigations are now run on a project basis, with the investigating officer tasking intelligence units with producing the necessary information on individuals and organisations. While some restructuring seems to be taking place, the basic process will remain essentially the same.

Buy-bust Operation: Another important investigative strategy revolves around the use of traps to catch criminals red-handed. While the legal requirements and most of the techniques remain obscure to the outsider, a typical form of trap is a 'buy-bust' operation in which a dealer in contraband is caught in the act of selling his or her product to either a police officer or an informer. This tactic is heavily relied on by police officers seeking to control street-level drug dealing, for instance.

The process can involve 'setting up a buy' from a dealer after getting his or her identity from an informer or in the course of another investigation, or by sending an officer/informer to a point known to be used by drug dealers and having them buy drugs. The suspect is usually arrested immediately after the transaction, because it is vital that he or she should still be in possession of the banknotes used by the buyer—the investigating officer would previously have recorded the serial numbers.

Such operations, though useful in giving law enforcement a presence in drug distribution, are not generally regarded as sufficiently effective to control the drug trade. However, this strategy is successfully used to combat a number of types of crime, including the purchase and sale of stolen goods. It is also a technique which can be quite precisely focused on problem individuals or groups.

What makes an effective detective?

Solid investigations require more than the mere existence of a detective service within the SAPS. The following sections detail much of what detectives themselves believe to be vital to their effectiveness. Of the six factors documented, by far the most commonly referred to were the logistical resources available to and the personal attributes and traits of, the individual detective.

Resources: There are currently about 24 000 detectives in the SAPS, divided between stations, specialised units and police intelligence. While a substantial number (45 per cent) had not received basic investigative training at the time this report was compiled, detectives have an average of eight or nine years' experience. Somewhat more than 50 per cent of detectives are white, with Africans making up most of the rest.

Years of Experience in the Detective Service

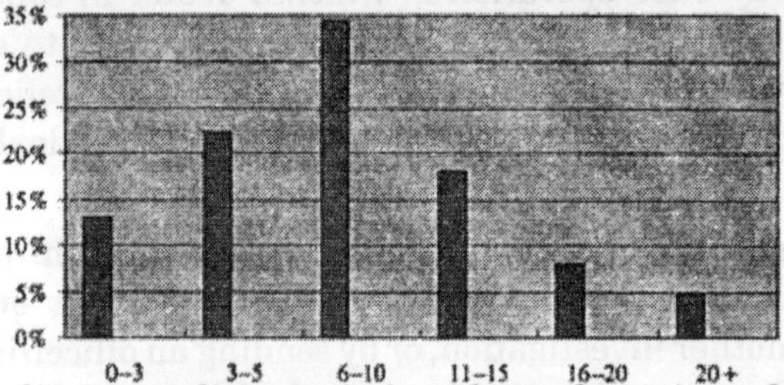

According to police statistics, these detectives dealt with just more than 2 million newly reported serious crimes in 1997, amounting to an average of nearly 90 cases each; besides this, about 500 000 older cases were still open. While it is impossible to determine conclusively whether these figures are correct, detectives and their commanders frequently complain about staff shortages, arguing that their human capacity has not kept up with the rise in crime or the change in the legal regime governing investigations.

The issue of the number of detectives does not, of course, exhaust the issue of resources and it is in the area of physical resources that detectives point to severe problems. Indeed, in some areas, such as the former Transkei, detectives talk of little else. They point to the lack of vehicles; that the vehicles they have are either old, ill-suited to the terrain or both; that their offices are falling apart; that their stations lack telephones; and so on. Of course, these constraints affect all detectives to a greater or lesser degree. No detectives are resourced to the point where they feel all their needs are met.

At the same time, detectives have generally been better resourced than their uniformed colleagues. Indeed, it was partly for this reason that many became detectives in the first place. However, detectives point out that their resource requirements are greater then those of their colleagues. A detective, for instance, requires ready access to a vehicle in order to visit crime scenes and witnesses. He or she also needs office space to compile dockets, make phone calls and interview witnesses.

Although there is no scientific basis for this, it seems there is a good case for increasing the resources of the detective service. Given the high level of crime, especially violent crimes, a call for raising the prosecution level of offenders seems to require an increase in the resourcing of detectives. This point will be examined in greater detail in the concluding section.

The Supportive Role of the Rest of the SAPS

Besides the size of the detective service and the physical resources they require to do their jobs, investigators require technical support in a range of areas: legal support in the investigation of cases; forensic and scientific support, including the maintenance of criminal records and fingerprints; specialised support such as surveillance teams; artists to build identikit pictures of suspects; etc. In general, detectives seem relatively satisfied with the quantity and quality of these services, although they are concerned about the speed and accuracy of replies to requests for identification of fingerprints.

Perhaps as important are the needs detectives have of the uniformed branch. Typically, when the police are called to a crime scene, it will be the uniformed branch that will be first to respond, either by deploying a patrol van or a rapid reaction unit. The officers who arrive first on the scene have a vital role to play in ensuring that the initial investigation, including the acquisition of physical evidence and taking of statements from witnesses, is successful. Similarly, the detective's work is enhanced and facilitated if officers staffing the community service centre at the police station or making an arrest are able to take statements adequately. The statements should cover the essential elements of the crime.

While detectives do seem to appreciate the difficulties confronting the uniformed branch, they insist that there is room for improvement. Detectives in major cities, for instance, recognise that uniformed members in patrol vans are often rushing from scene to scene because they themselves are underresourced. The effect is that they are not able to spend the requisite time on the scene and, in effect, lack ownership of the initial investigation. This has the consequence that the initial police work may not be satisfactory. For instance, physical evidence may be gathered but no record made of where it was taken from; or initial statements may be so confused that they need to be retaken, sometimes well after the event. Detectives also complain that uniformed members will not always accept their instructions at the scene of crime, adding to the difficulties of the initial investigation.

Besides these requirements, detectives would obviously prefer evidence to be secure during the initial and subsequent investigations and that prisoners do not escape from police cells.

These are not the only requirements that detectives have of the rest of the organisation. Greater intelligence resources would help, as would greater clarity on command and control structures. This latter would reduce the present levels of confusion about who is responsible for detectives at station level.

Personal Qualities: Given the nature of their work, including the fact that investigating officers must work long hours without being directly supervised by their commanding officers, detectives must be self-managed. Again, this is one of the reasons why some police officers join the detective service in the first place. However, the Nature of the Work means that it is possible for detectives to get away with not working. While solid management can alleviate this problem—especially if the commanding officer is well informed about the nature and facts of the cases a detective is working on—the reality is that if detectives are unmotivated, uncommitted and unproductive, it is possible for them to slip through the system.

Thus the first requirement of a good detective is that he or she be committed to the job and be self-disciplined. Besides these qualities, however, a good detective must be persistent and honest, must know the law, have the requisite skills and must be able to learn. The ability to communicate is also vital, as is a degree of personal authority—the latter being required in order to ensure that witnesses and complainants have confidence in the detective and cooperate willingly. Detectives must also be able to handle people at a crime scene and in other stressful situations.

Perhaps the most frequently mentioned quality required by a detective, however, is pride—which is all too frequently described through its absence. Almost every respondent stated that members of the organisation did not have enough pride in their work; were not personally committed to the conviction of criminals; or did not do their work efficiently or with an eye to the final outcome. While it is impossible for an outsider to comment authoritatively on this, it seems as if morale in the detective service is at a low point and has been declining for years.

At the same time, good detectives seem to be motivated by a view that crime and criminals are some sort of personal affront. What really seemed to motivate them was a sense of being personally insulted by crimes in their areas. As such, they were motivated by a personal desire to assert their authority and eliminate these insults.

This attitude might be described as a manifestation of a macho police culture which prides strength, confidence and aggression and it may be concluded that such attitudes are dangerous. In response, it might be unrealistic to expect dedicated investigative work without some sort of personal stake in the process. If it is the case that 'personalising' investigative work is necessary, as it probably is, then the question becomes whether and how this can be achieved outside the framework of machismo or a similar ideology.

These issues will have to be examined at some stage in the future. The question of pride will, however, be discussed again in a later section.

Management: Precisely because the work of an investigating officer requires considerable freedom and self-discipline, managing detectives is both easier and more difficult than managing uniformed members. When an individual detective is honest, industrious and self-disciplined and has personal integrity, managing him or her is relatively easy. But when an individual does not have these qualities, management is extremely difficult.

In general, detectives are regarded as poor managers by everyone in the SAPS, including many senior detectives themselves. That said, 'management'—in the sense of strategic planning, coordination and administration—is not one of the most essential requirements of a commanding officer. This is because most cases are separate entities which do not require too much coordinated effort. Thus regarding the commanding officer of an investigative unit as a manager of a business, responsible for coordinating the activities of his or her personnel into producing a single product, is incorrect. The branch commander should be regarded more as the administrator of a hospital—ensuring that the necessary support systems and resources are in place so that each individual professional can make decisions about the appropriate course of action in a variety of unique cases. Therefore, the management task has less to do with vision-setting and pursuing a corporate strategy than with ensuring that each individual detective has the support required to take actions that they will decide on themselves.

This analogy, though better than conceptualising the commanding officer as the manager of a company, does fall down in one area: it is the commanding officer's primary duty to ensure that his or her personnel are equipped with the essential attitude, knowledge and skills and to transfer such knowledge and skills to them. Thus the commanding officer has a crucial educative or mentoring role.

Success in this role obviously requires that the commanding officer himself has the necessary skills and experience, as well as the ability to transfer these. Traditionally, there are two primary ways in which skills are transferred among detectives: by means of training and by providing guidance to detectives in the course of their investigations. While the former has an important role, detectives argue that practical guidance is far more valuable than theoretical training (though such practical guidance does require a sound understanding of the basic rules and strategies of detective work).

Training is partly done by periodically inspecting dockets, but the transfer of skills may also require advice and assistance outside of this process. In this, the relationship between a detective and his or her commanding officer is very important. Detectives want and need managers who command respect for their knowledge, commitment and achievements. Indeed, many—though not all—detectives want commanders 'with hair on their teeth', commanders who demand and expect high performance and whom 'underperformers' fear.

On the face of it, this is quite surprising—one would have expected quite the opposite. Nonetheless, a number of detectives stated that there were many commanders who, being ill-suited to the job, were held in contempt by their staff, with the effect that morale and productivity decline (as does skills transfer). There is no doubt that leaders with authoritarian streaks create difficulties—not least because this has the potential to play into existing problems of racism, when it is used arbitrarily or in a discriminatory manner.

A more open managerial style may also have positive benefits in terms of morale, productivity and skills transfer—benefits which detectives may not be able to perceive, because such a style differs so much from the common practices of the past.

At the same time, however, the common complaint that managers no longer command the respect of their staff—because they are perceived to lack the requisite skills as investigators and managers—remains a problem which needs to be overcome.

The Role of the Community

Investigative work is one of the most obvious areas in which the attitude of the community and its willingness to assist the police is a resource to be prized and cultivated. This is also the area where the transition to democracy has the most potential for rapidly improving the quality of dockets going to court, as the legitimacy of the CJS in general and the police in particular improves.

Of course, taking advantage of the potential for increased legitimacy of the police is not the sole responsibility of the detective service.

In fact, the nature of the community policing model advocated and adopted in South Africa stresses the role of the police in preventing, as opposed to investigating, crime. This has meant that, to some extent, the willingness of the public to assist investigations depends on the performance of the rest of the SAPS in building police-community relations.

But community attitudes are also shaped by their perceptions of the functioning of the CJS and the police—perceptions shaped more by the media and the comments of politicians and other leaders than by the experience of individuals engaging with the police. Thus, to a great extent, the willingness of members of the community to assist the police is a factor beyond the control of the police, or, indeed, of investigating officers.

That said, there are a number of avenues which could be explored to help investigators gain the trust and assistance of the community. In this regard, an understanding of community attitudes to the police, perceptions of criminal justice and the nature of South Africa's diverse cultures appear to be potentially valuable, as is the development of better witness-management techniques.

At present, because of the lack of transport, witnesses living far from court must sometimes be fetched by the investigating officer in order to go to court. Where the officer is unable to do this, as in many rural areas, cases are sometimes struck off the roll simply because the witnesses do not arrive. Managing cases through court and ensuring that witnesses do not arrive simply to see a case remanded may improve the chances that cases will result in convictions. Similarly, the fact that many witnesses fear testifying and its consequences may be ameliorated if the process were better understood.

The Criminal Justice System

The last of the key prerequisites for successful investigations is a solid, reliable, legitimate CJS. A CJS which has these attributes will enhance investigations, both by making witnesses and victims feel more confident and by raising morale among investigators.

Surprisingly, given public perceptions that the CJS is collapsing, detectives are generally quite complimentary about the rest of the CJS. They are not, for instance, overly concerned about prosecutors being inexperienced or incompetent. Nor do they think sentences are too lenient—though they do tend to favour the reintroduction of the death penalty and in some cases of corporal punishment too.

There are, of course, exceptions to this rule: investigating officers are convinced that the CJS as a whole is underresourced and that this plays itself out in the inordinate delays between the arrest of a suspect and his or her trial. This, they argue, undermines community confidence, as well as creating a perception in the minds of criminals and potential criminals that the CJS is ineffective. A further concern in this regard relates to the human rights orientation of the courts and the application of laws and rules governing criminal trials, with detectives often voicing the view that the law has become too 'criminal-friendly'. This is discussed in detail in the next section.

Detective Tactics for the Hidden Job Market

Despite all the hype about the multitude of job sites on the internet and scanning the local and national newspapers, the fact remains that 60-75 per cent of vacancies are not advertised through the media. The best opportunities are less likely than ever to be signposted with neon lights and the sooner you learn how to uncover these opportunities the closer you are to successfully finding not just any job, but the 'right' job!

Having said this however, do continue to read newspaper vacancy advertisements, check with university Career Services, student job search and job websites—all options should be used; leave no stone unturned.

The key to successfully uncovering the hidden job market is to be proactive. The work you put in is what you get out. The new world of work has actually opened up more opportunities than ever before.

Here are some key tips to help you get started:

- Remain positive—perseverance is critical and accepting rejection is an important part of the process. Employers hire people who are confident, show enthusiasm and demonstrate a positive attitude.
- Be realistic—looking for work is a long-term investment. Develop key skills such as telephone technique, high-level research and networking skills. It may be necessary to accept a temporary or entry-level position to get your foot in the door.
- Get as many people as possible looking for you—this means telling everyone you know that you are looking and giving them a clear idea of what your skills are. Everyone means family, friends, neighbours, colleagues, current and/or past lecturers, current and past employers, even the owner of your corner store!
- Check the newspaper for articles about companies that are expanding, new developments, government tenders or awards. Make contact before new jobs are advertised.
- Identify two or three sectors you would ideally like to work in and do your market research. Check out their suppliers, distributors, customers and competitors. Check if there are any small businesses growing within these sectors
- Create ways of expanding your network—join a professional association, volunteer for community projects, attend meetings of your local Chamber of Commerce (this is a great way to tap into small businesses).
- Keep in touch with people who have given you any job-hunting assistance; provide them with feedback on your progress.
- Familiarise yourself with the range of resources available: trade association directories, professional journals and industry training organisations. Your local reference librarian is worth their weight in gold and don't forget about the yellow pages—an undervalued tremendous source of information.

Police and Detective Careers

People depend on police officers and detectives to protect their lives and property. Law enforcement officers, some of whom are State or Federal special agents or inspectors, perform these duties in a variety of ways, depending on the size and type of their organization. In most jurisdictions, they are expected to exercise authority when necessary, whether on or off duty. According to the U.S. Bureau of Justice Statistics, about 65 percent of State and local law enforcement officers are uniformed personnel.

Potential Jobs

Uniformed police officers who work in municipal police departments of various sizes, small communities and rural areas have general law enforcement duties including maintaining regular patrols and responding to calls for service.

Sheriffs and deputy sheriffs enforce the law on the county level.

State police officers (sometimes called State troopers or highway patrol officers) arrest criminals Statewide and patrol highways to enforce motor vehicle laws and regulations.

Detectives are plainclothes investigators who gather facts and collect evidence for criminal cases.

The Federal Government maintains a high profile in many areas of law enforcement. The U.S. Department of Justice is the largest employer of sworn Federal officers.

U.S. Drug Enforcement Administration (DEA) agents enforce laws and regulations relating to illegal drugs.

U.S. marshals and deputy marshals protect the Federal courts and ensure the effective operation of the judicial system.

U.S. Immigration and Naturalization Service (INS) agents and inspectors facilitate the entry of legal visitors and immigrants to the United States and detain and deport those arriving illegally.

U.S. Border Patrol agents protect more than 8,000 miles of international land and water boundaries.

Bureau of Alcohol, Tobacco and Firearms (ATF) agents regulate and investigate violations of Federal firearms and explosives laws, as well as Federal alcohol and tobacco tax regulations.

Customs agents investigate violations of narcotics smuggling, money laundering, child pornography, customs fraud and enforcement of the Arms Export Control Act.

Customs inspectors inspect cargo, baggage and articles worn or carried by people and carriers including vessels, vehicles, trains and aircraft entering or leaving the United States to enforce laws governing imports and exports.

U.S. Secret Service special agents protect the President, Vice President and their immediate families; Presidential candidates; former Presidents; and foreign dignitaries visiting the United States. Secret Service agents also investigate counterfeiting, forgery of Government checks or bonds and fraudulent use of credit cards.

The U.S. Department of State Bureau of Diplomatic Security special agents are engaged in the battle against terrorism.

Other Federal agencies employ police and special agents with sworn arrest powers and the authority to carry firearms. These agencies include the U.S. Postal Service, the Bureau of Indian Affairs Office of Law Enforcement under the U.S. Department of the Interior, the U.S. Forest Service under the U.S. Department of Agriculture, the National Park Service under the U.S. Department of the Interior and Federal Air Marshals under the U.S. Department of Transportation.

Working Conditions: Police work can be very dangerous and stressful. In addition to the obvious dangers of confrontations with criminals, officers need to be constantly alert and ready to deal appropriately with a number of other threatening situations. Many law enforcement officers witness death and suffering resulting from accidents and criminal behaviour. A career in law enforcement may take a toll on officers' private lives.

Uniformed officers, detectives, agents and inspectors are usually scheduled to work 40-hour weeks, but paid overtime is common. Shiftwork is necessary because protection must be provided around the clock. Junior officers frequently work weekends, holidays and nights. Police officers and detectives are required to work at any time their services are needed and may work long hours during investigations. In most jurisdictions, whether on or off duty, officers are expected to be armed and to exercise their arrest authority whenever necessary.

The jobs of some Federal agents such as U.S. Secret Service and DEA special agents require extensive travel, often on very short notice. They may relocate a number of times over the course of their careers.

Employment: Police and detectives held about 834,000 jobs in 2000. About 80 percent were employed by local governments. State police agencies employed about 13 percent and various Federal agencies employed about 6 percent. A small proportion worked for schools, railroads, transit agencies, or private detective, guard and armoured car services.

According to the U.S. Bureau of Justice Statistics, police and detectives employed by local governments primarily worked in cities with more than 25,000 inhabitants. Some cities have very large police forces, while thousands of small communities employ fewer than 25 officers each. Forty-six local, special and State agencies employed 1,000 or more full-time sworn officers, while approximately 7,000 departments employed fewer than 10 each.

Training, Other Qualifications and Advancement: Civil service regulations govern the appointment of police and detectives in practically all States, large municipalities and special police agencies, as well as in many smaller ones. Candidates must be U.S. citizens, usually at least 20 years of age and must meet rigorous physical and personal qualifications. In the Federal Government, candidates must be at least 21 years of age but less than 37 years of age at the time of appointment. Physical examinations for entrance into law enforcement often include tests of vision, hearing, strength and agility. Eligibility for appointment usually depends on performance in competitive written examinations and previous education and experience. In larger departments, where the majority of law enforcement jobs are found, applicants usually must have at least a high school education. Federal and State agencies typically require a college degree. Candidates should enjoy working with people and meeting the public.

Because personal characteristics such as honesty, sound judgment, integrity and a sense of responsibility are especially important in law enforcement, candidates are interviewed by senior officers and their character traits and backgrounds are investigated. In some agencies, candidates are interviewed by a psychiatrist or a psychologist, or given a personality test. Most applicants are subjected to lie detector examinations or drug testing. Some agencies subject sworn personnel to random drug testing as a condition of continuing employment.

Before their first assignments, officers usually go through a period of training. In State and large local departments, recruits get training in their agency's police academy, often for 12 to 14 weeks.

In small agencies, recruits often attend a regional or State academy. Training includes classroom instruction in constitutional law and civil rights, State laws and local ordinances and accident investigation. Recruits also receive training and supervised experience in patrol, traffic control, use of firearms, self-defense, first aid and emergency response. Police departments in some large cities hire high school graduates who are still in their teens as police cadets or trainees. They do clerical work and attend classes, usually for 1 to 2 years, at which point they reach the minimum age requirement and may be appointed to the regular force.

Job Outlook: The opportunity for public service through law enforcement work is attractive to many because the job is challenging and involves much personal responsibility. Furthermore, law enforcement officers in many agencies may retire with a pension after 20 or 25 years of service, allowing them to pursue a second career while still in their 40s. Because of relatively attractive salaries and benefits, the number of qualified candidates exceeds the number of job openings in Federal law enforcement agencies and in most State police departments-resulting in increased hiring standards and selectivity by employers. Competition is expected to remain keen for the higher paying jobs with State and Federal agencies and police departments in more affluent areas. Opportunities will be better in local and special police departments, especially in departments that offer relatively low salaries or urban communities where the crime rate is relatively high.

Employment of police and detectives is expected to increase faster than the average for all occupations through 2010. A more security-conscious society and concern about drug-related crimes should contribute to the increasing demand for police services. At the local and State levels, growth is likely to continue as long as crime remains a serious concern. However, employment growth at the Federal level will be tempered by continuing budgetary constraints faced by law enforcement agencies.

Total earnings for local, State and special police and detectives frequently exceed the stated salary because of payments for overtime, which can be significant. In addition to the common benefits-paid vacation, sick leave and medical and life insurance-most police and sheriffs' departments provide officers with special allowances for uniforms. Because police officers usually are covered by liberal pension plans, many retire at half-pay after 20 or 25 years of service.

Private Detectives and Investigators

Significant Points: Work hours are often irregular and the work can be dangerous.

About 1 in 4 are self-employed.

Applicants typically have related experience in areas such as law enforcement, insurance, the military, or government investigative or intelligence jobs. Despite faster-than-average employment growth, keen competition is expected because of the large number of qualified people who are attracted to this occupation; the most opportunities will be found in entry-level jobs with detective agencies or in stores that hire detectives on a part-time basis.

Nature of the Work: Private detectives and investigators use many methods to determine the facts in a variety of matters.

To carry out investigations, they may use various types of surveillance or searches. To verify facts, such as an individual's place of employment or income, they may make phone calls or visit a subject's workplace. In other cases, especially those involving missing persons and background checks, investigators often interview people to gather as much information as possible about an individual. In all cases, private detectives and investigators assist attorneys, businesses and the public with legal, financial and personal problems.

Private detectives and investigators offer many services, including executive, corporate and celebrity protection; pre-employment verification; and individual background profiles. They investigate computer crimes, such as identity theft, harassing e-mails and illegal downloading of copyrighted material. They also provide assistance in civil liability and personal injury cases, insurance claims and fraud, child custody and protection cases, missing persons cases and premarital screening. They are sometimes hired to investigate individuals to prove or disprove infidelity.

Most detectives and investigators are trained to perform physical surveillance. They may observe a site, such as the home of a subject, from an inconspicuous location or a vehicle. They continue the surveillance, which is often carried out using still and video cameras, binoculars and a cell phone, until the desired evidence is obtained. This watching and waiting often continues for a long time.

Detectives also may perform computer database searches or work with someone who does. Computers allow investigators to quickly obtain massive amounts of information on individuals' prior arrests, convictions and civil legal judgments; telephone numbers; motor vehicle registrations; association and club memberships; and other matters.

The duties of private detectives and investigators depend on the needs of their clients. In cases for employers that involve fraudulent workers' compensation claims, for example, investigators may carry out long-term covert observation of subjects. If an investigator observes a subject performing an activity that contradicts injuries stated in a worker's compensation claim, the investigator would take video or still photographs to document the activity and report it to the client.

Private detectives and investigators often specialize. Those who focus on intellectual property theft, for example, investigate and document acts of piracy, help clients stop illegal activity and provide intelligence for prosecution and civil action. Other investigators specialize in developing financial profiles and asset searches. Their reports reflect information gathered through interviews, investigation and surveillance and research, including review of public documents.

Legal investigators specialize in cases involving the courts and are normally employed by law firms or lawyers. They frequently assist in preparing criminal defenses, locating witnesses, serving legal documents, interviewing police and prospective witnesses and gathering and reviewing evidence. Legal investigators also may collect information on the parties to the litigation, take photographs, testify in court and assemble evidence and reports for trials.

Corporate investigators conduct internal and external investigations for corporations. In internal investigations, they may investigate drug use in the workplace, ensure that expense accounts are not abused, or determine whether employees are stealing merchandise or information. External investigations are typically done to uncover criminal schemes originating outside the corporation, such as theft of company assets through fraudulent billing of products by suppliers.

Financial investigators may be hired to develop confidential financial profiles of individuals or companies that are prospective parties to large financial transactions. These investigators often are certified public accountants (CPAs) who work closely with investment bankers and other accountants. They search for assets in order to recover damages awarded by a court in fraud or theft cases.

Detectives who work for retail stores or hotels are responsible for controlling losses and protecting assets. Store detectives, also known as loss prevention agents, safeguard the assets of retail stores by apprehending anyone attempting to steal merchandise or destroy store property. They prevent theft by shoplifters, vendor representatives, delivery personnel and even store employees. Store detectives also conduct periodic inspections of stock areas, dressing rooms and restrooms and sometimes assist in opening and closing the store. They may prepare loss prevention and security reports for management and testify in court against persons they apprehend. Hotel detectives protect guests of the establishment from theft of their belongings and preserve order in hotel restaurants and bars. They also may keep undesirable individuals, such as known thieves, off the premises.

Working Conditions: Private detectives and investigators often work irregular hours because of the need to conduct surveillance and contact people who are not available during normal working hours. Early morning, evening, weekend and holiday work is common.

Many detectives and investigators spend time away from their offices conducting interviews or doing surveillance, but some work in their office most of the day conducting computer searches and making phone calls. Those who have their own agencies and employ other investigators may work primarily in an office and have normal business hours.

When the investigator is working on a case away from the office, the environment might range from plush boardrooms to seedy bars. Store and hotel detectives work in the businesses that they protect. Investigators generally work alone, but they sometimes work with others during surveillance or when following a subject in order to avoid detection by the subject.

Some of the work involves confrontation, so the job can be stressful and dangerous. Some situations call for the investigator to be armed, such as certain bodyguard assignments for corporate or celebrity clients.

Detectives and investigators who carry handguns must be licensed by the appropriate authority. In most cases, however, a weapon is not necessary, because the purpose of the work is gathering information and not law enforcement or criminal apprehension. Owners of investigative agencies have the added stress of having to deal with demanding and sometimes distraught clients.

Training, Other Qualifications and Advancement: There are no formal education requirements for most private detective and investigator jobs, although many private detectives have college degrees. Private detectives and investigators typically have previous experience in other occupations. Some work initially for insurance or collections companies, in the private security industry, or as paralegals. Many investigators enter the field after serving in law enforcement, the military, government auditing and investigative positions, or Federal intelligence jobs.

Former law enforcement officers, military investigators and government agents, who are frequently able to retire after 25 years of service, often become private detectives or investigators in a second career. Others enter from such diverse fields as finance, accounting, commercial credit, investigative reporting, insurance and law. These individuals often can apply their prior work experience in a related investigative specialty. A few enter the occupation directly after graduation from college, generally with associate's or bachelor's degrees in criminal justice or police science.

The majority of States and the District of Colombia require private detectives and investigators to be licensed. Licensing requirements vary, however. Seven States-Alabama, Alaska, Colorado, Idaho, Mississippi, Missouri and South Dakota-have no statewide licensing requirements, some States have few requirements and many other States have stringent regulations. A growing number of States are enacting mandatory training programmes for private detectives and investigators.

For example, the Bureau of Security and Investigative Services of the California Department of Consumer Affairs requires private investigators to be 18 years of age or older; have a combination of education in police science, criminal law, or justice and experience equaling 3 years (6,000 hours) of investigative experience; pass a criminal history background check by the California Department of Justice and the FBI (in most States, convicted felons cannot be issued a license); and receive a qualifying score on a 2-hour written examination covering laws and regulations. There are additional requirements for a firearms permit.

For private detective and investigator jobs, most employers look for individuals with ingenuity, persistence and assertiveness. A candidate must not be afraid of confrontation, should communicate well and should be able to think on his or her feet. Good interviewing and interrogation skills also are important and usually are acquired in earlier careers in law enforcement or other fields. Because the courts often are the ultimate judge of a properly conducted investigation, the investigator must be able to present the facts in a manner that a jury will believe.

Training in subjects such as criminal justice and police science is helpful to aspiring private detectives and investigators. Most corporate investigators must have a bachelor's degree, preferably in a business-related field. Some corporate investigators have a master's degree in business administration or a law degree, while others are CPAs. Corporate investigators hired by large companies may receive formal training from their employers on business practices, management structure and various finance-related topics. The screening process for potential employees typically includes a background check for a criminal history.

Some investigators receive certification from a professional organization to demonstrate competency in a field. For example, the National Association of Legal Investigators (NALI) confers the Certified Legal Investigator designation to licensed investigators who devote a majority of their practice to negligence or criminal defense investigations. To receive the designation, applicants must satisfy experience, educational and continuing-training requirements and must pass written and oral exams administered by the NALI.

Most private-detective agencies are small, with little room for advancement. Usually, there are no defined ranks or steps, so advancement takes the form of increases in salary and assignment status. Many detectives and investigators work for detective agencies at the beginning of their careers and, after a few years, start their own firms. Corporate and legal investigators may rise to supervisor or manager of the security or investigations department.

Employment: Private detectives and investigators held about 43,000 jobs in 2004. About 26 percent were self-employed, including many who held a secondary job as a self-employed private detective. Around 27 percent of jobs were in investigation and security services, including private detective agencies, while another 15 percent were in department or other general merchandise stores. The rest worked mostly in State and local government, legal services firms, employment services companies, insurance agencies and credit mediation establishments, including banks and other depository institutions.

Job Outlook: Keen competition is expected because private detective and investigator careers attract many qualified people, including relatively young retirees from law enforcement and military careers. The best opportunities will be in entry-level jobs with detective agencies or in stores that hire detectives on a part-time basis. The best prospects for those seeking store detective jobs will be with large chains and discount stores.

Employment of private detectives and investigators is expected to grow faster than the average for all occupations through 2014. In addition to growth, replacement of those who retire or leave the occupation for other reasons should create many job openings. Increased demand for private detectives and investigators will result from fear of crime, increased litigation and the need to protect confidential information and property of all kinds. The proliferation of criminal activity on the Internet, such as identity theft, spamming, e-mail harassment and illegal downloading of copyrighted materials, will increase the demand for private investigators. Employee background checks, conducted by private investigators, will become standard for an increasing number of jobs. Growing financial activity worldwide will increase the demand for investigators to control internal and external financial losses and to monitor competitors and prevent industrial spying.

Earnings: Median annual earnings of salaried private detectives and investigators were $32,110 in May 2004. The middle 50 percent earned between $24,080 and $43,260. The lowest 10 percent earned less than $19,260 and the highest 10 percent earned more than $58,470. Earnings of private detectives and investigators vary greatly by employer, specialty and geographic area.

Private Investigation

Think of being a private eye and you have visions of Hercules Poirot, James Bond, or Sherlock Holmes. The need for a professional security services industry has emerged mainly to supplement the efforts of law enforcement agencies, especially from a less-obvious, informal angle. Individuals, lawyers and organisations may hire private investigators.

Private investigators provide any kind of investigative or protective service that clients want. The work could involve locating/ tracing missing persons, witnesses, debtors, assets (cash and/ or property) documents, or information; performing background checks on individuals, businesses or groups; video and photographic surveillance for matrimonial or insurance fraud; gathering evidence for criminal or civil trials; protecting clients or their property from theft, robbery, personal harm or other danger; determining if any criminal activity had occurred and road traffic and industrial accident investigations. Some private detectives/ agencies specialise in niche services like personal protection services, or background investigations.

Work Environment: Today the industry is high-tech and improved electronic aids and systems contribute to getting the private eye recognised as a professional service provider. Hidden cameras and recording devices and other sophisticated gadgets are increasingly being used. In keeping with their fictional counterparts, private investigators do use disguises when the occasion demands. An outdoor and hazardous work environment is an occupational hazard for any investigator.

Most aspirants are attracted to this profession as they feel it is fascinating, challenging, varied and full of thrills. While this may well be true, it is also true that during an investigation, there is quite a bit of monotony and routine work like maintaining a close watch on a suspect, maintaining accurate, well-detailed notes and providing verbal or written progress reports even when there is not much headway. While the work entails travel and meeting new people, it also translates into long, irregular hours, including nights, weekends and holidays.

Skills Required: Problem solving, organisational and self-management skills, strong interpersonal communication and writing/ reporting skills, research and computer skills are the special skills that will mark out your potential for effectiveness and success in this industry. Honesty, integrity and discretion are vital.

As a private eye you will need to be patient, persevering, adaptable and self-motivated. You should have the ability to work on your own initiative and possess an outgoing personality. Having linguistic skills helps. A background in psychology, sociology, law, physical education andbusiness can be helpful.

Entry: Lack of formal training and education need not be a stumbling block for entry. Aspirants should, however, be familiar with the realities rather than allow romanticism to lead them to this occupation. Private detective agencies will not open their doors to all and sundry.

In most agencies, the screening process for potential employees includes a background check to confirm education and work experience, to inquire about criminal history and to interview references and others who know the applicant. Rather than look for an employer, you may become an entrepreneur. Most of today's established names in the business did exactly that.

Employment: A private detective can be self-employed and work alone, or as part of an agency. Many have ventured into the field in a small way by helping friends, or neighbours and carried on from there, allowing word-of-mouth publicity to get them more work. Today, with the proliferation of various professional security service agencies, there are choices of entry at various levels.

Specialist skills can also play a role in securing a suitable position. For example, ex-police department or ex-defence personnel constitute a breed of professionals who can find it easier to gain entry into this industry. Some of the important agencies in the business have also been set up by retired defence or police officers.

Typical training is provided by the employers of security personnel at various levels. Eligibility requirements vary but physical and psychological requirements, prior related work experience are deciding factors for acceptance. In-house training is expected for new recruits at all levels.

Although meant to provide security to clients in many ways, being a private eye is not a secure profession. There is always an element of danger and uncertainty, the unknown quantity of what an investigation may unearth. Advancement opportunities and growth are not really defined, but those who have proved themselves remain in demand and can quote their price.

Investigation and Security Service Providers

- International Institute of Security and Safety Management, 85-A Humayunpur, B-5 Block, Safdurjang Enclave, New Delhi-110029
- Security and Intelligence Services (India) Ltd, 85-A Humayunpur, B-5 Block, Safdurjang Enclave, New Delhi-110029
- National Security and Allied Services, 1492, Wazir Nagar, Opp P.T. College, Defence Colony, New Delhi-110003
- National Institute of Pvt Investigation, S-2/ D-3, Alaknanda Complex, New Delhi

Private Detective and Investigator

Careers, Jobs and Training Information: Private Investigator and Detective Career and Job Highlights:

- Work can be hazardous and often may involve late or weekend hours.
- One-third are self-employed.
- Many have prior military, law enforcement, insurance, or government intelligence experience.

- Part-time store detectives and detective agencies will provide the greatest opportunities for new applicants; due to the many qualified people interested in this field, competition is quite intense.

Private Detective and Investigator Career Overview

Investigators and private detectives discover facts employing a number of different methods. Different types of surveillance and search techniques are used to conduct investigations. Detectives or investigators may place phone calls or visit places of employment to verify facts about someone's work or income. They conduct interviews in order to generate as much background information on someone as possible, especially when conducting background checks or searching for missing persons. Private individuals, lawyers and businesses all receive assistance from private investigators and detectives regarding a number of money-, law-and personal-related issues.

Personal protection services for celebrities, businesses and corporate executives by investigators and private detectives. They may also aid in background checks, fact verification for employment, investigations concerning injury law suits and liability, child support and custody battles, fraudulent insurance claims investigations and a variety of other situations. An increasing number are being hired to investigate a spouse or partner's fidelity.

Detectives and investigators typically have received some training with regards to on-site surveillance, often stationed for long hours in a car observing a property or person. They pursue the required evidence by using cell phones, binoculars or scopes and video recording equipment. Computers provide instant access to much personal information that may be relevant to an investigation-namely, phone numbers, criminal history, club or group memberships; car registrations; etc.

What exactly a detective or investigator does depends on the client. In an investigation sponsored by an employer into a suspected fraudulent compensation claim, detectives may observe the employee for long periods of time; when the employee did something that provided evidence that the claim was fraudulent, the investigator would take video or photographs to report the findings to the employer.

Many detectives and investigators choose to specialize. For example, those specializing in intellectual property theft track pirates and assist their clients in stopping the illegal activities. They also provide evidence for lawyers in court proceedings. Others focus on financial and estate affairs, conducting interviews, researching public documents and carrying out investigations to profile someone's assets or resources.

Legal investigators typically work with court cases and are paid by attorneys and law firms. The assist with preparing defense cases, conducting interviews of the police that handled the incident and witnesses, collect and analyze evidence and deliver papers and files. These investigators also prepare documents for courts, conduct background investigations on persons involved in the court case and may even give testimony in court.

Corporations may employ investigators, aptly named corporate investigators, to investigate internal and external circumstances and situations. In-house, these investigators may look into suspected workplace drug use, merchandise theft, or misuse of company funds. The primary focus of external investigations involves crimes committed against the company, such as false billing by suppliers.

When a large amount of money is involved with a company transaction, financial investigators may be hired to look into the financial backgrounds of individuals and businesses involved. Many of these investigators are Certified Public Accountants (CPAs) and have experience with banking and accountancy. Court-mandated damages to be paid may be recovered by careful investigations conducted by financial investigators into financial assets.

The primary focus of store detectives is to protect merchandise from theft and hinder thieves and shoplifters from successfully stealing company property. Loss prevention agents, as some store detectives are known, also help stop suspects from destroying store property. They are responsible for apprehending anyone caught stealing, including store employees, product representatives visiting the store and delivery persons. As part of their duties, they may inspect areas of the store as well as help close and open the store each day. Store detectives help prepare security reports and testify against shoplifters they have apprehended. Hotel detectives ensure safety and order on hotel premises, as well as protect hotel guests' belongings. These detectives may prohibit certain known thieves or otherwise undesirable persons from entering hotel property.

Private Detective and Investigator Training and Job Qualifications

While no formal private investigator training requirements exist to obtain employment as an investigator or private detective, many private investigators have earned a college degree and have some work experience in a related field-law enforcement, government intelligence, insurance, military, auditing, etc. Others gain experience through employment with private security or a collections agency. Private investigator many also complete a vocational private investigator training programme to prepare for their career.

Due to the early retirement possibilities (some after only 20 years) of military personnel, government agents and police officers, many of these people make private investigation their second career. Individuals from fields like law, insurance, investigative journalism and credit or collections apply their knowledge as investigators in a related field. Some begin their investigation careers immediately following their graduation from college with a degree in law enforcement or criminal justice.

Investigators and private detectives must have a license in most States and the District of Columbia. In many of these States, convicted felons are prohibited from becoming private detectives and many more States are requiring minimum, mandatory training for investigators. While many States maintain strict licensing requirements, 6 States have no standardized requirements-South Dakota, Mississippi, Idaho,

Colorado, Alaska and Alabama. One example of stringent licensing practice comes from the Bureau of Security and Investigative Services of the California Department of Consumer Affairs.

Private investigators must: pass a personal background check; pass a 2-hour legal examination; be at least 18 years old; and possess an education in criminal law, justice, or police science or work experience as a detective, or a combination of both equaling 6,000 hours (approximately 3 years). In order to be able to carry a weapon on the job, prospective investigators must meet additional regulations.

Ambition, diligence and creativity are important characteristics employers look for when hiring investigators. Good communication skills, quick thinking and an ability to confront problems are crucial. Earlier law enforcement careers help candidates develop essential interrogation techniques and interviewing methods. Private detectives must be able to show the facts they have obtained in their investigation in a convincing way to juries, since they are the ones that ultimately decide the validity of a case.

A college education is a valuable asset for prospective detectives, especially in courses related to law enforcement or criminal justice. The majority of corporate investigators are required to hold a degree, typically in finance or some other business-related subject. Other corporate investigators hold master's degrees in law and business or have professional certifications, like CPAs. Large companies often provide training for newly hired investigators regarding the company's management hierarchy, policies and finance practices. Prospective employees must usually pass a criminal background check to be considered seriously for the job.

Investigators who do the largest portion of their work in the fields of criminal defense and negligence can use the title Certified Legal Investigator, a title conferred on them by the National Association of Legal Investigators (NALI) after they meet education and experience requirements and pass the oral and written tests that the organization gives. Other investigators seek certification by other professional organizations.

Because there is not a lot opportunity to be promoted in the small detective agencies that are most common, advancement usually involves only a raise or increased responsibility; there are typically no ranks or hierarchies to rise in. Many private detectives start their own agencies after learning skills and techniques working in established firms at the commencement of their careers. Management and administration personnel may be promoted from within in a corporate investigative department.

Private Detective and Investigator Job and Employment Opportunities

Because of the high numbers of relatively young retired military and police officers who enter this profession, competition is keen. Part-time jobs with stores and detective agencies will supply the most beginning positions. Specifically, chain stores and discount stores will provide the most detective employment opportunities.

Despite the competition, job growth in the private detective and investigator industry is projected to be faster than average through 2012. Retiring investigators will create additional job opportunities. Public fear of crime, security needs related to business documents and information and an increase in the total number of law suits all lend themselves to creating more demand for investigative services. Lawyers will hire more detectives for their assistance with cases related to litigation and criminal cases. The increase in business activity and financial transactions will increase the need for investigators to protect company assets from theft and to prevent intellectual property theft by competitors.

Historical Earnings Information

The median yearly salary in 2002 for investigators and private detectives was $29,300. The lowest 10 percent made less than $17,290 while the highest 10 percent earned more than $57,370. The second and third quartiles earned $21,980 and $41,710, respectively. Investigation and security services warranted a median $29,030 in 2002 with $22,250 being the median at department stores. Higher annual earnings are possible with experience and employment in the most profitable fields.

Private Detective and Investigators Career Highlights

Private detectives and investigators offer many services for individual, corporate and government clients, including executive, corporate and celebrity protection; pre-employment verification; and individual background profiles.

The career education information presented here will help you learn more about careers in private investigation, the job outlook, the career training required and the career opportunities.

- Work hours for Private Detectives and Investigators are usually irregular and could include nights, weekends and holidays; the work can be dangerous, as well.
- About 25 percent of the persons in this occupation are self-employed.
- Candidates often have related experience in law enforcement, insurance, the military, or government investigative or intelligence jobs and some type of formal training.
- In spite of faster-than-average employment growth, intense competition in this industry is expected due to the large number of highly qualified people who are attracted to this career; most available opportunities will be entry-level positions with detective agencies or in stores that hire detectives on a part-time basis.

Nature of the Work: Private detectives and investigators use various methods to discover the facts. Investigations may involve the use of various types of surveillance or searches. To verify facts, for example an individual's place of employment or income, they could make phone calls or visit a subject's workplace. In other investigations, such as those involving missing persons or background checks, investigators frequently interview people to gather information about an individual. Private detectives and investigators aid attorneys, businesses and the general public with legal, financial and personal problems.

Private detectives and investigators provide many services. They may provide executive, corporate and celebrity protection; pre-employment verification; and individual background profiles, for example. They may handle computer crimes, such as identity theft, harassing e-mails and illegal downloading of copyrighted material, or provide assistance in civil liability and personal injury cases, insurance claims and fraud, child custody and protection cases, missing persons cases and premarital screening. In some cases they are hired to investigate individuals to prove or disprove infidelity.

Most detectives and investigators obtain training to perform physical surveillance; they may observe a site, such as the residence of a subject, from an inconspicuous location or a vehicle. They must persist with the surveillance, carried out using still and video cameras, binoculars and a cell phone, until the necessary evidence is obtained. This watching and waiting frequently lasts for a long time.

Detectives sometimes perform computer database searches or work with someone who does. With computers, investigators can quickly compile massive amounts of information on individuals' prior arrests, convictions and civil legal judgments; telephone numbers; motor vehicle registrations; association and club memberships; and many other material facts.

Duties of private detectives and investigators depend on what their clients need. In investigations for employers involving fraudulent workers' compensation claims, investigators may make long-term covert observation of subjects. If a subject is observed performing an activity that contradicts injuries claimed in a worker's compensation case, the investigator would take video or still photographs to document the activity and report it to their client.

Frequently, private detectives and investigators specialize in certain types of investigations. They might focus on intellectual property theft, for example, investigate and document acts of piracy, help clients stop illegal activity and provide evidence for prosecution and civil action. Other investigators may specialize in developing financial profiles and asset searches on individuals and entities. Their reports reflect information compiled through interviews, investigation and surveillance and research, including review of available public documents.

Legal investigators specialize in cases involving the courts. They are generally employed by law firms or lawyers. They often help to prepare criminal defenses, locating witnesses, serving legal documents, interviewing police and prospective witnesses and gathering and reviewing evidence. Legal investigators sometimes gather information on the parties to a litigation, take photographs, testify in court and assemble evidence and reports for trials.

Corporate investigators carry out internal and external investigations for corporations. Internal investigations may involve uncovering drug use in the workplace, ensure that expense accounts are not abused, or determine whether employees are stealing merchandise or proprietary information. External investigations are done to reveal criminal schemes originating outside the corporation. An example would be theft of company assets through fraudulent billing of products by suppliers.

Financial investigators are sometimes hired to report confidential financial profiles of individuals or companies that are prospective parties to large financial transactions. These investigators many times are certified public accountants (CPAs) working closely with investment bankers and other accountants. They search for hidden assets in order to recover damages awarded by a court in fraud or theft cases, for example.

Retail stores or hotels hire dectectives who are responsible for controlling losses and protecting assets. Store detectives are also known as loss prevention agents. They safeguard the assets of retail stores by catching anyone attempting to steal merchandise or destroy store property. They prevent theft by shoplifters, vendor representatives, delivery personnel and even store employees; store detectives may also conduct periodic inspections of stock areas, dressing rooms and restrooms and sometimes assist in opening and closing the store. They sometimes prepare loss prevention and security reports for store management and may testify in court against persons they apprehend. Hotel detectives protect guests from theft of their belongings and keep order in hotel restaurants and bars.

Working Conditions: Private detectives and investigators commonly work irregular hours, nights, weekends and holidays because of the need to conduct surveillance and contact people who are often not available during normal working hours.

Most detectives and investigators spend time away from their offices conducting interviews or surveillance, while others work in their office most of the day conducting computer searches and making phone calls. Those with their own agencies, who employ other investigators, often work primarily in an office during normal business hours.

When the investigator is working on a case away from the office, the environment will vary. Retail store and hotel detectives work on the premises that they protect. Investigators normally work alone, although sometimes they work with others during surveillance or when following a subject in order to avoid detection by the subject.

The work might involve confrontation, so the occupation can be stressful and dangerous. In some situations the investigator may need to be armed, such as certain bodyguard assignments for high profile or celebrity clients. Of course, detectives and investigators carrying handguns must be licensed by the appropriate authority. However, in most cases, a weapon is not necessary since the purpose of the work is gathering information and not law enforcement or criminal apprehension. Agency owners have the additional stress of having to cope with demanding and often distraught clients.

Training, Other Qualifications and Advancement: Although there are no formal education requirements for most private detective and investigator jobs, many private detectives have college degrees or some type of formal training or certification. Private detectives and investigators often have previous experience in other occupations, working initially for insurance or collections companies, in the private security industry, or as paralegals. Some investigators enter the field after serving in law enforcement, the military, government auditing and investigative positions, or Federal intelligence jobs.

Law enforcement officers, military investigators and government agents, who may retire after 20-25 years of service, often become private detectives or investigators in their second career, while others enter from such diverse fields as finance, accounting, commercial credit, investigative reporting, insurance and law. Frequently they are able to apply their prior work experience in a related investigative specialty. Some enter the occupation directly after completion of a formal training or certification programme, or after graduation from college, generally with associate's or bachelor's degrees in criminal justice or police science.

Most States and the District of Colombia require private detectives and investigators to be licensed. Licensing requirements vary by State, however: seven States-Alabama, Alaska, Colorado, Idaho, Mississippi, Missouri and South Dakota-have no statewide licensing requirements, some States have relatively few requirements, while many other States have stringent regulations. More States are requiring mandatory training programmes for private detectives and investigators.

For example, the Bureau of Security and Investigative Services of the California Department of Consumer Affairs now requires private investigators to be 18 years of age or older; have a combination of education in police science, criminal law, or criminal justice and experience equaling 3 years (6,000 hours) of investigative experience; they must pass a criminal history background check by the California Department of Justice and the FBI (in most States, convicted felons cannot be issued a license); and earn a minimum qualifying score on a 2-hour written examination covering laws and regulations. Also, there are additional requirements for firearms permits.

Most employers look for candidates with ingenuity, persistence and assertiveness. An applicant can not be afraid of confrontation, must communicate well and should be able to think quickly on his or her feet. Interviewing and interrogation skills are also important. Since the courts are usually the ultimate judge of a properly conducted investigation, the investigator must be able to present the facts in a manner will convince a jury.

Formal training in criminal justice or police science is beneficial to aspiring private detectives and investigators. Usually corporate investigators must have a bachelor's degree, preferably in a business-related field, although related experience and some formal training may be acceptable. Often, corporate investigators have a master's degree in business administration or a law degree, or others are CPAs. Corporate investigators working for large companies sometimes receive formal training from their employers on business practices, management structure and various finance-related topics. Typically, the screening process for potential corporate investigators will include a background check for a criminal history.

Many investigators earn certification from a professional organization to demonstrate competency in their field. The National Association of Legal Investigators (NALI) offers the Certified Legal Investigator designation to licensed investigators who work on negligence or criminal defense investigations. To earn the designation, applicants must meet experience, educational and continuing-training requirements and must pass written and oral exams administered by the NALI.

Most private detective agencies are small, with little room for advancement. Usually there are no defined ranks or steps, so advancement takes the form of increases in salary and assignment status. Many detectives and investigators work for detective agencies at the beginning of their careers and after a few years start their own firms. Corporate and legal investigators may rise to supervisor or manager of the security or investigations department.

Employment: According to the U.S. Department of Labour Statistics, private detectives and investigators held about 43,000 jobs in 2004. Approximately 26 percent were self-employed, including those who held a second jobs as a self-employed private detective. About 27 percent of jobs were in investigation and security services, while another 15 percent were in retail stores. The remainder worked mostly in State and local government, legal services firms, employment services companies, insurance agencies and credit mediation establishments, including banks and other depository institutions.

Job Outlook: Intense competition is expected. Private detective and investigator careers attract many qualified people, including relatively young retirees from law enforcement and military careers. The best job prospects will be in entry-level jobs with detective agencies or in part-time opportunities in stores. The best opportunities for those seeking store detective jobs will be with larger chains and discount stores.

Employment of private detectives and investigators is projected to grow faster than average for all occupations through 2014. Replacement of those who retire or leave the occupation should create many job openings. Higher demand for private detectives and investigators will come about as a result of fear of crime, increased litigation and the need to protect confidential information and property of all kinds. Increased criminal activity on the Internet, such as identity theft, spamming, e-mail harassment and illegal downloading of copyrighted materials, will increase the demand for private investigators specializing in technology. Employee background checks will become standard for an increasing number of jobs and growing financial activity worldwide will increase the demand in corporations to control internal and external financial losses and to monitor competitors and prevent industrial spying.

Salary Expectations: Median annual earnings of salaried private detectives and investigators were $26,750 in 2000. The middle 50 percent earned between $20,040 and $38,240. The lowest 10 percent earned less than $16,210 and the highest 10 percent earned more than $52,200. Median annual earnings were $21,180 in department stores, the industry employing the largest numbers of private detectives and investigators.

Earnings of private detectives and investigators vary greatly depending on their employer, specialty and the geographic area in which they work. According to a study by Abbott, Langer & Associates, security/loss prevention directors and vice presidents had a median income of $77,500 per year in 2000;

investigators, $39,800; and store detectives, $25,000. In addition to typical benefits, most corporate investigators received profit-sharing plans.

Related Occupations: Private detectives and investigators often collect information and protect the property and other assets of companies. Others with related duties include bill and account collectors; claims adjusters, appraisers, examiners and investigators; police and detectives; and security guards and gaming surveillance officers. Investigators who specialize in conducting financial profiles and asset searches perform work closely related to that of accountants and auditors and financial analysts and personal finance advisors.

Private Investigator

A private investigator, private detective, PI, or private eye, is a person who undertakes investigations, usually for a private citizen or some other entity not involved with a government or police organization. They often work for attorneys in civil cases or on behalf of a defense attorney. Many work for insurance companies to investigate suspicious claims. Before the advent of no-fault divorce, many private investigators were hired to search out evidence of adultery or other illegal conduct within marriage to establish grounds for a divorce. Despite the lack of legal necessity for such evidence in many jurisdictions, according to press reports collecting evidence of adultery or other "bad behaviour" by spouses and partners is still one of the most profitable activities investigators undertake.

Many jurisdictions require PIs to be licensed and they may or may not carry firearms depending on local laws. Some are ex-police officers. They are expected to keep detailed notes and to be prepared to testify in court regarding any of their observations on behalf of their clients. Taking great care to remain within the law (*e.g.*, being forbidden to trespass on private property or break into homes) is also required, on pain of losing their licenses as well as facing criminal charges. Irregular hours may also be required when performing surveillance work (*e.g.*, outside someone's house during the early hours of the morning).

PIs also undertake a large variety of work that is not usually associated with the industry in the mind of the public. For example, many PIs are involved in process serving, the personal delivery of summons, subpoenas and other legal documents to parties in a legal case. The tracing of absconding debtors can also form a large part of a PI's work load. Many agencies specialize in a particular field of expertise. For example, some PI agencies deal only in tracing. Others may specialize in technical surveillance countermeasures, or TSCM, which is the locating and dealing with unwanted forms of electronic surveillance (for example, a bugged boardroom for industrial espionage purposes).

Increasingly, modern PIs prefer to be known as "professional investigators" rather than "private investigators" or "private detectives". This is a response to the seedy image that is sometimes attributed to the profession and an effort to establish and demonstrate the industry to be a proper and respectable profession.

Global Focus

In some countries throughout the world private investigations are illegal. In the following countries private investigations thrive; United States of America, Mexico, Canada, United Kingdom, France, Spain, South Africa, Australia and Japan. In South Africa, private investigators are in very high demand due to poor police work and high crime. Other countries throughout the world have private investigators, but a lot of their duties are restricted. In South Korea, surveillance is allowed only in insurance fraud situations. In India, working the same case may involve speaking with a large network of people, driving long distances and contacting several companies over extended periods of time to solve the case. Some countries in the world require licensing of private detectives, but most do not.

Working Conditions: Private detectives and investigators often work irregular hours because of the need to conduct surveillance and contact people who are not available during normal working hours. Early morning, evening, weekend and holiday work is common.

Many detectives and investigators spend time away from their offices conducting interviews or doing surveillance, but some work in their office most of the day conducting computer searches and making phone calls. Those who have their own agencies and employ other investigators may work primarily in an office and have normal business hours.

When the private investigator is working on a case away from the office, the environment might range from plush boardrooms to seedy bars. Store and hotel detectives work in the businesses that they protect. Investigators generally work alone, but they sometimes work with others during surveillance or when following a subject in order to avoid detection by the subject.

Some of the work involves confrontation, so the job can be stressful and dangerous. Some situations call for the investigator to be armed, such as certain bodyguard assignments for corporate or celebrity clients. Detectives and investigators who carry handguns must be licensed by the appropriate authority. In most cases, however, a weapon is not necessary, because the purpose of the work is gathering information and not law enforcement or criminal apprehension. Owners of investigative agencies have the added stress of having to deal with demanding and sometimes distraught clients.

Training, Other Qualifications and Advancement: There are no formal education requirements for most private detective and investigator jobs, although many private detectives have college degrees or have taken legal or criminal investigation courses. Private detectives and investigators typically have previous experience in other occupations. Some work initially for insurance or collections companies, in the private security industry, or as paralegals. Many investigators enter the field after serving in law enforcement, the military, government auditing and investigative positions, or federal intelligence jobs.

Former law enforcement officers, military investigators and government agents, who are frequently able to retire after 25 years of service, often become private detectives or investigators in a second career. Others enter from such diverse fields as finance, accounting, commercial credit, investigative reporting, insurance and law. These individuals often can apply their prior work experience in a related investigative specialty. A few enter the occupation directly after graduation from college, generally with associate's or bachelor's degrees in criminal justice, police science or with a private investigation diploma.

The majority of United States states and the District of Columbia require private detectives and investigators to be licensed. Licensing requirements vary, however. Seven states-Alabama, Alaska, Colorado, Idaho, Mississippi, Missouri and South Dakota--have no statewide licensing requirements, some states have very few requirements and many other states have stringent regulations. A growing number of states are enacting mandatory training programmes for private detectives and investigators. For example, the Bureau of Security and Investigative Services of the California Department of Consumer Affairs requires private investigators to be 18 years of age or older, have a combination of education in police science, criminal law, or justice and experience equaling 3 years (6,000 hours) of investigative experience, pass a criminal history background check by the California Department of Justice and the FBI (in most States, convicted felons cannot be issued a license) and receive a qualifying score on a two-hour written examination covering laws and regulations. There are additional requirements for a firearms permit.

For private detective and investigative jobs, most employers look for individuals with ingenuity, persistence and assertiveness. A candidate must not be afraid of confrontation, should communicate well and should be able to think on his or her feet. Good interviewing and interrogation skills also are important and usually are acquired in earlier careers in law enforcement or other fields. Because the courts often are the ultimate judge of a properly conducted investigation, the investigator must be able to present the facts in a manner that a jury will believe.

Training in subjects such as criminal justice and police science can be helpful to aspiring private detectives and investigators. Most corporate investigators must have a bachelor's degree, preferably in a business-related field. Some corporate investigators have a master's degree in business administration or a law degree, while others are CPAs. Corporate investigators hired by large companies may receive formal training from their employers on business practices, management structure and various finance-related topics. The screening process for potential employees typically includes a background check for a criminal history.

Some investigators receive certification from a professional organization to demonstrate competency in a field. For example, the National Association of Legal Investigators (NALI) confers the Certified Legal Investigator designation to licensed investigators who devote a majority of their practice to negligence or criminal defense investigations. To receive the designation, applicants must satisfy experience, educational and continuing-training requirements and must pass written and oral exams administered by the NALI.

Most private-detective agencies are small, with little room for advancement. Usually, there are no defined ranks or steps, so advancement takes the form of increases in salary and assignment status. Many detectives and investigators work for detective agencies at the beginning of their careers and, after a few years, start their own firms. Corporate and legal investigators may rise to supervisor or manager of the security or investigations department.

The median salary for a private investigator in the U.S. is $32,000 USD, according to 2005 data.

History of the Private Investigator

In 1833 Eugène François Vidocq, a French soldier, criminal and privateer, founded the first known private detective agency, Le bureau des renseignments (Office of Intelligence) and hired ex-cons. Official law enforcement tried many times to shut it down. In 1842 police arrested him in suspicion of unlawful imprisonment and taking money on false pretenses after he had solved an embezzling case. Vidocq later suspected that it had been a set-up. He was sentenced for five years with a 3,000-franc fine but the Court of Appeals released him. Vidocq is credited with having introduced record-keeping, criminology and ballistics to criminal investigation. He made the first plaster casts of shoe impressions. He created indelible ink and unalterable bond paper with his printing company. His form of anthropometrics is still partially used by French police. He is also credited for philanthropic pursuits—he claimed he never informed on anyone who had stolen for real need.

After Vidocq, the industry was born. Much of what private investigators did in the early days was to act as the police in matters that their clients felt the police were not equipped for or willing to do. A larger role for this new private investigative industry to was to act as pseudo law-men, particularly when dealing with labour and employee issues.

The wealthy found that the need to help control large numbers of workers, particularly ones who had developed new ideas as a result of the French Revolution, did not sit well with the wealth resource owners. Some early private investigators were nothing short of mercenaries and/or professional military companies helping private entities with problems that could be solved with force or the show of force, usually in foreign countries.

In the US, the Pinkerton National Detective Agency was a security guard and detective agency, established in 1850 by Allan Pinkerton. Pinkerton had become famous when he foiled a plot to assassinate then President-Elect Abraham Lincoln. Pinkerton's agents performed services which ranged from the equivalent of both a private military contractor to that of security guards. During the height of its existence, the Pinkerton Detective Agency had more agents than the standing army of the United States of America, causing the state of Ohio to outlaw the agency, due to the possibility of its being hired out as a "private army" or militia.

During the labour unrest of the late 19th century, businessmen hired Pinkerton guards to keep strikers and suspected unionists out of their factories. The most notorious example of this was the Homestead Strike of 1892, where Pinkerton agents ended up killing several people by enforcing the strikebreaking measures of Henry Clay Frick, (acting on behalf of Andrew Carnegie, who was abroad). The agency's logo, an eye embellished with the words "We Never Sleep" inspired the term "private eye."

Pinkerton agents were hired to track western outlaws Jesse James, the Reno brothers and the Wild Bunch, including Butch Cassidy and the Sundance Kid.

It was not until the prosperity of the 1920s that the private investigator became a person accessible to the average American. With the wealth of the 20s and the expanding of the middle class came the need for middle America.

Since then the private detective industry has grown with the changing needs of the public. Social issues like infidelity and unionization have impacted the industry and created new types of work, as has the need for insurance and with it insurance fraud, criminal defense investigations, the invention of low cost listening devices and more.

PIs in Fiction

Perhaps the most famous fictional PI is the Sherlock Holmes character created by Arthur Conan Doyle, who would refer to himself in the jargon of his age as a "private inquiries agent."

Since about the 1940s, PIs have also been frequently found in fiction as a stock character; they are a hero archetype who stumbles into detective stories to solve a mystery case, whether it be a whodunit murder or other crime activity. The PI is usually cool, relaxed and intelligent. A stereotypical look would have him drink whiskey, smoke, dress in a trenchcoat and fedora and be a good marksman.

PIs are also popular in television fiction, including such hit series as Magnum P.I., Tropical Heat, Veronica Mars, Moonlighting, Remington Steele, The Rockford Files, Monk and Spenser: For Hire; both TV and movie PI fiction often utilize the device of the main character first-person voiceover to make up for the fact that visual fiction is rarely ever shot in the true first-person, as well as to provide exposition about the detective's thoughts. Meanwhile filmmakers like Joel and Ethan Coen (The Big Lebowski), David O. Russell (I? Huckabees) and writers like Jennifer Colt (The Butcher of Beverly Hills),

Laura Anne Gilman (Staying Dead) and Jim Butcher (The Dresden Files) have moved the traditional PI protagonist towards new genres.

PIs in Reality Television

Since 2000, the syndicated television show Cheaters has been on the air. The show focuses on infidelity cases, investigated by the Cheaters Detective Agency.

Parco PI was a cable reality television show. The show featured Vinny Parco, a private investigator in New York City, New York.

Coastguard

Coastguards are civil servants who coordinate civil maritime search and rescue operations around the UK. They use high technology equipment to maintain watch. Coastguards maintain communications with all parties during emergencies. They have various other duties, e.g., pollution control.

Work Activities: HM Coastguard co-ordinates all civil search and rescue operations around the UK coastline and 1000 miles into the North Atlantic. Coastguard stations around the coast use high technology equipment to maintain watch 24 hours a day. They also respond to '999' emergency phone calls.

HM Coastguard is a part of the Maritime and Coastguard Agency, which is responsible for:

- developing, promoting and enforcing high standards of marine safety
- minimising the loss of life among seafarers and coastal users
- minimising the risk of pollution from ships
- where pollution occurs, minimising the impact on UK interests
- providing support to the Receiver of Wrecks.

In an emergency, the coastguard acts immediately to plan what help is needed. In addition to over 400 coastguard rescue teams and helicopters, the coastguard may call on:

- the Royal National Lifeboat Institution (RNLI)

- the Royal Navy
- the Royal Air Force (using fixed-wing aircraft and helicopters).

HM Coastguard employs regular watch officers, watch assistants and auxiliary coastguards.

Coastguard watch officers maintain constant watch on international distress signals. They carry out coastal searches and are also responsible for leading and supervising mud rescue and cliff rescue teams. They also help to staff busy operational centres, using advanced communication systems. Coastguard watch officers may have to travel to other districts, including remote coastguard stations.

Watch assistants have a support and administrative role in the operational centres. They respond to emergency calls, monitor equipment, update logs and provide information to the general public.

Members of the Coastguard Auxiliary Service are volunteers with an interest in and concern for safety of life at sea. They receive training to respond to coastal incidents.

Personal Qualities and Skills: You should be quick thinking and decisive. You'll need to remain calm in emergencies, have good organisational skills and high levels of concentration. Good communication skills are vital, as coastguards need to relay information quickly and accurately.

You must be reliable and have a strong sense of responsibility.

Supervisory skills may be required at times of emergency, when volunteers and coastguard rescue teams are assisting.

You should have good general fitness to cope with a range of activities such as cliff rescues and boat work. You should have normal sight and hearing.

All watch officers must be qualified to drive group A-E vehicles and hold a valid UK driving licence.

Pay and Opportunities: Coastguard personnel are paid on a rising scale. Coastguard personnel are paid on a rising scale. Coastguard watch assistants earn in the range of £11,735-

£14,133 a year. Coastguard watch officers earn in the range of £14,183-£18,349 a year. Earnings may increase with a shift allowance of up to 25% of basic salary.

Coastguard officers work a basic 42-hour week in 12 hour shifts. Early starts, late finishes, shift work and work on weekends and public holidays are normally required.

Coastguards are civil servants employed by the Maritime and Coastguard Agency. HM Coastguard is made up of around 600 regular officers, about 150 of whom are graded as Watch Officers and around 3,000 members of coastguard rescue teams who work as volunteers, providing a local back-up network.

The following information is sourced from government statistics. The government's definition of types of job is slightly different to that used in this programme. For this type of job, the most relevant Government-defined occupation is 'Protective service associate professionals not classified elsewhere'.

In 2001 there were 1,100 people working as 'Protective service associate professionals not classified elsewhere' in Scotland. 5 in every 10,000 employees working in Scotland were employed as 'Protective service associate professionals not classified elsewhere'.

Entry Routes and Training: To become a watch officer you must have at least six years maritime experience or three years search and rescue experience. Relevant practical experience might be for the Royal or Merchant Navy, RAF Search and Rescue, or Air Traffic Control.

The training consists of a month-long induction, followed by three two-week courses during the following year. At the end of this period exams are taken and you must pass an interview. If you are successful and you have satisfactory probation reports, your appointment will be confirmed.

It may be possible to enter this job after experience as a coastguard watch assistant or a member of a coastguard rescue team. Rescue team members are volunteers who are required to pass an interview before serving.

Qualifications; For entry to HM Coastguard as a watch officer, the minimum requirement is 3 Standard Grades (1-3) to include English and Maths.

Between three and six years relevant work experience is also required.

Adult Opportunities: Extensive experience of the sea is necessary for entry to become a watch officer, for example, in the Merchant Navy, the Royal Navy or the fishing industry.

For entry to watch assistant work, you will need an interest in maritime affairs plus the ability to use a visual display unit (VDU) and communication equipment.

Relevant voluntary experience includes membership of a local Coastguard/Lifeboat Rescue Team.

- 3% of people who work in occupations such as coastguard work part-time.
- 21% have flexible hours.

Bliss, Edward and James L. Hoyt: *Writing News for Broadcast*, New York, Columbia University Press, 1994.

Boella, Michael John: *Principles of Hospitality Law*, London, Cassell, 1999.

Bone, Jan, & Ana Fernandez: *Opportunities in Film Careers*, New York, VGM Career Books, 2004.

Bowers, C. A.: *The Cultural Dimension of Educational Computing: Understanding the Non-neutrality of Technology*, New York, Teachers' College Press; 1988.

Boyd, Andrew: *Broadcast Journalism: Techniques of Radio and TV News*, Woburn, Focal Press, 2001.

Brown, Douglas Robert: *The Restaurant Managers Handbook: How to Set Up, Operate, and Manage a Financially Successful Restaurant.* Lauderhill, Atlantic Pub., 1991.

Brown, James and Quaal Ward: *Radio-Television-Cable Management*, New York, McGraw Hill, 1998.

Bryant, Jennings: *Television and the American Family*, Hillsdale, Lawrence Erlbaum, 1990.

Buckingham, David: *Young People and the Media*, New York, Manchester University Press, 1993.

Buckner, Robert W.: *Site Selection: New Advancements in Methods and Technology*, New York, Lebhar-Friedman Books, 1998.

Caldwell, J. T.: *Electronic Media and Technoculture*, New Brusnwick, Rutgers University Press, 2000.

Careers in Focus: *Photography*, New York, Ferguson, 2004.

Carmouche, Rita: *Behavioural Studies in Hospitality Management*, New York, Chapman & Hall, 1995.

Carroll, Victoria: *Writing News for Television*, Ames, Iowa State University Press, 1997.

Cassiday, Doris, and Bruce Cassiday: *Careers in the Beauty Industry*, New York, Franklin Watts, 1978.

Clark, Mona: *Interpersonal Skills for Hospitality Managers*, London, Chapman Hill, 1995.

Clark, Roy Peter: *A Journalist Teaches Young Writers*, Portsmouth, Heinemann, 1987.

Cockburn, C. and Ormrod, S.: *Gender and Technology in the Making*, London, Sage, 1993.

Cohler, David Keith: *Broadcast Newswriting*, Englewood Cliffs, Prentice Hall, 1990.

Cracknell, H. L.: *Escoffier: The Complete Guide to the Art of Modern Cookery*, New York, John Wiley, 1979.

Craig, James: *Graphic Design Career Guide*, New York, Watson-Guptill, 1992.

Crawford, Tad: *Starting Your Career As a Freelance Photographer*, New York, Allworth Press, 2003.

Crouse, Chuck: *Reporting for Radio*, Chicago, Bonus Books, 1998.

Davidson, M. J. and Cooper, C. L.: *Women and Information Technology*, New York, John Wiley & Sons, 1987.

Delaney, Chuck: *Photography Your Way*, New York, Allworth Press, 2005.

Dennis, Everette E. and Edward C. Pease: *Children and the Media*, New Brunswick, Transaction Publishers, 1996.

Diamond, S. Taylor's Way: *Women, Cultures and Technology*, New York: Routledge; 1997.

Donald, Ralph and Thomas Spann: *Fundamentals of Television Production*, Ames, Iowa State University Press, 2000.

Dornenburg, Andrew: *Culinary Artistry*, New York, John Wiley & Sons, 1996.

Douglas, George H.: *The Early Days of Radio Broadcasting*, Jefferson, NC: McFarland, 1987.

Easlea, B.: *Fathering the Unthinkable: Masculinity, Scientists and the Nuclear Arms Race*, London, Pluto Press, 1982.

Ellis, Elmo: *Opportunities in Broadcasting Careers*, Chicago, VGM Career Books, 2005.

Faulkner, W. and Arnold, E.: *Smothered by Invention: Technology in Women's Lives*, London, Pluto Press, 1985.

Fensch, Thomas: *Television News Anchors*, Jefferson, McFarland, 1993.

Field, Shelly: *Career Opportunities in Advertising and Public Relations*, New York, Ferguson, 2006.

Foster, Timothy R. V.: *How to Succeed As an Independent Consultant*, London: Kogan, Page, 2002.

Fox Keller, E.: *Reflections on Gender and Science*, New Haven, Yale University Press, 1985.

Gardner, Garth: *Careers in Computer Graphics and Animation*, Fairfax, GGC, 2001.

Gibbs, Jenny: *Interior Design*, New York, H. N. Abrams, 2005.

Go, Frank M.: *Human Resource Management in the Hospitality Industry*, New York, Wiley, 1996.

Goldfarb, Roz: *Careers by Design*, New York, Allworth Press, 2001.

Gordon, Sandra R.: *Great Jobs for Film Majors*, Chicago, VGM Career Books, 2004.

Graham, Duane: *The Remarkable Story of Otto Graham*, Wayne, Immortal Investments Publishing, 2004.

Green, E. and Adam, A. Virtual Gender: *Technology, Consumption, and Identity*, New York, Routledge, 2001.

Greenman, Robert: *The Adviser's Companion*, New York, Columbia Scholastic Press Association, 1991.

Griffiths, D.: *The Exclusion of Women from Technology*, London, Pluto Press, 1985.

Hall, Ken G.: *Australian Film: the Inside Story*, Sydney, Summit Books, 1980.

Hewitt, John: *Airwords: Writing for Broadcast News, Mountain View*, Oxford, Mayfield Pub. Company, 2002.

Higham, Robin: *A Guide to the Sources of United States Military History*, Hamden, Archon Books, 1975.

Hilliard, Robert L. and Michael C. Keith: *The Broadcast Century and Beyond*, Boston: Focal Press, 2001.

Hinkin, Timothy R.: *Cases in Hospitality Management: A Critical Incident Approach*, New York, Wiley, 1995.

Holloway, J. C. : *Towards a Core Curriculum for Tourism: A Discussion Paper*, London, The National Liaison Group for Higher Education in Tourism, 1995.

Horstede, G.: *Cultures and Organizations: Software of the Mind*, London, McGraw-Hill Book Company, 1991.

Hungerland, Buff: *Marketing Your Creative Portfolio*, Upper Saddle River, Prentice Hall, 2003

Jain, S. C.: *Women and Technology*, Jaipur, Rawat Publications, 1985.

Jefferson, Michael: *Breaking into Graphic Design*, New York, Allworth Press, 2005.

Jensen, Clayne R.: *Opportunities in Recreation and Leisure Careers*, Lincolnwood, VGM Career Horizons, 2000.

Jones, Sue Jenklyn: *Fashion Design*, New York, Watson-Guptill, 2002.

Kieffer, John: *The Photographer's Assistant*, New York, Allworth, 2001.

Kirkham, P.: *The Gendered Object*, Manchester, Manchester University Press, 1996.

Kissane, Sharon F.: *Career Success for People with Physical Disabilities*, Lincolnwood, VGM Career Horizons, 1997.

Kring, Robin: *Party Creations: Book of Theme Event Design*, Denver, Clear Creek Pub., 1993.

Kurzweil, R.: *The Age of Spiritual Machines*, New York, Viking, 1999.

Lavery, P.: *Tourism Marketing and Management Handbook*, New York, Prentice Hall, 1989.

Lewis, Robert C.: *Cases in Hospitality Marketing and Management*, New York, John Wiley, 1997.

MacCloskey, Monro: *How to Qualify for the Service Academies*, New York, Richards Rosen Press, 1964.

Maclay, Edgar Stanton: *A History of the United States Navy 1771-1893*, New York, Appleton Co., 1894.

Mauro, Lucia: *Careers for Fashion Plates and Other Trendsetters*, Chicago, VGM Career Horizons, 2003.

McGuire-Lytle, Erin: *Careers in Graphic Arts and Computer Graphics*, New York, Rosen, 1999.

Miller, Samuel D.: *An Aerospace Bibliography*, Washington. Office of Air Force History, 1978.

Mitchell, Leslie Scott: *Freelancing for Television and Radio*, London; Routledge, 2005.

Mogel, Leonard: *Creating Your Career in Communications and Entertainment*, Sewickley, GATF Press, 1998.

Noronha, Shonan F. R.: *Opportunities in Television and Video Careers*, Chicago: VGM Career Books, 2003.

Orlik, Peter B.: *Career Perspectives in Electronic Media*, Ames, Blackwell Pub., 2004.

Packard, Sidney: *The Fashion Business: Dynamics and Careers*, New York, Holt, Rinehart, and Winston, 1983.

Parks, Peggy J.: *The News Media*, San Diego, Lucent Books, 2002.

Paullin, C.O.: *The Navy of the American Revolution*, Cleveland, The Burrows Brothers Co., 1906.

Perna, Rita: *Fashion Forecasting*, New York, Fairchild Publications, 1987.

Rachlis, Eugene: *The Story of the U.S. Coast Guard*, New York, Random House, 1961.

Reis, Ronald A.: *Careers in Art and Graphic Design*, Hauppage, Barrons, 2001.

Rocha, Tony L.: *Careers in Magazine Publishing*, New York, Rosen, 2001.

Rubinstein, Donna: *The Modeling Life*, New York, Berkeley Publishing Group, 1998.

Satterthwaite, Frank: *The Career Portfolio Workbook*, New York, McGraw-Hill, 2003.

Seguin, James: *Media Career Guide*, Boston, St. Martin's, 2006.

Sones, Melissa: *Getting into Fashion: A Career Guide*, New York, Ballantine, 1984.

Vogt, Peter: *Career Opportunities in the Fashion Industry*, New York, Facts on File, 2002.

Wilson, Wayne: *Careers in Publishing and Communications*, Bear, Mitchell Lane, 2002.

Yager, Fred, & Jan Yager: *Career Opportunities in the Film Industry*, New York, Ferguson, 2003.

Zahler, Karen Gantz.: *Superchefs: Signature Recipes From America's New Royalty*, New York, John Wiley & Sons, 1996.

Index

A

B

C

P

R

S

T

U

V

W

Y

❑❑❑